CULTURE AND IDENTITY

X

SKILLS-BASED SOCIOLOGY

Series Editors: Tim Heaton and Tony Lawson

The *Skills-Based Sociology* series is designed to cover the Core Skills for Sociology A Level (and equivalent courses) and to bring students up to date with recent sociological thought in all the key areas. Students are given the opportunity to develop their skills through exercises which they can carry out by themselves or in groups, as well as given practice in answering exam questions. The series also emphasises contemporary developments in sociological knowledge, with a focus on recent social theories such as postmodernism, the New Right and the New Left.

Published

THEORY AND METHOD
Mel Churton

EDUCATION AND TRAINING
Tim Heaton and Tony Lawson

MASS MEDIA
Marsha Jones and Emma Jones

CULTURE AND IDENTITY
Warren Kidd

STRATIFICATION AND DIFFERENTIATION
Mark Kirby

CRIME AND DEVIANCE
Tony Lawson and Tim Heaton

HEALTH AND ILLNESS
Michael Senior with Bruce Viveash

THE FAMILY
Liz Steel and Warren Kidd

Forthcoming

RELIGION
Joan Garrod and Marsha Jones

WEALTH, POVERTY AND WELFARE
Sharon Kane and Mark Kirby

POLITICS
Warren Kidd and Karen Legge

Skills-Based Sociology
Series Standing Order ISBN 0–333–69350–7
(outside North America only)

You can receive future titles in this series as they are published. To place a standing order please contact your bookseller or, in the case of difficulty, write to us at the address below with your name and address, the title of the series and the ISBN quoted above.

Customer Services Department, Macmillan Distribution Ltd, Houndmills, Basingstoke, Hampshire, RG21 6XS, England

CULTURE AND IDENTITY

Warren Kidd

palgrave

First published 2002 by
PALGRAVE
Houndmills, Basingstoke, Hampshire RG21 6XS and
175 Fifth Avenue, New York, N.Y. 10010
Companies and representatives throughout the world

PALGRAVE is the new global academic imprint of
St. Martin's Press LLC Scholarly and Reference Division and
Palgrave Publishers Ltd (formerly Macmillan Press Ltd).

ISBN 0–333–79002–2

This book is printed on paper suitable for recycling and made from fully managed and sustained forest sources.

A catalogue record for this book is available from the British Library.

10   9   8   7   6   5   4   3   2   1
11   10   09   08   07   06   05   04   03   02

Printed in Great Britain by Antony Rowe Ltd, Chippenham, Wilts

For **Jane**, **Joan**, **Eddie**, **Fred** and **Barbara**

Thank you for your love and support

Contents

Acknowledgements

When writing a book such as this, one becomes indebted to a great many people for their help, support and friendship, and it seems only right that those people should be mentioned here. While the final responsibility for this work is my own, I would like to thank the series editors, Tony Lawson and Tim Heaton, for their continued support and guidance. I would also like to thank Catherine Gray at Palgrave.

Since the topic of culture and identity is a contemporary one it is much discussed, and I would like to thank David Abbott and John Bird for various discussions I have had with them at different times: I have found their ideas and opinions very helpful, both on the topic itself and on the tricky issue of how to teach it.

Continued thanks must go to both Mark Kirby and Dave King for their guidance, friendship and many a late night phone call trying to sort out, amongst other matters, the problems of postmodernism and poststructuralism. Thank you also to Gerry Czerniawski for making teaching sociology such a pleasure. Finally, this book is, as always, dedicated to my friends, colleagues, loved ones and students.

WARREN KIDD

1 Introduction

The philosophy behind the book

The *Skills-Based Sociology* series has three main aims: to provide a thorough and comprehensive coverage of topic areas for all sociology specifications (including the AS and A2 awards offered by AQA and OCR) – in this case 'culture and identity'; to provide students with activities and exercises, worked into the text of the book, to help them develop the required skills of sociology, with a particular focus on examination skills; and to update teachers' and students' knowledge of the topics in question.

The world of sociology is a rapidly changing and ever expanding one. Each month, new trends are established, old traditions are continued and recent fads and fashions are replaced by newer ones. Each month, new research is completed and new articles, journals and books are published. There is a wealth and rich variety of sociological information 'out there' for the interested consumer, and in recent years there have been moves by textbook writers, academics and exam boards to try to keep Advanced Level sociology as up to date as possible with theoretical and empirical developments.

Given that the use of theory is at the heart of what sociology does, a key feature of this book – and the *Skills-Based* series in general – is its emphasis on the newer sociological theories, which are given an equal footing with more traditional ideas and concepts. Given its current popularity, this is especially important in the case of 'culture and identity'.

The role of 'culture and identity' in the new AS and A2 specifications

This book has been written for students of the AQA and OCR sociology specifications, aimed at the 16–19 post-compulsory age group – the new AS and A2 levels known as Curriculum 2000. In the new sociology specifications that accompany the wider changes to post-16 education in schools and colleges, the role of culture and identity has changed, yet it remains vital to the AQA and OCR courses as it is a core theme of the QCA sociology criteria.

This book covers issues of culture and identity that are central to all sociological debates and discussions, as illustrated in Chapters 2 and 3. To show how these link to the new Curriculum 2000 sociology specifications an appendix is provided at the back of the book (pages 210–11). This appendix maps Chapters 2–13 of the book against the AQA and OCR specifications, showing which chapters link to which topic areas currently being taught for the new AS and A2 examinations.

AQA

The AQA specification has interwoven issues of culture and identity throughout the units/topics on offer – at both year 1 AS level and into year 2 A2 level. This decision is based on the observation that, like theory and methods, issues of culture and identity are absolutely central to all sociology. Every unit/topic on offer requires students to think about contemporary debates on culture and identity and, in the case of A2 level in particular, to use contemporary theories that are based on discussions of the role of culture and identity in society. In particular, issues of culture and identity within the AQA specification link well with the topics of:

- Mass media.
- Education.
- Religion.
- Crime and deviance.
- Power and politics.
- World sociology.

OCR

The OCR specification has placed issues of culture and identity into three main areas of the two-year programme. At AS level the introductory unit, *The Individual and Society*, is based entirely on culture and identity, as are the topics of 'youth and culture' in AS unit 2 and 'popular culture' in A2 unit 6.

In common with the AQA specification above, issues of culture and identity also link well with many other topics/units.

What are culture and identity?

By culture sociologists generally mean 'the way of life of a group' and by identity we usually mean 'knowing who you are', although, as

Chapter 2 will illustrate, there is great controversy over the precise definition of these key concepts. The study of culture and identity therefore involves debates on a wide range of important issues:

- The relationship of the individual to the wider group.
- The degree of freedom individuals have in their day-to-day life.
- The type and degree of self-consciousness individuals have in respect of the way they behave.
- The amount of control that the wider social framework into which we are born has over our life.

The importance and origins of culture and identity

Adoption of the topic of 'culture and identity' is a major theoretical and empirical development in contemporary sociology. Although the topic is a relatively recent addition to sociology syllabuses it would be a great mistake to assume that sociologists have only recently become interested in the issues with which it is concerned. One of the aims of this book is to demonstrate that sociology has, since its beginning and the work of its founders, been concerned with the relationship between the individual and society, the role of culture in social life and how identity develops in a social context.

However, as well as acknowledging the traditional roots of culture and identity in older theories, it is important to pay attention to newer ideas. Hence this book will not just consider the ideas of Durkheim, Marx and Weber, but will also look at the theories that developed after their time (the interactionist schools, neo-Marxism, the various branches of feminism and the Frankfurt School), relating these older ideas to the 'new sociology' of post-structuralism, postmodernism, the new right, structurational sociology, and the idea of reflexive modernity and the risk society, amongst others.

Using the skills of sociology

Learning sociology is not just a question of remembering ideas and concepts – although memory is, of course, an important aspect of revising for examinations. In order to be successful at sociology you have to be able to apply the ideas you have learnt in appropriate ways, to interpret questions correctly and to develop the skill of evaluation – to be able to discuss both the strengths and the weaknesses of the ideas contained within the sociological 'world-view', as well as the claims made by the proponents of various theoretical positions. The 'Curriculum 2000' restructuring of the post-16 curriculum in the wake of the Dearing Review has specified some central skills that all students will be examined on at the AS and A2 levels in all subjects. Students will be examined on:

- Knowledge
- Understanding
- Identification
- Analysis
- Interpretation
- Evaluation

This set of essential skills form the Assessment Objectives (AOs) for the AS and A Level awards. The skills of knowledge and understanding are referred to as AO1; in combination the other skills are referred to as AO2. The AS examination places more emphasis on knowledge and understanding, whereas the A2 examination places greater emphasis on the AO2 skills to reflect the fact that the second year is of a more advanced level than the first.

In order to help you develop the above skills, exercises are provided in each chapter of this book. Each exercise is accompanied by symbols denoting the particular skill or skills it seeks to help you develop: *k* for knowledge, *u* for understanding (for AO1); *id* for identification, *in* for interpretation, *a* for analysis and *e* for evaluation (for AO2).

Where appropriate some chapters conclude with a sample examination question for you to practice. As with the general exercises in each chapter, they encourage you to reflect on the contents of this book in an active fashion.

Subject content

Chapter 2 introduces key issues in the study of culture and identity, plus the relevant definitions and concepts.

Chapters 3–6 outline various key theoretical perspectives that sociologists draw on to consider matters of culture and identity, including functionalism, Marxism, neo-Marxism, interactionist sociologies, postmodernism, poststructuralism, feminisms and structurational sociology.

After this review of theory, Chapters 7–13 take these theories and apply them to related topics and debates, including mass culture, youth culture, work and class, gender, sexuality and the body, ethnicity, and nationality and globalisation.

2 Key issues in the study of culture and identity

By the end of this chapter you should be able to:

- define the concepts of culture and identity;
- evaluate the problems involved in the definition of the concepts of culture and identity;
- understand why issues of culture and identity are of importance in sociology;
- compare sociological and non-sociological ideas on culture and identity.

Introduction

Consider for a moment how you came to be reading this book. Glad though I obviously am that you are reading it, the act of purchasing and reading a book is not as 'normal' or 'simplistic' as it may at first seem. Did you buy the book, or was it bought for you? Was it ordered by post, over the telephone or via the Internet, or was it bought in a book shop? Was the book given to you by a teacher at your school or college? Are you expected to use it in lessons or at home as part of your private study? Why are you studying this subject – assuming of course that you are not simply an interested reader, or even a teacher? Is it 'normal' or 'natural' to conduct one's life in this way? Why do we take these patterns of behaviour for granted in our day-to-day lives? Do we read books in order to obtain knowledge, pass an examination, help us get a job, earn money and so on? Could society – and therefore our lives – be organised any other way?

By thinking about our lives in this way, we bring ourselves to the sociological study of what we call 'culture' and 'identity'.

What is 'culture'?

To start with a simple definition, culture means '*the way of life of a group of people*'. In other words – how they live their lives. The patterns of social organisation and the 'normal' ways in which we are expected to behave in society touch all aspects of our daily lives. However we should not assume that all cultures are the same. For example, simply because social life, for us, happens to be structured in a particular way, does not mean that it has to be like this, nor that it was like this in the past – or is even like this in other societies around the world. Given its importance in every aspect of our social life, the concept of culture is central to the subject of sociology.

Exercise 2.1

Consider what we mean by the phrase 'way of life'. Copy out and complete the following table, and then answer the question that follows it.

	Way of life on an average Saturday
Myself	
Someone of my age living 100 years ago	
Someone living today who is elderly	
Someone living in a poor area of India	

Question:

How do 'ways of life' vary amongst cultural groups? (*Answer this question in about 300 words.*)

Now consider what you have done since you awoke this morning. Consider the reasons, or rather the 'motivations' – the 'meanings' – that lie behind the acts you have performed. Why do you behave as you do? Who says you should act as you do? How do you know how to behave? These questions relate to our culture and prompt other questions that are seemingly simple but sociologically vital:

- How is culture patterned?
- How is culture maintained?
- Why is culture as it is – could it be any different?

These three questions run through the topic of 'culture and identity' and answers to them are to be found throughout this book. They are also fundamental to sociology in general and sociological theories in particular. The study of culture is therefore vital to sociology, and to our lives as a whole. Culture is part and parcel of all that we do, all that we are, all that we can and might become.

What is 'identity'?

If culture is how we behave as a member of a group, then the word 'identity' relates to how we think about ourselves as people, how we think about other people around us, and what we think others think of us. 'Identity' means being able to 'fix' or 'figure out' who we are as people.

Exercise 2.2

Using the Internet or CD-ROMs, find pictures of five different youth cultural groups, – such as skinheads, heavy metal, indie-kids, nu-metal, punk, hip hop and so on. For each picture, describe how you think they see themselves – what you think their identity is, based on the cultural groups they belong to. Describe each one in about 100 words.

Culture and identity are frequently linked – but they should not be seen as exactly the same. While our culture often establishes our sense of identity or even identities, sociologists usually separate the two concepts, with 'culture' representing the 'macro' pattern – the 'big picture' – and 'identity' representing the smaller, more 'micro' meanings we have as individuals.

Exercise 2.3

Look up the definition of 'culture' in any good English language dictionary. Take a note of all the different meanings this concept has – you might be surprised at how many there are! When you have completed your list of meanings, divide them into four types, according to the four ways in which the word 'culture' tends to be used:

1. Social scientific uses – these, as in sociology, tend to look at group behaviour and patterns.

2. Artistic uses.

3. Scientific uses.

4. Any others.

It is from the definitions in your first group that a sociological definition of the word 'culture' will come. Using these to help you, and the brief introductory discussion, write your own definition of the concept of 'culture'. Use your own words, and try to write a definition that you think might be of use to sociologists.

In his famous book *The Sociological Imagination*, C. Wright Mills (1959) writes:

The sociological imagination enables its possessor to understand the larger historical scene in terms of its meaning for the inner life and the external career of a variety of individuals. . . . The sociological imagination enables us to grasp history and biography and the relations between the two within society. That is its task and its promise.

By 'the sociological imagination' Mills means that a key feature of all sociological thinking is the ability not to take ordinary life for granted – not to allow the culture we are brought up in to affect how we understand the world as sociologists. Yet although we should try to step back from our culture, sociology can help us to understand our own life better if we think in a detached fashion about how culture operates. We can, as sociologists, reflect on the function culture performs for society, and therefore think about how it has shaped our own lives.

Exercise 2.4

Using your 'sociological imagination', brainstorm what you think the functions of culture are for society as a whole.

Later in the same book, Mills (1959) suggests that '*No social study that does not come back to the problems of biography, of history and of their intersections within a society, has completed its intellectual journey.*' Here we have a very clear statement about the key role that both culture and identity should have in sociology. Mills suggests that the task and the purpose of sociology is to study the way in which individuals fit into the cultures that produce them, and that they themselves maintain and recreate over time.

We are thus shaped by culture: who we think we are – our 'identity' – is related to what society says we should do and be. During the course of our lives – our 'biography' – we should be able to look at what we do and how we behave, and attempt to see how our identities and the social structure, or culture, fit together. By 'biography' sociologists tend to mean the history of who we have become and how we have become who we are – the process and experiences of socialisation. One's self-identity or biography (who we think we are) is developed over a long period of time and is seen by many sociologists as a resource: we can draw on it to determine how to act in particular situations. It is something we can reflect upon.

Exercise 2.5

Consider the ideas of C. Wright Mills above. Key features of the 'sociological imagination' are the ability to be critical about social life, and when studying it to detach yourself from the values you have been brought up to believe in.

Brainstorm why it is important for the sociologist to be as critical as possible about society.

Attempts to define 'culture'

The sociologist Raymond Williams (1983), in his book *Key Words: a vocabulary of culture and society*, says:

> Culture is one of the two or three most complicated words in the English language. This is partly so because of its intricate historical development, in several European languages, but mainly because it has now come to be used for important concepts in several distinct intellectual disciplines and in several distinct and incompatible systems of thought.

From your work in Exercise 2.4, you may have already come to the same conclusion as Williams regarding the word culture. Although for sociologists 'culture' is often taken to mean 'the way of life of a group', this short-hand definition hardly does the concept justice, given that what it stands for is often regarded as a vital, if not *the most vital*, feature of all social life. For example the 'way of life of a group' would need to include:

- The dominant values of a society.
- The values that guide the direction that social change might take.
- Shared linguistic symbols (language).
- Religious beliefs.
- What is considered to be the correct way for people to behave in their day-to-day lives.
- What is considered to be the highest intellectual and artistic achievements of a group, including science, art, literature, music and so on.
- Formal behavioural traditions and rituals.
- Dominant patterns of living, including styles of architecture and patterns of land use.

As can be seen from this list, the way of life of a group, its culture, is the product of a massive social undertaking: the result of the collective, combined and interrelated efforts of all its members.

Exercise 2.6

In order to explore the idea of what culture means in more detail, write a list of examples of each of the above characteristics of the 'way of life of a group'. Base your list on what happens in present-day British society.

In order to use the concept of culture in a detailed, precise and fruitful way we need to take our basic definition and expand it. Consider the following interpretations.

Culture as a 'system'

In this interpretation, culture is seen as the cement that bonds individuals together. It is made up of shared or collective symbols and it shapes our lives. It gives us the rules by which to live our lives. It hovers over us, structuring the world around us.

Exercise 2.7

One way of looking at culture is to see it as providing rules by which to live. In a group, write a list of your school/college rules. Then produce a written answer to each of the following questions:

1. Do you agree with your school/college rules? Why? Why not?

2. Does everyone follow the rules? What happens if they do not?

3. How do these rules create a shared 'identity' in the school/college?

4. How does the school/college encourage you to feel as though you belong to a group?

Culture as a 'map of meaning'

In this view, culture is that which we carry around inside us, created by our interactions with others. It still provides us with symbols and rules, but we have a much more active role in its creation. Culture creates the world we live in. It also allows us to understand and interpret our own actions and the actions of others.

These two interpretations of culture (culture as a system, and culture as a map of meaning) offer different yet related views on what culture is, what it does, and why it is important.

- Cultures allow us to build the reality we live in, usually through the meanings we give to symbols, passed down in language.
- Cultures are shared and are also a form of constraint since they predate those who are brought up in them. Nonetheless they are a 'human enterprise' – they exist because of humans.
- Culture allows us to interact with others, to share common meanings, patterns of behaviour and ways of communicating.

- Cultures exist both subjectively and objectively: they are objective because they are concerned with material things – they shape styles of dress, food, art, music and so on; and they are subjective because they are concerned with individuals' interpretations – they exist in the mind and allow us to make sense of the world around us.

Although culture is shared, in any one society there may be more than one culture or many small subcultures, the sum of which influences the individual. For many sociologists, humans are both cultural beings and social beings: we are shaped by our culture, and we shape it and perpetuate it in our day-to-day lives when we interact with others.

Exercise 2.8

In the eyes of many sociologists, culture creates a 'bond' between people in society. How might this be achieved? Write down as many examples as you can think of. To start you off, here are two examples:

- Culture gives shared rules.
- Culture provides a shared language.

A key question for sociologists and other interested commentators – such as sociobiologists, anthropologists and psychologists – is: to what extent does our culture constrain us? Or to put it another way: are humans the puppets of culture or do they have free will?

These questions are very profound and have preoccupied philosophers since the beginning of intellectual inquiry. In sociology we can make a very rough and simplistic division into two basic positions, between which a whole range of other views might exist:

View one: 'structural sociology'	View two: 'action sociology'
Culture as constraint/order	Culture as meaning
Looks at the 'big picture' (macro/positivism)	Looks at the 'small picture' (micro/phenomenology)
Humans are puppets of society	Humans have 'agency', or free will
Humans are passive	Humans are active
Concerned with the wider system or social structure	More concerned with looking at action and interaction
Determinism (humans are made, or 'determined' by social forces)	Voluntarism (humans can think for themselves)
More interested in 'culture'	More interested in 'identity'

On the one hand we have a sociological view that sees humans as manipulated by their culture, while the other view suggests that humans themselves manipulate their own identities in an active way. Although these are extreme views, they are reflected in the differences between the structural sociology (view one) of perspectives such as functionalism and some forms of Marxism, and the more action sociology (view two) of the various interactionist or interpretive schools of thought. These distinctions will be explored in more depth in later chapters, as will theories that attempt to bridge this divide.

Exercise 2.9

Copy out the following passage and fill in the gaps with the words provided at the end.

Many sociologists have studied culture and how it operates in society, although they often .... its role in different ways. Although it can be seen in different ways, it is usually regarded within sociology as a vital aspect of social .... – providing meaning, ... , socialisation and so on. For some, culture is that which .... us together and constrains our actions – it is vital for the effective running of society, it is essential for social order. Others give more .... to humans and describe them as 'actors'. In this view culture is created by .... in order to create a stable sense of reality in everyday life, full of meaning that is shared.

Missing words

- interpret   • humans   • reality   • norms   • free will   • bonds

Non-sociological uses of the concept of 'culture'

Since culture plays an important role in social life, the concept should have an equally important place in sociological study. Interestingly, however, as syllabus topics 'culture and identity', 'popular culture' and 'the individual and society' have only appeared at advanced level during the past few years. This is not to say that the terms have only just been invented or that sociologists have only just begun to take an interest in these topics. Rather there has been renewed interest in these ideas due to changes in the theories used by sociologists to make sense of society – in particular the rise of ideas known under the rather broad heading of 'postmodernism'.

Sociology is not, however, the only academic discipline to be interested in such ideas.

Sociobiology

Sociology can be seen as a challenge to the ideas of sociobiology. The latter, which dates back to the ideas put forward by Charles Darwin (1871) in *The Descent of Man and Selection in Relation to Sex* on the evolution of the human species, suggests that everything that humans do is the result of their biological make-up. As a species evolves its biological needs may change, and so too will the culture of the species. For example Tiger and Fox (1972) claim that social action is the direct result of the satisfying of preprogrammed biological needs and appetites. Equally Desmond Morris (1968), a noted zoologist of whom you may have heard due to his television documentary work, claims in his book *The Naked Ape* that although culture is a human creation and is shared, the need for culture is primarily the in-built biological need to continue the life of the group over time. In this sense humans, the 'naked apes', are no less animal-like than other apes: our biology rules our culture.

A more recent example of this type of theorising is to be found in the work of Goldschmidt (1990), who claims that the human sense of self-identity, given by the cultures to which we belong, is the result of humans' neurophysical impulses and their drive for self-gratification. In other words, identity is a biological need to seek pleasure, to satisfy our own needs in order to survive, and we compete with others to do so.

Exercise 2.10

 Write down four strengths and four weaknesses of the sociobiológical approach.

Exercise 2.11

 In a group, list all the arguments sociologists would level against the sociobiological approach in order to criticise it.

Psychoanalytic theory

Whereas a great deal of sociology and anthropology seriously questions the notion that humans act according to instincts (in-born behaviour), the tradition of psychological thought known as 'psycho-analysis' looks at how instinct might affect how we think and act. This view, developed by Sigmund Freud (1923), suggests that throughout life all human action is based on the interrelationship between natural biological needs and learnt social or cultural rules. Freud divided the human mind into three separate but interrelated elements: the id, the ego and the superego. In the id we find humans as they naturally are

– having biological drives that seek to maximise pleasure; in the ego we reflect upon who we are and how we behave; and in the super-ego we learn to follow the cultural rules of the particular society in which we have been brought up.

Freud claimed that psychological disorders and problems result from culture and biology clashing in the individual's mind. Freud saw culture – or what he called 'civilisation' – and natural needs and drives as often producing neuroses and 'perversions'. This is where humans act according to their unconscious biological needs, yet the culture they have learnt might define such behaviour as wrong or immoral.

Exercise 2.12

Identify which of the following statements are (1) sociological, (2) sociobiological, (3) psychoanalytic or (4) a combination of two or all three. Copy out the statements and write down your answers.

1. Culture exists because it is a product of how we behave as humans: it is natural.

2. Culture allows us to create a stable reality in which to act.

3. Humans are in a constant state of tension between learnt behaviour and natural instincts.

4. Society and culture are only real inasmuch as humans act as though they are real.

5. Culture bonds individuals to the group, but each group may have its own rules, customs and identity.

6. All cultures perform the same functions – even if they appear to be different in content – since they all serve human nature.

Are sociologists influenced by freud?

Although many sociologists take issue with Freud's notion of the id in respect of human biological instincts, some have been influenced by his ideas on the theme of civilisation. In *Civilisation and its Discontents*, Freud (1930) argued that although humans, by their nature, seek pleasure (known as the 'pleasure principle'), many people in modern society are in fact unhappy. Freud asked why this should be so, given that humans instinctually seek pleasure. The answer to this question lies in the idea of 'civilisation' (or 'culture'): modern living has placed new demands on humans and set new rules for how they should live their lives. The rules of supposedly 'civilised' societies are in fact massive social constraints that lead to unhappiness – or 'discontents' – since they prevent people from acting in 'truly human' ways.

This theme of civilisation has influenced the work of some sociologists in very different ways.

Norbert Elias

In his book *The Civilizing Process* (originally written in 1939), Elias (1978) provides a history of how manners have changed and developed over time. Elias argues that manners are a clear indication of cultural tastes and standards, and that they provide a clear insight into the personalities and psychologies of the individuals who live in society in particular times, and who are expected to behave in particular ways. Elias's central thesis is that as time goes by society becomes increasingly more 'civilised'. There is increased pressure to conform to a larger set of rules, and this pressure changes and affects personality and identity. Elias argues that this evolutionary civilising process has its modern expression in state regulation of many aspects of day-to-day life. This view appears to reflect Freud's concern that modern life constrains the nature of the individual through cultural change.

Elias uses the development of rules in sport as evidence for his views. Elias and Dunning (1986) suggest that the organisation of both sport and government have experienced a similar and historically parallel cultural evolution away from violence and towards rules to control and outlaw violence.

Exercise 2.13

k u id in

This exercise requires you to think about how manners or rules in sport have changed over time. Copy out and complete the following table.

Name of the sport	What was the sport like?	How have the introduction of manners/rules made the sport more 'civilised' today?
1.		
2.		
3.		
4.		
5.		
6.		
7.		
8.		

The Frankfurt School: Herbert Marcuse

Many writers at the Institute of Social Research at Frankfurt University, Germany (established in 1923), adopted an interdisciplinary approach to social theorising; that is, they combined the different ideas of various thinkers, including Marx (see Chapter 3) and Freud. In *Eros and Civilization*, Herbert Marcuse (1969) wrote, with the Second World War in mind:

> the fact that the destruction of life (human and animal) has progressed with the progress of civilisation, that cruelty and hatred and the scientific extermination of men have increased in relation to the real possibility of the elimination of oppression – this feature of late industrial civilisation would have instinctual roots which perpetuate destructiveness beyond all rationality.

This is a more pessimistic use of Freud's notion of civilisation than that of Elias. For Marcuse, the so-called civilised culture of the modern age had simply resulted in ever more technologically enhanced means by which humans could kill with ever increasing efficiency. This pessimistic and critical view of science, technology and other aspects of the cultural 'civilising process' was echoed in Max Weber's famous declaration that modern times would unleash an *'iron cage of bureaucracy'* from which it would be very hard to escape.

For Marcuse and other members of the Frankfurt School, civilisation had resulted in capitalist exploitation of the masses and their alienation. Humans' natural need for pleasure seeking had been stripped away by the factory – depriving them of their humanity in the search for profit by the capitalist class. Thus culture only serves the interests of the powerful, and in doing so it supresses the instinctual human need for work as a source of pleasure, not profit – a key idea in the work of Marx himself. Marcuse's concern that culture and its developments – technology and science – might lead to further destruction due to the instinctual nature of humans is reflected in the work of Freud (1930):

> The fateful question for the human species seems to me to be whether and to what extent their cultural development will succeed in mastering the disturbance of their communal life by the human instinct of aggression and self-destruction.

Socialisation, norms and values

The learning of a culture – the process whereby the traditions of a community are passed down the generations – is known as 'socialisation'. This process is usually seen as involving the transmission of the *norms* and *values* of a given culture.

- *Norms* are the culturally prescribed ways or patterns of behaviour that a society expects of its 'normal' members. Going against the norm is usually referred to as 'deviant' behaviour.
- *Values* are the ends that 'normal' behavioural patterns attempt to achieve. For example, queuing for a bus in our society is a norm designed to achieve an 'orderly' society.

Exercise 2.14

Copy out the table below and complete it by listing some examples of norms and values in your day-to-day life. One example has been provided to start you off.

Examples of norms	Examples of values
1. We should queue for the bus	
2.	
3.	
4.	
5.	
6.	
7.	
8.	

Exercise 2.15

Why is socialisation important for (1) the individual, (2) society, and (3) how sociologists understand what goes on in society? Write your answers in a table copied from the one below.

The individual	Society	Sociology
1.		
2.		
3.		
4.		
5.		

Perspectives on socialisation

Sociological perspectives differ in how they interpret the role of socialisation in society. Whereas some sociologists emphasise the passivity of humans in the socialisation of their culture and regard individuals as 'cultural robots', others emphasise the more active part played by humans in the creation of the reality in which they live. The latter sociologists claim that humans are not puppets of society, but are endowed with 'agency'. To summarise:

- Functionalist sociologists tend to see socialisation as a positive means by which to ensure that the individual conforms to the rules of the wider group (see Chapter 3).
- Marxist sociologists see socialisation as a form of social control whereby the masses are expected to conform to dominant rules of the capitalist class (see Chapter 3).
- Interactionist sociologists see socialisation as the process by which a symbolic set of meanings about what social reality is like for those involved come to be shared (see Chapter 4).
- In a more contemporary argument, Anthony Giddens' 'structurational sociology' suggests that although the existing culture is instilled in individuals through the socialisation process, these same individuals contribute to the changing nature of this reality through their daily lives. For Giddens (1984) both structure and action should be combined if sociologists are to see the bigger picture of the relationship of the individual to society – to see how both cultural socialisation and individual free will contribute to the lives of those in society (see Chapter 5).

Exercise 2.16

In a copy of the following table, match the following statements to the theoretical views held by functionalists, Marxists, interactionists and structurational sociology:

Statement	Theoretical view
Culture is created by social actors, yet it also constrains them.	
Norms and values tell us how to live – we do not decide them, and we are punished if we do not follow them.	
Humans have agency or 'free will', they are not passive victims of culture.	
Individuals need to create a culture in order to interact with others.	
Culture and socialisation are tools designed and used by the powerful to retain their dominance over society.	
Norms and values are created through a process of agreement.	
Socialisation bonds individuals together.	

The nature versus nurture debate

When comparing the ideas of sociologists with those of sociobiology and Freud's psychoanalysis we can glimpse a key intellectual debate within many disciplines in the social sciences – the 'nature versus nurture debate'. Central questions are:

- Are we the product of culture or instinct?
- Do we learn how to behave or is behaviour inborn?

Within this debate we can identify two positions, as illustrated in the table below.

Nature	Nurture
This position is held by biologists, some psychologists, sociobiologists	This position is held by sociologists (although in different ways) and some psychologists
Action is inborn	Action is learnt/taught
Instincts shape culture	Culture is learned and therefore changes and varies a great deal between societies
Behaviour is preprogrammed	Behaviour is socialised (learnt)
Known as 'biological determinism'	Known as 'social determinism'

This debate is of central concern within sociology. Even if individual sociologists disagree over whether cultural constraint is positive or negative, all-embracing or limited, they all tend to favour the idea of culture over instinct, and focus on the idea of socialisation.

Feminism and 'being a women'

Early feminist thinker and philosopher Simone de Beauvoir wrote in her book *The Second Sex* (1972, first published in 1953) that '*One is not born, but rather, becomes a woman.*' What this means is that women are taught how to behave; that what we understand by 'femininity' is the product of culturally learnt behaviour rather than the result of biological preprogramming. This inspired a key theme in feminist thinking: that men and women might be biologically different in terms of their reproductive organs (their 'sex'), but the behavioural differences between men and women (called 'gender') are cultural creations, and therefore can be challenged and eventually changed. The Feminist views on the divide between 'sex' and 'gender' – between nature and culture – places feminist thought in direct opposition to the claims made by sociobiologists.

Exercise 2.17

The following statements are traditionally associated with either masculinity or femininity. Copy out the table and identify which statement is associated with masculinity and which with feminity.

Statement	Traditionally associated with masculinity or femininity?
Over-emotional	
More interested in sex than in love	
Concerned about their appearance	
Unable to make decisions	
Caring	
Good leaders	
Better at solving problems	
Better at making objects/products	
Physically strong	

Sociobiological ideas on the superiority of nature over nurture continue to this day, especially among some in the social scientific community, despite many years of feminist intellectual thought. Steve Jones (1994), in his book *The Language of the Genes*, suggests that what we often call the 'battle of the sexes' is not only real but is also rooted in the human genetic code: it is a fundamental feature of all animal species and is the basis of many features of evolution. Jones argues that conflicts over sex are behind all human society:

- Males and females are the result of a complex biological conflict within the womb of the biological mother.
- There is conflict between men to find a sex partner – and between women to find a sex partner.
- Men and women themselves conflict in society since they seek different things from life.

While Jones warns against comparing humans too closely with animals, he stresses that the fact that humans are animals should not be forgotten: nature is still more important than nurture. It is this type of argument against which many feminist thinkers protest. To state that the social and behavioural differences between men and women are natural is to justify male dominance and female subordination – known as 'patriarchy'.

Exercise 2.18

Imagine that you are a feminist sociologist. How would you respond to the types of argument raised by writers such as Steve Jones? Write a detailed answer of about 500 words.

Understanding the individual and society

Many modern sociological thinkers have suggested that the central issue or problem for sociological study is the relationship between the individual and society. In other words, the point of much sociological inquiry is to investigate the following questions:

- How is collective culture possible given that we are all individual beings?
- How is individuality possible, given that we share a common culture?
- Or, to use the terms used previously in this chapter, how does structure – the social system – control individuality?

In the words of Margaret Archer (1995), 'Necessarily then, the problem of the relationship between individual and society was *the* central sociological problem from the beginning. The ... task of understanding the linkage between "structure and agency" will always retain this centrality because it derives from what society intrinsically is.' This means that studying both culture and identity is vital for the sociologist:

- Studying culture allows an insight into the bigger picture, the social structure, how society is patterned and is thought of as a 'thing' by those who live in it.
- Studying identity, or rather identities, allows us to think about the meaningful role of humans as thinking beings who make up society.

Issues of 'structure' and 'action' or 'agency' have been the focus of much sociology since its foundation. This is due, as Archer states above, to this being the prime concern of many early sociologists. For example Bryan Turner (1984) suggests that early sociologists such as Emile Durkheim (see Chapter 3) operated with a view of the individual and society in which humans were seen as a product of natural desires that needed to be controlled by culture – not dissimilar, perhaps, from some of the themes that run through the work of Freud.

'Since man is both a member of nature by virtue of being an organism and a member of society by virtue of culture, some solution has to be found to this Jekyll-and-Hyde duplexity' (Turner, 1984). Turner suggests that, just like Freud and his psychoanalytic theory, many founding sociologists – including Emile Durkheim (1982) – were interested in the possible tensions between 'nature' and 'culture':

- For Freud, if culture prevents people behaving according to their nature this may lead to many psychological problems for the individual.

- For Durkheim, the function of culture is to act as a vital form of social constraint, keeping the individual bonded to the wider social group by supressing the natural desire for individuality.

As Durkheim argued in his classic text *The Elementary Forms of the Religious Life* (1982, originally published in 1912), 'Man is double. There are two beings in him: an individual being . . . and a social being which represents the highest reality in the intellectual and moral order that we can know by observation – I mean society.'

Evaluating the concept of 'culture': three problems

Problem 1: value judgement

In *The Myth of Mass Culture*, Alan Swingewood (1977, p. 26) suggests that 'Culture is not a neutral concept; it is historical, specific and ideological.' What Swingewood means by this is that when using the concept of culture we must be sure to consider whether all sociologists take the word to mean the same thing, even if they are using it in a similar way. Sociologists tend to look at the social world in different ways and therefore draw some very different conclusions. Often the concept of culture (like many others in sociology) has a political orientation or value judgement attached to its use. For example, whereas functionalists might see culture as vital since it bonds social members together, Marxists may see culture as a mechanism by which some groups maintain power over other groups. We should therefore be very careful when considering any sociological debate to ask ourselves the following question: what political values are used by this thinker, and how might this affect how he or she sees the world?

Link exercise 2.1

The next chapter (Chapter 3) deals in more detail with different theoretical interpretations of culture and identity (we shall also return to the subject later on in this chapter). For the time being, think about the two theoretical interpretations of culture raised in the text above:

- Culture as social bond.
- Culture as social control.

For each of the two, describe in writing how culture might act in this way. Then state which interpretation you favour the most and explain why. Complete this exercise in about 300 words.

Problem 2: choosing between cultures

When discussing the role of culture in society, and particularly when comparing different cultures and subcultures, sociologists tend to adopt one of two positions.

Firstly, one might believe there are absolute standards of taste and that some values are better than others. According to this view, some cultures and subcultures are better, more elite or more advanced/ developed than others because they are based on higher standards. This absolutism often leads to quite controversial political positions since if one culture is judged better than another, should the lesser culture be taught better values? In the past this argument was used to justify the Western world's colonial expansion and even slavery. It also has parallels in modern forms of racism (and even ethnic cleansing in modern Eastern Europe), where some people object to another group simply because they have different values. It is problematic to 'prove' in an objective fashion that one set of cultural ideas are better than another, since who is to say which cultural values are superior, and on what basis do they term their judgement?

The political and moral problems involved in valuing some cultures above others has led many sociologists to adopt a more relativisitic position when thinking about and comparing cultures. In this view, no one culture is 'correct' – rather, different cultures are simply different and should be tolerated as such. However this relativist position also raises many political and moral questions: if a culture is based on the oppression of a minority group, should we still value that culture as much as one that is based on tolerance and freedom? Or, are we simply judging other cultures by standards that should not be applied to them?

Problem 3: the myth of cultural integration

Margaret Archer (1996), echoing some of Raymond Williams's (1963) concerns about the word 'culture', suggests that the concept suffers from two main problems in modern sociological thought:

- The concept is too vague: there are too many unclear definitions and it means different things to different thinkers.
- The concept is interpreted by thinkers in two very different, extreme ways: either as a supreme power ruling over all and controlling all actions; or as shared meanings that individuals have the power to manipulate as they wish.

Archer suggests that modern sociology should clarify what it means by culture and what it thinks culture does. It is time to think again about the classical problem of the relationship of the individual to society. Archer argues that this problem stems from a wider problem that she calls the 'myth of cultural integration'. What she means by this is that while the various sociological theories interpret the role of culture in society differently, they all agree that culture is unifying, bonding everyone together into an integrated whole. Archer suggests that this assumed integration is a core myth of sociology, and it is a myth that has been perpetuated over time by many different sociologists and types of sociological theory: Marxism, functionalism and interactionism, to name but a few, although they use the idea of integration in different ways.

Exercise 2.19

Archers' ideas are important for two reasons:

- They identify a key theme that runs through the whole of sociology.
- They serve as a good criticism of the idea that we are all 'swamped' by our culture and are totally integrated into it.

Since her ideas are quite difficult to understand at first, reread the above passage and conduct the following tasks:

1. Write out Archer's ideas in your own words (approximately 100 words).

2. Describe how Archer's ideas can be seen as a criticism of functionalism and Marxism (approximately 100 words).

Understanding the concept of 'identity': do not lose sight of the individual

When we, as sociologists, talk about the culture of a whole society and about the subcultures of the smaller groups who make up this whole, we are in danger of losing sight of the role of the individual in society. In order to consider what individuals themselves think – both about themselves and about others – sociologists employ the concept of 'identity': the characteristics of thinking, reflection and self-perception that are held by people in society.

Defining 'identity'

A useful starting point when thinking about what 'identity', or rather 'social identity' might mean, is to view it as simply being able to 'know who you are'.

Exercise 2.20

Identity means 'knowing who you are'. Copy out the following table and list the things you think you are – the aspects of you as a person that make you who you are.

Feature of you as a person	Why is it important to who you think you are?
1.	
2.	
3.	
4.	
5.	
6.	

Compare your list with that of a friend.

1. How similar and how different are they?

2. What do you consider to be important to 'who you are as a person'?

Knowing who you are is a massive undertaking, requiring great mental reflection and contemplation, yet most of us probably 'know who we are'. That this can happen, that humans have a sense of who they are as a person, can be seen as vital for all social life. Without knowing who I am, how can I begin to understand what I do, and therefore what others around me do?

Richard Jenkins (1966) takes this theme of 'knowing who we are' further and defines social identity as:

> our understanding of who we are and of who other people are, and, reciprocally, other people's understanding of themselves and of others (which includes us). Social identity, is, therefore, no more essential than meaning; it too is the product of agreement and disagreement, it too is negotiable.

Jenkins suggests that social identity is so important to society that social life is unimaginable without it: we simply need to know who we are:

> Whether in the abstract or the concrete, with reference to ourselves or to others, in personal depth or during superficial casual chat, with reference to individuality, nationality, social class, gender or age . . . it seems that we cannot do without some concepts with which to think about social identity, with which to query and confirm who we are and who others are. . . . Without frameworks for delineating social identity and identities, I would be the same as you and neither of us could relate to the other meaningfully or consistently. Without social identity, there is, in fact, no society (ibid.).

Identity as an active construction

What is important about Jenkins' definition is his claim that identity is negotiable. The importance of the concept of identity for modern sociology is that it allows us to see humans as active, thinking beings, rather than the passive victims or 'robots' of the culture that controls them.

It is possible to distinguish between three related but subtly different forms of identity:

- *Individual identity*. Although in one sense this sort of identity is social since it is believed by many to be created through social interaction with others, individual identity is the unique sense of personhood held by each social actor in her or his own right.
- *Social identity*. By 'social identity' many sociologists mean a collective sense of belonging to a group, of individuals identifying themselves as being similiar to or having something in common with the other members of the group.
- *Cultural identity*. This concept refers to a sense of belonging to a distinct ethnic, cultural or subcultural group.

Exercise 2.21

in id a

Some sociologists think that we cannot act as we wish to – that we do not have free will or the right to make choices. Others insist that we are not controlled by society and are free to make choices. Which view do you find the most realistic and why?

1. List the situations in society where you are free to make choices (for example choosing your own clothes).

2. Now list the situations where you can make choices but they are very limited (for example choosing a school for your children).

3. Now make a final list of situations where you are forced to act in a certain way and have no choice in the matter (for example conforming to the law).

4. Which is the longer list? Write down what you think this might mean for the degree of freedom we do or do not have as members of a society.

Stuart Hall (1990) notes that 'Identity is not as transparent or unproblematic as we think. Perhaps instead of thinking of identity as an already accomplished fact, which the new cultural practices then represent, we should think, instead, of identity as a "production", which is never complete . . .' This image of a moving, fluid and dynamic identity is far removed from the idea held by some of the more traditional schools of sociological thought that humans are 'puppets of culture'. In Hall's view, identity is as much a process of becoming, as it is about what one is.

Identity and 'difference'

In 'knowing who we are' we not only call up notions of 'similarity' with others, but also notions of 'difference' from others. By noting that difference is as important an aspect of identity as similarity, we are able to draw an important distinction between what Kathryn Woodward (1997) refers to as 'essentialist' and 'non-essentialist' definitions of identity:

- *Essentialist definitions*. Such definitions suggest that each ethnic/cultural group has an absolute and rigidly fixed set of historical characteristics that make up its identity and are shared by all members of the group. Furthermore each cultural identity has one important and essential defining characteristic.
- *Non-essentialist definitions*. These focus on the characteristics shared by those in an ethnic/cultural group and the differences within the group – and between this group and others. These definitions also take into consideration the fact that identities change over time.

Imagined communities and postmodernism

Identity has been taken to mean 'knowing who one is' – having a sense of similarity with some people and a sense of difference from others. Due to the instilling of cultural values we can speak of identity as giving one a sense of belonging to a 'symbolic community' or an 'imagined community'.

As Anthony Cohen (1989) argues, the notions of 'community' that give rise to a sense of identity cannot be plotted on a geographical map nor can a community be understood as a common group of people controlled by the same state. Instead, the identification with a community is largely a symbolic process. It is based not on territorial lines but on the establishment of shared sets of meaning, the use of which enables people to act and interact with others, and with whom they can identify.

Some sociologists and philosophers, under the banner of postmodernism, claim that in the contemporary age identities are changing and are very different from those in the past. Postmodern writers – and writers who reject some of the claims of postmodernism, such as Anthony Giddens (1991) – have suggested that identities are become increasingly freer, ambiguous and plural in the postmodern age (see Chapters 5 and 6). Many postmodernist writers suggest that the (as David Harris, 1996, calls them) 'master identities' of class, age, gender and ethnicity are 'decomposing': they are falling away, to be replaced by new identities based on a whole range of sources, including consumerism, the body and sexuality.

Conclusion

Culture and identity have been key issues in sociology since its inception. They allow sociologists to discuss who we think we are and how we behave as individuals and groups. The concept of culture allows us to explain how and why different societies behave in different and unfamiliar ways. It also allows us to think about what it means to be human – are we the product of biology or of socialisation? Do we have free will or are we puppets of our culture? In what way are humans 'symbolic creatures'?

When discussing culture and identity we can engage in a debate with the 'ghosts' of the founders of sociology. We can look at the ideas that led to the birth of the subject and at the newer ideas that challenge many of the assumptions held by the founders. This postmodern challenge to the traditional sociology of identity will be explored later in this book, but first we need to consider how classical sociology and its founders viewed culture and identity.

Examination advice

The new Curriculum 2000 specifications offered by OCR and AQA both deal with issues of culture and identity, but differently. Whereas the OCR specification has clearly identifiable culture- and identity-related topic areas – with titles such as 'culture and socialisation', 'the individual, culture and society' and 'popular culture' – the AQA specification draws on culture and identity issues as general themes that run throughout the two-year course. For example in the topic areas of the media, education and deviance it is impossible not to discuss issues of culture and identity, but they are also central to all sociology.

For the AS examination, both examination boards use a mixture of stimulus or data-response questions plus extended writing questions. The A2 examations require essay-writing skills. Essentially, A2 answers should build on and extend the depth of AS work.

The key to getting a good overall mark in AS sociology is to:

- Use sources (if applicable) directly – make reference to them, and discuss and evaluate them.
- Make sure that the length and depth of your answer to each question are in accordance with the number of marks on offer.
- Use key sociological words for depth and detail.
- Make sure you understand the 'command' words used at the start of each question – that is, you should understand the differences and/or similarities between words such as evaluate, outline and assess, and phrases such as 'to what extent'.

The key to getting a good mark for AS questions with higher marks – extended writing questions – is to concentrate on the following – this is also true for the OCR essay questions at the AS level of assessment:

- Answer the question directly. Provide a conclusion at the end that directly addresses the actual point of the question – that is, whatever it is that the 'command' word at the start of the question asks you to do.
- Use key words and try to define or explain them within the 'flow' of what you are writing – this will considerably add to the depth of your answer.
- Try to quote studies and fit them into the question being asked – don't just list them, apply them to the specific issues in question.
- Link studies to theories or particular sociologists. Try to compare different types of sociology for evaluation purposes.
- Make evaluative criticisms of the data or source/stimulus provided (when relevant or applicable) and of studies and sociological ideas.

In the A2 examination your essay answers should:

- Be much more extensive in terms of length and points made.
- Have greater focus on the role that sociological theory has in the debate on and discussion of the topics in question asked.
- Be more evaluative.
- Have strong introductions and conclusions that weigh up the evidence and address the different sides of or solutions to the concepts in question.
- Make very clear links between theories, studies and key concepts.
- Demonstrate different interpretations of the same question, or even ideas or concepts from the viewpoint of more than one sociological theory.
- Demonstrate the interconnectedness of all sociological ideas and debates, in that an idea or concept applied in one topic area can be applied to another area – but ensure that you make its relevance clear.

Bearing this advice in mind, try writing an answer to the following mini-essay questions – the sort of questions you might find at the end of an AS stimulus or data-response question. Use the ideas presented in this chapter to help you.

(a) How important is socialisation for human societies?

(b) Evaluate the usefulness of the idea of 'culture' in helping us to understand the role of the individual within society.

3 Classical views on culture and identity

> By the end of this chapter you should:
>
> - be familiar with the classical/founding ideas of Marx and Durkheim;
> - be able to discuss the importance of the ideas of Marx and Durkheim to a modern sociology of culture and identity;
> - be able to apply functionalist and Marxist ideas to the modern world;
> - be able to evaluate functionalism and Marxism.

Introduction

Although the French thinker Auguste Comte (1798–1857), writing in the mid 1800s, is credited for coining the term 'sociology' to describe the scientific study of society, the modern discipline with which we are familiar owes a great deal to the legacy of three key thinkers, known collectively as the 'founders': the German political philosopher and economist Karl Marx (1818–83), the French sociologist Emile Durkheim (1858–1917), who was influenced by Comte's version of sociology, and the German social historian Max Weber (1864–1920), whose intellectual legacy we shall discuss in Chapter 4.

When first conceived, sociology was both macro (looking at the 'big picture') and scientific in nature. It was concerned to study the whole of social life – society was seen as a living, growing system made up of parts or elements that all contributed towards the whole in some way. The study of such a system, in order to understand the larger structure and pattern, was originally intended by Comte and Durkheim to be scientific in nature. This early sociology was known as 'positivism' – a term that still exists today. As Comte (1957) suggested in *A General View of Positivism*, first published in France in the mid 1800s, 'The primary object . . . of Positivism is two-fold: to generalize our scientific conceptions, and to systematize the art of social life.'

From its earliest days the purpose of sociology was to understand how society operates as a whole in order to help society to progress and develop further. According to Comte, his sociology was both *philosophy* and *polity*: both a scientific intellectual endeavour and a means by which to suggest ways forward to policy makers. This sociology was born out of the industrial revolution and the general personal, moral and intellectual upheavals this dramatic social change left in its wake.

Karl Marx suggested that his particular system of intellectual thought (he would not have actually used the word 'sociology' himself) was a scientific means by which to understand the key currents of social change that move the whole structure of society through history. As Marx noted in one of his numerous letters, the work by Charles Darwin on the evolution of the human species (see Chapter 2) 'serves me as a natural scientific basis for the class-struggle in history' (Marx, quoted in Beer, 1985). Equally, standing at Marx's grave at Highgate Cementry, London, in 1883 Friedrick Engels – Marx's friend and intellectual companion – said, 'just as Darwin discovered the law of development of organic nature, so Marx discovered the law of development of human history' (Engels, quoted in Kumar, 1986).

Marx believed, then, like Comte that intellectual study of the ways in which societies evolve and develop could be used to improve the nature of society. However the two writers drew very different conclusions as to how society could best be helped, given their very different political value judgements.

Exercise 3.1

The ideas of Marx and Durkheim are central to modern sociology and they influenced many sociologists writing after them. In a two-column table, list what you can remember from your studies so far of the ideas of Marx (column 1) of your table and those of Durkheim (column 2).

The 'classical sociology' of the founders had the following key features:

- A belief in social progress.
- An image of society as a system.
- The view that societies evolve through history.
- The idea that sociology can understand and solve social problems by scientific means.

These features have been labelled 'modernist' since the founders believed that modern industrial society represented the end achievement of all human history: the ultimate social progression.

Exercise 3.2

Sociology was born at the time of what historians refer to as the 'industrial revolution', which brought about major social change. Look up information on the industrial revolution in history books, other sociology books, CD-ROMs, the Internet and any other likely sources.

1. Take some notes on what happened.

2. How do you think this social change might have influenced the origins of sociology?

Modernist scientific sociology, which looked at the overall pattern of society as a system and at how structures controlled the individual, might seem far removed from the study of culture and identity. But this is not the case. Within these classical traditions of early sociological thought we find the basis of all of modern sociology. Most, if not all, contemporary thinkers have felt the need to 'debate with the ghosts of the founders'. Whether or not such debate might lead to agreement with the classical ideas, modern sociology has a huge debt to pay to the ideas of Marx and Durkheim and their views on culture and identity.

However, many of today's thinkers believe that society has moved on and changed in significant ways that were not foreseen by the founders, and that this social change has discredited a great deal of what the founders stood for. Some of these critics of the founders' 'modernity' use the term 'postmodern' for their particular type of theorising. Through the use of this term they are trying to indicate that profound change has recently taken place, especially with regard to culture and identity (see Chapter 6).

Introducing two classical views on culture

By studying first Durkheim and then Marx it is possible to identify two 'classical' or 'modernist' interpretations of the role that culture plays in social life – both from a position of structural sociology.

Interpretation one: Emile Durkheim

- Culture bonds the individual to the wider group through the socialisation process.
- Culture keeps potentially disruptive individuality at bay.
- Individual identity must be replaced by a collective group identity for society to 'work' in a state of consensus.
- Collective identity and culture are necessary for social order to be established and maintained.

Exercise 3.3

The ideas of Durkheim are essential to sociology, despite the fact that they were written a long time ago. Rephrase the above list in your own words, in detail.

Interpretation two: Karl Marx

- Culture – or 'ruling ideas and values' – is produced by a ruling group in order to justify its dominance over others.
- Culture acts as a constraint on the individual, leading to social order and control.
- Individuals must realise their true class identity in order to break free from ruling-class oppression.
- Class consciousness and identity leads to revolutionary social change, and to the creation of a new social type and a new social culture.

Exercise 3.4

Like those of Durkheim, Marx's ideas are still essential to sociology. Rephrase the above list in your own words, in detail.

Exercise 3.5

On the basis of the ideas presented so far in this chapter, and your answers to Exercises 3.3 and 3.4, which theory do you think is the most realistic – that of Durkheim or that of Marx? In order to help you decide, copy out and complete the table below.

List the ideas of Durkheim that you find most satisfactory	1. 2. 3. 4. 5.	Explain why:	
List the ideas of Marx that you find most satisfactory	1. 2. 3. 4. 5.	Explain why:	
What do you find unsatisfactory about the ideas of Durkheim?		What do you find unsatisfactory about the ideas of Marx?	
Which of the two theories do you prefer and why?			

The ideas of Durkheim and Marx: similarities and differences

Similarities

- Both Durkheim and Marx adopted a structural position – they saw society as a system made up of smaller parts.
- They both saw society as characterised by the existence of order, control and the constraint of individuals.
- Individuals were viewed as less important than groups.
- Individuals were seen as the 'puppets' of culture.

Differences

- Whereas Durkheim saw order as a necessary part of society, Marx believed that order was established through unequal power relations between the ruling class and the masses.
- Durkheim saw individual identity as a 'problem' (that is, it was disruptive) for the group to solve so that order and harmony could continue, whereas Marx thought that individual identity should be replaced by class identity so that class groups could overthrow the oppressive ruling elite through revolutionary struggle and conflict.
- Both believed that the social structure controlled the individual through the socialisation of values, but for Durkheim this was a positive situation, whereas for Marx it was a negative one.

Exercise 3.6

Copy out the following table and decide for each statement whether Marx, Durkheim or both would be most associated with it.

Statement	Marx, Durkheim or both?
Culture is a form of constraint	
Elite rules and values lead to power inequality in society	
Identity is most associated with one's role in the productive process and the economy	
People need to be bonded together	
Culture is a form of social control	
Cultural constraint is necessary for society	
Culture is a form of social cement	

Statement	Marx, Durkheim or both?
Culture exists as a structure over and above individuals	
Without culture there will be chaos	
Culture is simply a reflection of the rules of the powerful	

We shall now consider these two views in more detail, as well as more recent expressions of these ideas.

View one: culture as order – functionalism

While it is universally accepted that Emile Durkheim was the founder of the functionalist movement in sociology, there is much debate over how we should 'read' or interpret his ideas. Much of what English-speaking sociologists know of Durkheim comes from the translations by Talcott Parsons (1951) (this is also true of the ideas of Max Weber). There is considerable disagreement over whether Parsons' interpretation of Durkheim is the 'correct' one, or whether Parsons understood Durkheim only within the context of the 1950s American society in which he was living.

In current sociology there is great debate over the contemporary and future relevance of Durkheim's ideas and the wider theory of functionalism. Whereas some see the rise of Marxist theories in the 1970s, feminism in the early 1980s and postmodern ideas in the 1990s as evidence of the death of functionalism, others point to the rise of New Right and New Left ideas, which have points of comparison with some functionalist ideas and can even be seen as neofunctionalism (new functionalism).

Functionalism before Durkheim

The term 'functionalism' – or as it is sometimes known, 'structural functionalism' – was coined in the 1950s, but the label covers the work of a wide range of thinkers who preceded or followed Durkheim: the anthropologist Bronislaw Malinowski, Talcott Parsons and the nineteenth-century English sociologist Herbert Spencer. Like Marx, Spencer was influenced by Darwin's theory of evolution, although in a very different sense. Marx was interested in the evolution of class struggle and conflict, while Spencer was interested in how society as a living, growing 'organic' whole slowly developed and became more complex with the onset of industrialisation. In fact the phrase 'survival of the fittest', which is often credited to Darwin, was actually first used by Herbert Spencer himself!

Spencer asked 'What is a society?' in his book *The Principles of Sociology* (1971, first published in 1876). His answer (and others like it) was couched in terms of an 'organic analogy', where society was compared to a living creature: usually a human body – a highly modernist image. Spencer claimed that society is like a living body since it is more than simply the sum of its parts. The combination of all the components of society, and how they fit together, is more important than the components themselves. This is also true of the human body. Individually the parts of a body can do nothing, but combined in the right way they work together to maintain the whole. This is what we mean by a 'system'.

Exercise 3.7

Spencer (and Durkheim) claimed that society is like a body in that both society and the body have basic needs that must be fulfilled. Draw up a two-column table and list what you think are the basic needs of the body and the basic needs of society. Try to identify six examples of each.

Spencer suggests that society is a living thing as it:

- Grows in size (this was especially true with the arrival of industrialisation).
- Develops additional component parts over time ('differentiation').
- Each separate part of the whole develops and performs a specific function or task for the whole.
- The various parts are mutually dependent on each other – they are no use on their own.

Exercise 3.8

Further to your answer to Exercise 3.7, how might culture meet the needs of society? Draw up a list, then compare your list with someone else's.

Exercise 3.9

Spencer (and a number of others since him) viewed society as a huge, interlinked entity where individuals are controlled by wider forces. How realistic is this notion? Draw up a list of the weaknesses of this 'organic analogy'.

Since all the parts of the living system of society fit together and perform a function for the whole, order and solidarity (being 'bonded together') are vital to the smooth operation of the system. Culture is that which cements individuals to the whole, through the socialisation of norms and values and a collective identity. Individualism is potentially damaging to such a system.

Spencer's 'organic analogy' has been taken up by other writers, including Durkheim.

The historical context of Durkheim's work

To understand Durkheim's views on the orderly function of culture – the key feature of his sociology – we must think for a moment about the sort of society in which Durkheim lived. Not only was Durkhiem's sociology instrumental to the creation of modernist sociology, but Durkheim *the person* was the product of the rapidly developing modernity of the French society around him.

As Colin Sumner (1994) notes, a number of key social events occurred in France in Durkheim's time:

- The governmental system was changing and the Third Republic was established.
- The early stages of industrialisation were taking place.
- This industrialisation was followed by a period of economic depression.
- France was rapidly expanding as a colonial power.
- French culture (art, music, literature and so on) was flourishing.
- The death sentence for criminals (public execution by guillotine) was replaced by more 'humane' imprisonment.

According to Sumner, 'the old sat uneasily with the new. Times were changing and consequently so were ways of seeing' (ibid.)

Exercise 3.10

It is often useful to consider sociologists themselves as people who live in society and are therefore influenced by what happens around them. Look again at the list of changes that took place in France during Durkheim's life time. How do you think these might have influenced his ideas? Copy out and complete the following table.

Historical events	How might these events have influenced Durkheim's views on the nature of society?
1. The governmental system was changing and the Third Republic was established	
2. The early stages of industrialisation were taking place	
3. This industrialisation was followed by a period of economic depression	
4. France was rapidly expanding as a colonial power	

Historical events	How might these events have influenced Durkheim's views on the nature of society?
5. French culture (art, music, literature and so on) was flourishing	
6. The death sentence for criminals (public execution by guillotine) was replaced by more 'humane' imprisonment	

In light of the above, Durkheim's views on the relationship between culture, social order and the individual can only be understood by considering Durkheim as a theorist of social change.

Exercise 3.11

Like Durkheim, Marx lived in a period of change and this probably influenced his ideas. With the help of history books, biographies, the Internet and CD-ROMs, investigate the period in which Marx was writing and draw up a list of the historical changes that you think would have most influenced his sociological ideas.

Durkheim: looking at order in a time of social change

Durkheim can be seen as trying to provide a solution to what is known as the 'Hobbesian problem of order'. This 'problem', first posed by the English philosopher Thomas Hobbes, asks: how is order possible, given that by nature humans are greedy, competitive and do not live in harmony with each other? Durkheim answered this question by turning his thoughts to the role that culture plays in society: culture socialises the individual into the group, and in so doing creates social order. We might suggest that Durkheim was directed to thinking about the problems of order because French society, at the time when he was writing, was experiencing rapid social change.

Exercise 3.12

How might identity be threatened by social change? Present your answer to this question as a list of examples.

Durkheim suggested that the socialisation process instils a 'conscience collective' in the minds of the social group. This is made up of 'collective representations': shared norms and values that place special significance upon the group, and in so doing create a group identity. According to Durkheim (1972):

When individual minds are not isolated, but enter into close relation with, and act upon, each other, from their synthesis arises a new kind of psychic life. It is clearly distinct from that led by the solitary individual because of its unusual intensity. Sentiments created and developed in the group have a greater energy than purely individual sentiments.

Identity and the group

In *The Elementary Forms of the Religious Life*, (1982, originally published in 1912) Durkheim suggested that group rituals are essential for the socialisation process to work. He claimed, using ideas on the psychology of crowd behaviour borrowed from fellow French thinker le Bon, that group membership creates the psychologically correct atmosphere for the successful socialisation of cultural norms and values. In such situations – for example tribal religious ceremonies – individuality is submerged under a collective sense of identity.

Exercise 3.13

Durkheim's views on group identity can be applied to many more groups than the religious groups in his own example. Consider the supporters at a football match. How do the home team's supporters identify themselves as a group, separate from the opposing team's supporters? *Discuss your ideas with someone else and draw up a list of your answers.*

Durkheim argued that a 'division of labour' exists in modern social life, which has changed significantly due to industrialisation. A division of labour is when tasks are divided between many different people. Durkheim noted that in 'traditional' societies solidarity – individuals being bonded together – was based on their essential similarity, yet in an industrial society this similarity gives way to job specialisation and therefore people become dissimilar. How then, asked Durkheim, could order – solidarity – still be possible?

Durkheim drew a distinction between two types of solidarity:

- *Organic solidarity*: this is found in 'traditional societies' and is based on similarity between members.
- *Mechanical solidarity*: this is found in industrial/'modernist' societies where a specialised division of labour exists. Solidarity is ensured as the members of the group become increasingly interdependent: they have to rely on each other.

Therefore social order is maintained in the industrial age through the creation of a whole range of identities, based on one's position in the division of labour, but these identities are integrated into a common culture and a 'value consensus' due to increasing interdependence.

Norms, anomie and freedom

As we have seen, culture acts as a form of 'social glue'. However if order breaks down, if the norms are not followed, we have a state of what Durkheim called 'anomie' – normlessness:

> [with anomie] . . . since the conscience collective is weaker, the frictions which are thus created can no longer be so completely nullified. Common sentiments no longer have the same capacity to keep the individual attached to the group under any circumstances. Subversive tendencies, no longer having the same counterweight, occur more frequently (Durkheim, 1972).

Durkheim was particularly worried about the potential for increased anomie with the rise of organic forms of solidarity. He was also worried about the increase of suicide at times of social change due to the rise of anomie and loss of the order normally provided by the socialisation of cultural values. Durkheim believed that order and control through culture ultimately leads to human freedom. What he meant by this is that if human desires are not checked – if humans are allowed to exist in their 'natural' state without culture to constrain them – then they are open to irrational individualism. However if their nature is controlled by culture, then they are able to think rationally about the world they inhabit. This nature/culture duality in human beings and humanity's need for the constraint of culture is a key theme in all of Durkheim's work.

Durkheim suggested that the individual is made up of two elements:

- The individual being with selfish, 'natural', desires.
- The collective social being – the product of control by culture and socialisation, giving up natural desires in favour of collective moral sentiments.

This shows that since early days sociology has been concerned with the problems of the relationship of the individual to society (see Chapters 1 and 5).

Functionalism after Durkheim: Talcott Parsons

The American sociologist Talcott Parsons – like Durkheim and Spencer before him – saw society as a system of interrelated parts. It is culture that keeps the individuals who make up this system in order, through the creation of 'value consensus' by socialisation. This social system is made up of four key elements, or rather four key functions that must be performed by the subsystems to ensure the survival of the whole:

- A = *adaptation*: fitting into the environment and delivering the basic necessities of life. Fulfilled by the economic subsystem.

- G = *goal-attainment*: providing standards for behaviour and the direction of social development and change. Fulfilled by the religious and political subsystems.
- I = *integration*: ensuring that everyone follows the rules and fits into the wider group. Fulfilled by the legal subsystem.
- L = *latent pattern maintenance (latency)*: keeping the whole together through collective sentiments. Fulfilled by the cultural subsystem.

According to Parsons, culture performs the function of *'pattern maintence'* – it creates the collective symbols (for example religious symbols) that people internalise through socialisation and that help to bring about a shared sense of identity in a harmonious society.

Exercise 3.14

Copy out the following passage and fill in the blanks with the words listed below.

Functionalism is often associated with the ideas of Spencer, Durkheim and .... , although there is some disagreement about the interpretation of what Durkheim 'really meant'. Functionalism, although there are some similarities, is usually viewed as the opposite of .... , in the sense that functionalists see society as stable and in .... , whereas Marxists concentrate on the existence of class conflict. Culture is seen by functionalists to .... the individual to the group, often through what is called value consensus. Individuality is often seen as a .... for the smooth running of a .... society, and the .... , brought together by 'moral unity', is seen as the most suitable way for society to function. This moral unity creates a sense of .... identity, which helps to avoid the problem of anomie or 'normlessness'.

Missing words

- bond
- Parsons
- stable
- problem
- harmony
- collective
- group
- Marxism

Neofunctionalism and the 'radical Durkheim'?

Jeffrey Alexander (1985) suggests that it might be time for sociological analysis to return to functionalist ideas, although what he is suggesting is more of a reworking of Parsons' work – a sort of neo-Parsonianism – than of the whole of functionalism. According to Alexander:

No one knows where such developments will lead, whether a neofunctionalist school will shape contemporary sociology in less conspicuous ways. In the past, Parsons' controversial reputation meant that even some of the participants in this revival were loathe to acknowledge his influence. The movement to reappropriate Parsons in a neofunctionalist way is gaining momentum. Whether it is simply old wine in new bottles, or a new brew, is something history will decide (ibid.)

This reworking would reject some elements of Parsons' work and retain others. In particular, Alexander wishes to reject the notion that the life and actions of people are totally shaped by structural forces. In this sense Alexander is rejecting the traditional argument that culture shapes the destiny of the individual through the internalisation of values through socialisation, in favour of a model where society is still seen as a system, but one that is in a state of change or flux.

In *The Radical Durkheim*, Pearce (1989) suggests a reworking not of Parsons' work but that of Durkheim. In this 'new Durkheimianism', Pearce suggests that Durkheim was not a theorist of consensus but of conflict, and in this sense his work can be seen as paralleling that of Marx. Although – mainly from Parsons – we have an interpretation of Durkheim as a theorist of the harmony and solidarity of society through culture, he does consider the problems of disorder, conflict and deviance – through his idea of anomie and his concern for the growth of individualism. This new 'radical' Durkheim would not be writing from a right-wing political position as Parsons did, but much more from a liberal or even a socialist stance – advocating the morality of the community for the good of the whole. This version of Durkheim has many parallels with the ideas of the New Left – especially those held by the 'New Labour' Party under Tony Blair.

It is interesting to note that Durkheim's work is so wide-ranging that it has influenced not only the New Left but also the New Right. The term New Right is a label given to the political thinking of the British Conservative Party in 1979–97 under the leadership of Margaret Thatcher and during the 'Reagan years' in American politics. The New Right are often seen as inheriting the intellectual legacy of functionalism because both theories stress the role of collective moral sentiments in the creation of harmony, order and discipline in society. The New Right claim that a moral rejuvenation of society is needed, otherwise order and 'traditional moral values' will collapse, to be replaced by a rising tide of normlessness – not too far from Durkhiem's own concern about the rise of anomie in society.

The strengths of functionalism

- It allows us to think about the nature of the social system as a whole.
- It explains the process of socialisation and how culture can create order in society.

Consider the two strengths of functionalism listed above. Draw up a list of further strengths.

The weaknesses of functionalism

- Marxist sociologists would suggest that functionalism overemphasises the role played by consensus in society at the expense of conflict.
- It treats humans as puppets or victims of their culture.
- It is often described as having an 'oversocialised' conception of the individual since it assumes that the socialisation process is able to subsume everyone into the group.
- It treats society as a living thing, more important than the individual.
- Interactionist sociologists would criticise the fact that functionalists see individuals as passive, ignoring their active role in creating culture through meaningful interaction.

View two: culture as ideological control – Marxism

Whereas Durkheim and the wider functionalist movement see society as a system based on harmony, consensus and order, for Marxists society is structured as a pattern of conflict – even if, for a great deal of the time, the individuals who live in a society might not consciously recognise this. According to this 'conflict structural' perspective, the existence of conflict and power inequalities in society are due to the existence of different classes and the struggle for power between these classes. For Marx, writing in the mid 1800s, the single most important feature of society was the existence of class. The opening line of his famous *Communist Manifesto*, written in 1872 with Friedrich Engels states: 'The history of all hitherto existing society is the history of class struggles.'

Marx's social theory was based on the prediction that class conflict would disappear after the fall of capitalism. Marx's ideas proved to be very powerful, not just in sociology but also in the world as a whole: governments were toppled, monarchies were overthrown and whole societies claiming to be 'Marxist' or 'communist' in character were created.

Class and conflict

Class is an economic category and usually refers to the amount of economic power and material wealth an individual has. Those who share a position of power in common with others – based on their material and economic wealth – can be said to be in the same class as each other. Marx himself defined class in a very succinct way: there are only two class groups – those who own 'the means of production' and those who do not. The latter have no choice but to sell their labour power to (work for) the former. Marx referred to the ruling class as the 'bourgeoisie' and the working class as the 'proletariat'. He saw the relationship between the classes as one of inequality: the oppression of the powerless masses by the powerful ruling class. Marx suggested that class forces move and shape the direction taken by the history of any given society. This was a highly 'modernist' claim (see Chapter 6), based on three key ideas:

- Evolution.
- 'Teleology'.
- 'Dialectical force'.

Marx was influenced by the ideas of Charles Darwin and his theory of evolution. When Marx was formulating his economic and philosophical ideas the concept of evolution – which is taken for granted today – was new and revolutionary. Darwin proposed that the historical evolution of all species is based on the principle of 'natural selection'. Individuals compete with each other for the resources required for survival, and only those with characteristics most suited to their environment will survive and pass on those favourable characteristics to their offspring. This process continues incrementally over time, each new species gradually developing out of earlier forms. Marx borrowed this notion of slow evolutionary change, where one change leads to the development of a second, and so on, and applied it to the evolution of human societies overtime. He claimed that as class power changes, so does the nature of the society in question. Essentially, social change is the result of the conflict between class groupings.

Marx's views on how societies change over time were highly 'teleological'. This concept was formulated by religious thinkers who saw the direction of universal change as a purposeful (rather than causal) movement towards a defined goal, usually directed by a God or gods. Marx's view of history was teleological in the sense that he saw change as having a purpose and a direction. Marx divided human social history into five stages, or social types, called 'modes of production':

- Primitive communism.
- Slavery.

- Feudalism.
- Capitalism.
- Communism.

Marx argued that it was conflict between classes that governed these changes and the direction they took. To explain this Marx borrowed an idea from the German philosopher Hegel – an idea known as the 'dialectic'. A dialectical force is when two opposites come together, conflict and produce a new outcome – a change. For Hegel:

- Thesis + antithesis = synthesis.

Or

- One idea + another idea = conflict/debate = new idea.

For Marx:

- Ruling class + subordinate class = class conflict = revolution.

Marx suggested that those who own the means of production conflict with those who do not, and the result of this conflict is dramatic or 'revolutionary' change and the creation of a new social type, where the previous subordinate class becomes the dominant class. The process continues until, finally, communism is reached. For Marx the word 'communism' meant the collective or communal ownership of the means of production. Since in this social type there is no dominant class – in fact there is no class at all – there can be no more social change through dialectical forces. This social type is therefore seen as the ultimate type, the evolutionary result of the march of history: a very teleological image.

Class consciousness and social identity

Marx argued that revolutionary change can occur only when the working classes become fully aware of the oppressive conditions in which they live. In other words, the working classes are exploited by the ruling or 'capitalist' class to the point where they simply cannot endure hardship and inequality any longer: 'What the bourgeoisie, therefore, produces, above all, is its own grave-diggers. Its fall and the victory of the proletariat are equally inevitable' (Marx and Engels, 1985).

This revolutionary change occurs only as a result of a change in consciousness and identity on the part of the working classes themselves. Marx referred to this as a movement from a class 'in itself' to a class 'for itself'. In other words the members of the working classes realise the nature of their situation and begin to develop a class identity that allows them to develop solidarity with their fellow members and act against their oppressors. Before the working class becomes a 'class for itself' with the development of a class identity, the realities and problems of society are largely hidden from them. This state of deluded consciousness, this illusory world in which they live, is referred to as a state of 'false class consciousness'. Marx believed culture serves to create and perpetuate this state of 'false consciousness' in society. The aim of Marxist sociology is therefore to expose society for what it really is, and in doing so to create 'true class consciousness'.

Economic forces and culture

Marx's views on class are known by the term 'historical materialism' since he believed that economic production ('materialism') has been responsible societal change throughout history. In terms of the structure of the social system, economic productive forces are also key. Marx divided the social system into two:

- The economic base (also known as the 'substructure' or 'infrastructure').
- The superstructure.

This division is based on the material and non-material components of the social system and can be further divided as follows:

<table>
<tr><td>Economic base</td><td>Superstructure</td></tr>
<tr><td>↓</td><td>↓</td></tr>
<tr><td>Material components
(how production is organised)</td><td>Non-material components
(how culture develops)</td></tr>
<tr><td>↓</td><td></td></tr>
</table>

1. Means of production
2. Social relations of production

'Means of production' refers to everything needed to produce goods: factories, machinery, raw materials and so on. 'Social relations of production' refers to the nature of the relationship between those involved in the productive process, namely the exploitation and oppression of the masses by the ruling class.

The economic base – how production is organised – shapes everything in the superstructure. This way of thinking is often referred to as 'economic determinism' since economic forces shape or 'determine' everything else – including the culture of a society. Hence those who control the productive process (the ruling classes, since they own the means of production) are those who have the power over society – the power to control and shape the nature of the values and norms of that society, its rules, religion, education and so on. Marx believed that the ruling classes use the superstructure (the culture of a society) for their own purpose: to hide the true nature of society from those they rule over.

The dominant ideology thesis

Since those who control the economic base control the society's culture, it follows that they control the dominant values of that culture, and the socialisation process is a mechanism with which to ensure the control of the working class through the creation of false consciousness.

In their classic work *The German Ideology*, written between 1845 and 1846, Marx and Engels (1974) stated that 'The ideas of the ruling class are in every epoch the ruling ideas, i.e. the class which is the ruling *material* force of society, is at the same time its ruling *intellectual* force.' In modern-day sociology this statement has become known as 'the dominant ideology thesis' since Marx and Engels argued that the ruling cultural ideas of a society are handed down, ready-made, by those who are dominant and powerful. They continued:

> The class which has means of material production at its disposal, has control at the same time over the means of mental production, so that thereby, generally speaking, the ideas of those who lack the means of mental production are subject to it (ibid.).

This is a theory of culture that sees culture as a form of constraint, as a form of control, and individuals as largely the puppets of this control if they suffer from false consciousness.

Culture as ideology

The key Marxist concept with which to understand this cultural control by 'ruling ideas' is 'ideology'. Culture is seen to contain a ruling-class ideology that is socialised into the consciousness of the individuals living in a society. In order to define 'ideology' we shall look at two sociologists' consideration of the term:

> The particular conception of ideology is implied when the term denotes that we are sceptical of the ideas and representations advanced by our opponent. They are regarded as more or less conscious disguises of the real nature of a situation, the true recognition of which would not be in accord with his interests (Mannheim, 1960).

In this view ideology consists of ideas that are purposefully incorrect. These ideas are used by their formulators to control others. Ideology is thus deliberately created by the powerful to ensure their continuing domination through the manipulation of others by means of false ideas:

> By ideology I mean the mental frameworks – the languages, the concepts, categories, imagery of thought, and the systems of representation – which different classes and social groups deploy in order to make sense of, define, figure out and render intelligible the way society works . . . the theory of ideology helps us to analyse how a particular set of ideas comes to dominate the social thinking of a historical bloc . . . and maintain its dominance and leadership over society as a whole. It has especially to do with the concepts and the languages of practical thought which stabilize a particular form of power and domination (Hall, 1996).

In this view, different groups (the powerful and the powerless) have their own ideologies – their own world views – and the battle between these ideologies is a struggle for power. An ideology, if it becomes dominant throughout society, gives people a language and rules, which they use to understand the world around them. Hence ideological struggle is a struggle over the 'correct' way to think.

Exercise 3.16

Consider the ideas of Karl Mannheim and Stuart Hall on ideology. Then rewrite their views in your own words and describe what 'ideology' is for each of these two writers.

In general, ideology refers to ideas, images, values and representations that justify a position of power. They are used by those in such a position to maintain their rule, at the expense of those they rule over. It is ideology that culture gives to the masses and that keeps them in a state of illusion – and even self-delusion – as to the real workings of the social system. It is ideology that Marxism seeks to fight against.

Exercise 3.17

When studying sociology for the first time it is very easy to become confused and worried by the range of specialist terms and difficult language. This language is important, however, since it provides an easy way – eventually – to think about and discuss some quite difficult but important ideas. Use the above discussion of Marxist views on culture and identity to define the following key Marxist words/terms:

- Class
- Mode of production
- Superstructure
- Ideology
- Means of production
- False class consciousness

Now use these words to write a summary paragraph of the Marxist view on the role of culture in society.

Examples of ideology: religion, education and the mass media

Religion

Writing in 1844, Marx contended that 'Religion is the sigh of the oppressed creature, the heart of a heartless world, just as it is the spirit of an unspiritual situation. It is the opium of the people' (Marx and Engels, 1984). In this view, religious values are a part of culture that instils an ideological view of the world to justify capitalist oppression. Marx compares these values to a drug – opium.

Education

Bowles and Gintis (1976) note that the values underpinning schooling in capitalist society – through what is described as the 'hidden curriculum' – are ideological since they represent the dominant ideology of the time. These values further the power of the ruling class by creating a false consciousness in the minds of the working classes: teaching them to obey authority, not to question the need to do mundane tasks and so on. Paul Willis (1977) includes a similar theme in his book *Learning to Labour*, where he argues that the function of schools in capitalist society is to prepare working-class children for a life of labour under capitalism.

The mass media

Adorno and Horkheimer (1993), who were members of the Frankfurt School (see Chapter 2) during the lead-up to the Second World War, suggested that the commercial development of the mass media had led to a 'mass culture' based on intellectual sameness, which prevented critical thought and in so doing sustained capitalist ideological rule (see Chapter 7).

Exercise 3.18

This exercise requires you to consider how religion, education and the mass media might control ideas in society. List your ideas in a three-column table with the following headings:

1. How does religion contribute to ideological control?

2. How does education contribute to ideological control?

3. How do the mass media contribute to ideological control?

in **id** **a**

Commodification and commodity fetishism

For the Frankfurt School, a key feature of modern culture was the creation of a 'culture industry', where cultural products lose their intellectual and critical value and become cheap, non-artistic and throwaway. The problems of consumerism also concerned Marx. He suggested that a process of 'commodification' of culture takes place under capitalism where cultural products are reduced to how much money they can be bought and sold for, rather than for the pleasure they can give to individuals.

Equally, Marx argued that if society becomes too obsessed with the purchase of cultural goods then humans enter into a state of 'fetishism' with 'things' and almost worship things for what they have come to stand for – that is, money, wealth and status. Because of this, capitalism is allowed to continue since it is seen to 'deliver the goods'. For Marx – and for the Frankfurt School – this fetishism is based on false ideological wants, manipulated by capitalism through advertising in the media.

The strengths and weaknesses of Marxism

Strengths

- Unlike functionalism, Marxism recognises the role played by conflict in social life.
- It illustrates the unequal nature of social life.
- It attempts to help those without power to think about their situation more clearly.
- Like functionalism it provides a way of thinking about the overall picture of the social system.

Weaknesses

- Marxism assumes that people live in a state of delusion about the world they live in.
- It resorts to a 'conspiracy theory' in order to explain how power inequality continues.
- It sees society as a system made up of two groups and does not really consider the role of the individual.
- Feminists would suggest that class inequality is focused on at the expense of gender.

Exercise 3.20

Consider the above strengths and weaknesses of the Marxist position. Which list outweighs the other? Do you see more of the strengths of Marxism or more of the weaknesses as important? Write an explanation of which list you think is more important, and why (about 150 words).

Marxism after Marx

Although Marx wrote in the 1800s and is considered to be one the of founders of sociology, his ideas did not become a popular or established part of the sociological world-view until the 1970s. Marxist theory today covers a wide range of ideas and variations. A distinction is usually made between classical/traditional Marxism, as discussed in this chapter, and what is called neo-Marxism or new Marxism.

Within neo-Marxism there are many different varieties and versions (see Chapters 7, 8 and 10), and many Marxist ideas have been taken up by other sociological branches, such as feminism (see Chapter 11) and interactionist sociology (see Chapter 4). Neo-Marxist ideas have developed for the following reasons:

- What many see as the failure of the 1917 Russian revolution to achieve true communism without resorting to the establishment of an oppressive regime.
- The discovery in the 1970s of previously unknown texts by Marx, which led to renewed interest in his ideas.
- Periods of economic depression in the 1970s in the West, which caused some to turn to the subject of class to explain such events.
- The predicted Marxist revolution in the UK failed to materialise.
- The constant updating and re-evaluation of ideas within academic sociology.

Exercise 3.21

In sociology at the moment there is considerable debate about the relevance of the founders' ideas in today's world. How relevant do you think their ideas are? Write an explanation of your view, stating the reasons why you think as you do (about 200 words).

Conclusion

The 'modernist' sociologies of Marx, Durkheim and their followers tend to view humans as being manipulated by their cultures. Identity is seen as something given by the group rather than created by the individual for him- or herself. The influence on sociology of Marxist and Durkheimian ideas has been massive – without these ideas sociology would not be the discipline it is today. However, many of the assumptions held by these thinkers have come under attack in contemporary sociology. The most serious challenge to the popularity of Marxist ideas has been the rise of theories described as 'postmodern', as will be explained in Chapter 6. However, along with the ideas of Durkheim and Max Weber, those of Marx will continue to feature in sociological debates on culture and identity because of their foundational role. In the next chapter we turn to the ideas of the last of the three founders – Weber – and his attempts to evaluate Marxism.

Examination questions

Use the advice on pages 28–9 to answer the following questions:

(a) Evaluate the Marxist view that dominant culture always reflects the interests of the powerful.

(b) Assess the argument that common cultural values lead to stability in society.

4 Socialisation, identity and the life-course: the development of 'action' sociology

By the end of this chapter you should:

- be able to evaluate the ideas of Marxism and functionalism from an 'action' standpoint;
- have knowledge of the contribution made by Max Weber to the understanding of culture and identity;
- understand the ideas of 'action' sociology;
- understand how action sociology has influenced the contemporary development of sociology as a whole.

Introduction

From our discussion of Durkheim and Marx in Chapter 3 we can identify two basic views on culture and identity. The first view, from Durkheim, suggests that culture binds the individual to the group and instils a collective identity. The second view, from Marx, is that culture is a form of constraint, used to justify inequality and to hide the true nature of an exploitative society. Both of these views, although different, come from a sociological tradition that can be described as 'structural' or adopting a 'systems' approach to viewing and studying society.

Exercise 4.1

In your own words (about 400 in all) briefly summarise the two views outlined above, based on knowledge you have gained from the previous chapters. Use named examples and the key words that each view would utilise. Explain what these words/ideas mean as you go along.

The work of the German social historian Max Weber at the turn of the twentieth century provided a very different interpretation of the role of culture and identity. Weber did not write from a 'structural' position, rather he adopted what we call an 'action' or a 'micro' approach. The basis of the action approach to sociology is:

- Humans are not passive victims of the social structure.
- 'Society' does not exist as a 'thing', but rather as a series of actions and interactions by individuals.
- Social life 'makes sense' – it is meaningful to those involved in its day-to-day creation.
- Sociology and sociologists can only study the reality of society by looking at the micro level – that is, by looking at the smaller picture: what people actually do, and what they think about what they do.

Exercise 4.2

Consider the above list of key ideas of the 'action' approach to sociology. Rewrite each one into your own words and give an example of each.

Exercise 4.3

The ideas of Max Weber – like those of Durkheim and Marx (Chapter 3) – are important to a great deal of sociological discussion. Brainstorm what you know about the ideas of Weber from your studies so far.

Weber was not interested in society as a 'thing', nor in humans as the puppets of culture. Rather he believed that humans make history and society through what they do – there are no underlying rules or 'logic' to the pattern of history. In this view culture is created by humans through the meanings and motives they hold, which allows them to make sense of what they do. Identity is important in interaction since it is the basis of how people think they should fit in, and therefore what they think they should be doing.

Exercise 4.4

In a copy of the following table, give an example of each of the observations made by Weber.

Observations made by Weber	Example
Humans make history and society through what they do	
There are no underlying rules or 'logic' to the pattern of history	
Culture is created by humans through the meanings and motives they hold	
Culture allows people to make sense of what they do	
Identity is important in interaction since it is the basis of how people think they should fit in	

With Weber's ideas we have a third view of culture and identity – that culture is made up of meanings and motives for action, and is created by individuals in an active fashion.

The role of meanings and motives in society

Although Weber's emphasis on the role of action, consciousness and meanings in culture place his ideas firmly within an 'action' sociology framework, his broader sociological ideas are less easy to label in this fashion. What makes Weber an interesting sociologist – and a powerful influence – is that many of his ideas appear to cross the divide between structure and action.

Weber argued that all sociological explanations should strive to be 'adequate' on two levels: at the level of 'meaning' – called '*verstehen*'; and at the level of 'causality' – called '*erklaren*'. Put another way, Weber advocated an approach to studying the individual and society that seeks to understand what individuals do (and what they think of what they do) – *verstehen* – and then to determine how this fits into the bigger picture of social life – *erklaren*. Weber's major contribution to sociology was the idea of trying to achieve *verstehen* in social research. This idea can be described as 'seeing the world through the eyes of those involved'. Many action sociologists since Weber have taken up the idea of *verstehen*. The claim is made that to understand the reality of what society is, and how it works, we must look at how individuals make sense of what they do, in an active fashion. The task of sociology is to see how culture socialises a collective set of symbols into a group of people, who then use these symbols to gain an understanding of what they do, what others do and what others expect them to do.

The aim of action sociology is to look at the meanings and motives of action and interaction through the eyes of those doing the acting. For Weber, individuals do not act unless they have a reason or 'motivation' for doing so. All action makes sense to those doing it, even if it might not to an outside observer. Individuals are seen to hold a 'subjective meaning' of what they do, and this meaning is created by the individual through interaction with others.

Exercise 4.5

Action sociologists – or as we some times call them, interactionists – are interested in the role played by individuals' meanings and motives.

1. In a two-column table, list your reasons (motivations) for attending school (column 1) and the reasons for doing your homework (column 2).

2. How do meanings and motives make action possible? (Approximately 150 words.)

According to action sociology, culture is the collective sets of meanings, values and motives that together make up the 'subjective understandings' of all those involved in the creation of society. In this interpretation, culture is not a 'thing', but something that individuals do. It is a process: dynamic and fluid and produced by individual consciousness. Individual identity is also important in the processes of action and interaction, since without a sense of who they are it will be difficult for individuals to think about:

- how they wish to behave;
- who other people are;
- why others behave as they do;
- how others expect them to behave towards them.

Identity is essential if meaningful interaction is to take place amongst a society of thinking, creative, conscious and active individuals.

Exercise 4.6

 Weber proposed that we should study the meanings and motives individuals have in their minds. Why do you think it might be useful for a sociologist to study these? Write out your answer and explain your view in about 150 words.

To summarise the ideas of Weber:

- Society is not a 'thing' that exercises control over the individual through culture. Instead it is actively created by individuals.
- Individuals need to have motivations for what they do, and they reflect upon these – they are not simply subsumed into the group identity and stripped of all individual consciousness.
- Culture has no overall pattern that controls and moulds the individual – such patterns only exist in the minds of those who, in their day-to-day life, create culture by interacting with each other.

The role of cultural ideas in history

In *The Protestant Ethic and the Spirit of Capitalism*, first published in 1905, Weber provides us with both an account of how values and meanings work within culture, and an evaluation of Marx's ideas about how classes affect the evolution of society (see Chapter 3). Marx argued that:

- Class division is the most important factor in a society.
- Societal evolution can be divided into five key stages, through which all cultures will travel.

- Class conflict moves society ever onward towards its ultimate destiny – communism.
- This historical pattern can be predicted in advance.

Whereas for Weber:

- Societal evolution is haphazard and accidental.
- It is human action and interaction that cause social change and societal evolution.
- The outcome of this interaction can never be predicted in advance.
- Cultural ideas and values are independent of the economy and of how production is organised (a key difference between Weber and Marx).

In order to evaluate Marx's contention that class conflict was the force behind social change, Weber looked at the formation of industrial capitalist societies in Western Europe. According to Marx, these were an inevitable feature of history, and had to come about through conflict between merchants and the aristocracy in the feudal mode of production. For Weber, however, capitalism was the accidental and unintended outcome of the meaningful actions and interactions of a group of Calvinist Protestants, following their particular religious values and trying to make life meaningful.

The Calvinists were a Protestant sect who broke away from the Roman Catholic Church because they felt that Catholicism was becoming too 'decadent' – too concerned with worldly and material goods and wealth. The Calvinists had a very particular set of ideas, with which they made sense of the world around them, and which, like any other meaningful set of motivations, allowed them to make sense of their action and interaction in society. The Calvinists believed that everyone should have a 'calling' in life: a pursuit that one should follow single-mindedly in order to show one's devotion to God. In this view hard work was a virtue. People should not waste time or be lazy, but should devote themselves to their calling. For the Calvinists, just who was destined to enter heaven after their death had been decided at the moment of 'creation' (of the earth) – only a select few (the 'elect') would meet God in the afterlife. Finally, success in one's calling was an indication of God's favour – a sign that one might be one of the elect.

Weber argued that the specific cultural values of this religious group led them to act in a very particular way that made sense to them: to work hard, and rather than spend their financial rewards, to plough them back into their businesses – back into their 'calling'. This meaningful set of motivations, this 'Protestant ethic', was responsible for the creation of what Weber termed 'the spirit of capitalism'. Not actually capitalist society as such, but the necessary cultural ideas needed for others to come along and use them as the basis of meaningful interaction. In this way the values of a small group – the Calvinists – accidentally led to the establishment of a whole society based on the pursuit of profit through reinvestment. Later the capitalist economic idea spread across the globe – from simple yet highly meaningful cultural values. Weber used this historical example to illustrate, in contradiction to Marx, that history cannot be predicted, and that culture is created and given meaning by those involved in its production.

Exercise 4.7

Copy out the following table and decide whether each statement would be said by Marx or by Weber.

Statement	Would this be said by Marx or Weber?
Class is the most important feature of society	
Culture is a structure above the individual	
We must understand the role of meanings in action	
We must understand the role of ideology in making people follow the rules of society	
History moves through five identifiable stages	
History is unpredictable	
Class causes all social change	
Capitalism will inevitably lead to communism	
Capitalism is a historical accident	
Humans cause social change through their actions	

Georg Simmel

Although in many respects Weber's sociology attempted to bridge the divide between action and structure, his idea of *verstehen* and the role played by meanings and motives in culture and identity have been taken up by a great number of action sociologists. Before we look at these ideas we shall discuss the work of a contemporary of Weber who shared with him an image of the active and creative interactional human in culture.

Simmel (1950) also saw society as being made up of individual members who acted with full consciousness. Rather than looking at society as a structure or system over and above the individual – as in Durkheim's image of the social system as a living thing – Simmel concentrated on the role played by humans in the creation of social life. To say that for Simmel social life did not display any sort of pattern is not true. Simmel (1955) used the term 'web of group affiliations' to denote the points of intersection between the lives of individuals that when added together could be seen as a giant map or web of interactions extending over the whole of society.

Simmel drew a distinction between the *form* of social life and the *content* of social life. By this he meant that some very stable patterns ('forms') appear in different cultures and within the same culture over time. In our society we call these patterns family, education, work, religion and so on. These continue to exist over time in an easily recognisable form, but within these common patterns the day-to-day lives that we live ('content') are highly unique. Therefore common *forms* exist in each culture, but the *content* of social life varies according to the individual in question. The key feature of this web of interactions that we call 'society' is that it is based on action and interaction. It is based on exchanges of meaning, and as such it is dynamic, open and fluid. Society is a process of exchange, a 'happening' made possible by the collective efforts of many.

For Durkheim (see Chapter 3), if social order is to be achieved individual identity has to be subsumed into the group through the process of socialisation. For Simmel, social life, for each individual involved in the wider 'web', is a tension between two forces: individual identity and social/group identity. Simmel saw individuals not as 'passive robots of culture' but as creative agents trying to work out the meaning of their lives, and in doing so, trying to retain a sense of who they are in the face of pressures from the group. This idea that the individual is split into two and needs to find a way to reconcile both identities in her or his day-to-day life is a popular theme in classical social theory, especially in the work of Freud and Durkheim. It is described as 'homo duplex': the two sides of humanity (see Chapters 2 and 3). One side is the 'natural' side, which is engaged in a struggle against the side created by culture or society.

One of the characteristics of Simmel's work was that his choice of topics was varied and he often chose some interesting themes to study. One of these was the significance of fashion for identity. Simmel (1957) suggested that social life is a struggle between individuality and group identity. Or in other words, between acting in a unique way and copying the actions of the wider group. The first is motivated by attempts to preserve one's individual identity, the second by attempts to 'fit in' with the others around us. Simmel suggested that this is a tension within all of us: the tension between being authentic to one's true wishes on the one hand, and feeling accepted by others and having a place in the group on the other. 'Identity' is thus not simply something that is handed down by culture or by the group, it is also something that we try to retain some control over through our actions.

In this context, fashion is seen as a means by which to establish who we are in an ever-changing world, a world where we enter into struggles with others on a daily basis, struggles over who we are, who we think we should be and how we are seen by others.

Exercise 4.8

Simmel described fashion as a mask behind which we can hide – a way we can convey to others what we want them to think who we are.

Copy out the following table and in the right-hand column describe how different items of fashion might say different things about who we think we are, and who we think others are.

Fashion item	What might this say about our identity?
A brand new pair of fashionable trainers	
A new MP3 player	
A leather jacket and torn jeans	
Basketball boots	
Lots of gold jewellery	
A Japanese character tattoo	
Combat trousers and a body warmer	
A pierced navel	
A shaven head	
A designer dress	

The 'dark side' of identity in the modern age

Unlike those of some of the other early sociologists, Weber's and Simmels' versions of what 'modernity' (see Chapter 6) or industrial society might do for individual identity are at times pessimistic. For example Weber suggested that in the modern age individual identity might find itself locked into an 'iron cage of bureaucracy'. Individuals could be trapped into a life of petty rules and procedures with no sense of creativity – an awful future for active and creative individuals.

Simmel suggested that day-to-day life in the city might have important effects on one's sense of identity. He noted that the city – or as he called it, the 'metropolis' – individuals can feel isolated and lonely precisely because they are surrounded by large numbers of other city dwellers, who tend not to have intimate personal relationships with all those around them:

> The feeling of isolation is rarely as decisive and intense when one actually finds oneself physically alone, as when one is a stranger, without relations, among many physically close persons, at a party, on the train, or in the traffic of a large city (Simmel, 1950).

Hence city life poses problems for individual identity. On the one hand, one is free to be who one wants to be, since the culture of cities tends to be more cosmopolitan, forgiving and fluid. The impersonal nature of city life often means there are fewer ties to the group so it is easier to break free. On the other hand, the increase in freedom due to reduced social constraint means that one's inner 'mental life' becomes even more important. With no all-encompassing group to turn to, what the individual thinks of him- or herself becomes even more important. With the constant ebb and flow of city life and the rapid turnover of people, ideas and identities, individuals might find the need to withdraw into themselves to find peace. This is what Simmel refers to as 'the separation of the subjective from the objective life'.

Exercise 4.9

Both Weber and Simmel identified the effects that the 'dark side' of modern life has on identify. Write a list of examples of this dark side – of the problems encountered in modern society, such as crime, cramped housing, loneliness and so on.

Simmel and 'modernity'

Simmel's concern with identity in the city reflected themes that were common among other classical social theorists. There are links between Simmel's thoughts on the subject and

- Durkheim's idea of 'anomie' or 'normlessness', which raises problems for who we think we are;
- Marx's idea of alienation – being separated and isolated from others;
- Freud's notion of the tension between who we want to be and the constraints of 'civilisation' that are imposed upon us.

Although we might call Simmel a 'modernist thinker', many of his ideas transcend this label. 'Modernity' (see Chapters 3 and 6) was the name given to the sort of thinking about society that was popular at the time of the founders, and Marx, Durkheim and Weber were all modernist thinkers.

'Modernity' was born at the time of the industrialisation of Western Europe, and the modernist outlook on society, as held by the founders and other classical theorists, tended to include the following beliefs:

- Society was heading in a particular direction.
- Social change represented the onward march of progress.
- Science and technology were of increasing benefit to humankind.
- Societies and humans were becoming more rational.

● The aim of sociology was to discover the ultimate truth of social life.

Exercise 4.10

How realistic were the beliefs of modernist sociology? Copy out and complete the following table. Make sure you include evidence for your view, for example a situation that suggests that the feature in question has or has not happened in society.

Key feature of modernist sociology	How realistic do you think use this was?	What evidence can you to prove your view?
Society was heading in a particular direction		
Social change represented the onward march of progress		
Science and technology were of increasing benefit to humankind		
Societies and humans were becoming more rational		
The aim of sociology was to discover the ultimate truth of social life		

Many of the contemporary thinkers known as 'postmodernists' claim that the modernist thinking about progress, reason and rationality was nothing more than illusion. Thinkers such as Jean Baudrillard (1993) contend that the contemporary age is not characterised by absolutes, but by:

● the fragmentation of many old ideas once held true;
● chaos;
● ambivalence;
● plurality;
● the rise of relativism (no more 'truths', no longer can we say anything absolute or certain about the nature of social life).

Postmodernists claim that identity in the postmodern world is very different from identity under modernity. Today there is much more freedom to do what we want and be who we want to be, to change our minds frequently and 'reinvent' ourselves from time to time. For example postmodern thinker Connie Zweig (1996) argues that there has been a 'death of the self':

Amid the relativism forced upon us by the experiences of living in a global civilisation . . . we are all challenged to look again in the mirror and rethink our assumptions about who and what we are. We face the discomfort – and the depth – of living with uncertainty, paradox, ambiguity, and constant change.

Life in the postmodern age is seen as being based on playing with images, having games with identity and living in chaos, and there is no true sense of who we are. However these themes are present in Simmel's writings. For example postmodern geographer Edward Soja (1996) describes the city as a huge, sprawling, out-of-control playground where there is chaos, a multiplicity of identities and a loss of sense of purpose and meaning. Yet we can find these themes in Simmel's work on the city and in his idea that fashion allows us to play with the outer identities we present to others. Given the fact that Simmel made his observations in the first decade of the twentieth century, we need to ask if the postmodernists really have any new insights to offer. This illustrates the continued importance of classical thinkers for sociology today. Even those who wrote over a century ago had insights that allow us to think about our own times more clearly.

Exercise 4.11

 The views and aims of modernist sociology have been criticised by postmodernists. Copy out and complete the following table. Use the information on modernism and postmodernism in this chapter to identify the key features of modernism criticised by postmodernists and what their actual criticisms would be.

Key feature of modernist sociology	How would postmodernists criticises this?
1.	
2.	
3.	
4.	
5.	

Contemporary forms of action sociology

When we consider action sociology – or any of its other labels, such as interactionism, micro sociology or interpretive sociology – we can identify three subtraditions of this approach that have been highly influential in the shaping of theory as a whole. These three are the 'modern classics' of sociological thought and date from approximately the 1920s through to the late 1960s in America and Britain.

Symbolic interactionism

This branch of interpretive sociology is based on the premise that humans are active agents who manipulate symbols that have meaning. The founders of this approach, which has significantly shaped present-day views in action sociology, worked at Chicago University in the 1920s and are referred to as the Chicago School. Symbolic interactionism sees humanity as creating – through meaningful interaction – a sense of 'society'. Culture is ready-made for us at birth. We are socialised into the dominant meanings that our culture gives to symbols such as language, and actively seek meaning in everyday life.

A key idea developed by the Chicago School is the notion that human activity is a process of interaction between self-aware, self-consciousness beings who are able to reflect upon what they do. The area of the human personality devoted to reflection on who one is has become known as 'the self' or sometimes 'the self-image'. Charles Cooley (1927) described the 'self' as a 'looking-glass self'. In other words, who we think we are is a mirrored reflection of the judgements that others make of us. We are, or become, what others make of us:

> Society is an interweaving and interworking of mental selves. I imagine your mind, and especially what your mind thinks about my mind, and what your mind thinks about what my mind thinks about your mind. I dress my mind before yours and expect that you will dress yours before mine. Whoever cannot or will not perform these feats is not properly in the game (Cooley, 1927).

Interaction is actually the combined efforts of self-aware, thinking beings whose sense of identity guides not only what they do but also how they perceive others, and think others perceive them. This idea of an active, creative and thinking self-identity was taken up by George Mead (1934) in his book *Mind, Self and Society*. According to Mead, the 'self' is divided into two halves: the 'I' – the inner self, which does not think about action, but simply performs it according to the individual's inner wishes; and the 'me' – the outer self, which takes into consideration what the individual thinks other people's wishes are. The 'me' is able to reflect upon the 'I' after interaction has taken place.

Exercise 4.12

 Identify two strengths and two weaknesses of symbolic interactionism.

Phenomenology

The second form of interpretive sociology, known as 'phenomenology', was originally developed as a philosophical perspective by

Edmund Husserl and later become incorporated into sociology by Alfred Schutz. Phenomenology is interested in how individuals go about the process of creating meaning, sharing meaning and classifying meaning through the use of symbols – especially language. Schutz suggests that we store in our minds 'typifications' and 'meaning contexts' that help us to categorise our day-to-day experiences. 'Typifications' are the mental pigeon holes into which we sort 'typical' examples of reality into similar sets. For example, in our minds the concept 'tree' is a typical example of all trees. Through the creation of typifications we build up sets of typifications into 'meaning contexts', which we hold, ready to be used in our daily life as a 'stock of knowledge at hand'. For example I have a typification in my mind called 'friendship', which I can use to try to understand my actions, the actions of others around me and my relationships with those others. Equally, I can compare the experience of 'friendship' with similar typifications such as love, sexual attraction and so on, all of which form a 'meaning context' that I can carry around with me. It is a resource that I can constantly draw on to try to give meaning to life.

Phenomenologists Peter Berger and Thomas Luckmann (1967) suggest that what each culture defines as 'real' is simply the product of the meanings of that culture. In other words, cultures created by human interaction shape how those humans perceive the world. Culture becomes a filter through which they interpret their experiences. What is seen to be 'real' is actually a product of negotiated and socially created meaning. Such cultures are human made, and are kept alive by human interaction. Culture is not a 'thing' that bears down on and controls the individual, despite the fact that when the individual is born, reality is ready-made for her or him.

Exercise 4.13

Identify two strengths and two weaknesses of phenomenology.

Ethnomethodology

The idea of 'ethnomethodology' was first developed by Harold Garfinkel (1967). The term refers to the methods used by people – 'lay actors' – to understand social reality in an active fashion through common-sense thought, which is itself a cultural product. Garfinkel is especially interested in how, although we are active in establishing with others a sense of shared meaning, we largely take interaction for granted. There are various rules on how we should and should not behave in each culture, but these go largely unspoken. They are ever present yet hidden at the same time. Culture gives us our common-sense, taken-for-granted thought and we use this to understand who we are and how we should act – our identity.

Exercise 4.14

a **e**   Identify two strengths and two weaknesses of ethnomethodology.

Strengths and weakneses of the action approach

Strengths

- Humans are seen as active and thinking beings.
- The concept of 'structure' is how individuals experience a ready-made reality – it does not exist as a 'thing' that controls the individual.
- Individuals think about self-identity and have some control over it.
- Culture is seen as the outcome of shared meanings.
- Humans are seen as 'social beings', but ones that remain as individuals within the wider group.

Weaknesses

- Humans are seen as having total free will in some versions of action sociology, yet one cannot truly do as one wishes in society without experiencing external control.
- Action sociology ignores the role that power and inequality play in shaping the outcome of interaction.
- It is often not clear in action sociology whether, in establishing our self-identity, we are passive victims of others, or able to reject others' definitions of us.

Exercise 4.15

Construct a diagram that illustrates how the following theories fit in with each other, for example which theories agree or disagree. Try to include the names of the sociologists most associated with the theories, and some of the key concepts they might use.

- modernism
- functionalism
- ethnomethodology
- postmodernism
- Weberian sociology
- Marxism
- interactionism
- neo-Marxism
- phenomenology

Hint: start off by drawing the macro/micro divide in sociological theory and work from there.

Self-identity and the map of one's life

As Richard Jenkins (1996) notes, at the moment of birth each and every individual is placed into a web of identity-defining moments, interactions and processes. These include:

- The naming of the child (this might even take place before the birth).
- The establishment of its sex.
- The establishment that the child is 'healthy'.
- The legal and bureaucratic process of birth registration.

The moment of birth, in modern Western societies, brings to the individual a whole host of cultural assumptions, legal rules and laws, and subjective meanings by the adults that interact with the individual during the early years. Yet despite all this instilling of group identity, during the course of their lifes individuals come to define themselves as persons in their own right, they achieve self-consciousness and develop a sense of identity. Although we as humans are group or 'social' beings, we eventually become people in our own right, not simply as defined by law and legally responsible for our actions and their consequences, but 'inside our head'. The process leading to a fully self-consciousness selfhood has been conceived as a series of stages initiated by others through socialisation. In early infanthood play – especially 'copying games' – is considered important to this process.

According to Jenkins (ibid.), at birth individuals are the victims of others' definitions of their identity. They learn from them who they are. Later they gain greater 'agency', that is, they gain greater control over their lives, and therefore over their personhood. The question is, however, how much agency do individuals really have in the overall process of knowing who they are, and when does this occur?

> Our own sense of humanity is a hostage to the categorising judgements of others . . . the social world is *always* a world of others, and, in the beginning, the balance is overwhelmingly in favour of the identificatory work that they do (Jenkins, 1996).

Exercise 4.16

a
1. The above quotation notes that in the early stages of our life, who we think we are is often defined for us by others. Think about this idea, and then write a list of the ways that individuals can be judged/labelled by others – the actual judgements they can make.

in e
2. Divide your list into those that you think are powerful and long lasting, and those that you think are not.

e
3. Answer the following question on the basis of your lists. Can our identity be shaped for us by others? Explain your view. Write a couple of paragraphs in all.

Dunn (1988) suggests that we start to become responsible for ourselves in early childhood. Awareness of others leads to concern for others, and through this a concern with who we might be ourselves.

Just when this self-concern develops in the child is still a matter of debate, but many commentators agree about the pattern of this journey of self-discovery. According to Poole (1994, cited in Jenkins, 1996):

- By 7 to 9 months infants have become attached to the adults who are responsible for their day-to-day care.
- At 12 months infants begin to recognise objects around them and understand adult's categorisation of these objects.
- By the age of two a basic familiarity with conversational language has been established.
- Children continue to learn about the actions of others – especially through copying play, which represents a form of 'abstract thought'.
- Between the ages of two and four children develop and elaborate on notions of community, and identify themselves as sharing group membership with the people in question.
- At this point, cultural pressures from others makes gender an important factor in the establishment of self-identity.
- From about five or six years children begin to develop a sense of moral responsibility for their actions and the consequences of their actions. They begin to learn to present a mask of their self to others.
- As children move towards adult hood they become members of wider and more varied groups and communities of identification.

Contained within this model of self-development are the two key features of action sociology in respect of the formation of self-identity:

- Identity is created through interaction with others.
- Humans are active and reflexive in the creation of who they are.

We have, then, within action sociology a model of humanity based on a range of 'differences' or 'opposites' that make up the individual:

- Humans are both individuals and members of a group.
- Humans are both active and passive receivers of group stimuli.
- Humans are both socialised into culture and have agency.

In other words, self-identity is created through what might appear a rather contradictory process: one's individuality originally comes from others. This observation has led to a reworking of action sociology in the work of Pierre Bourdieu, and this will be further examined in Chapter 5 by looking at the ideas of Anthony Giddens.

While self-identity is seen to be the product of both socialisation and interaction – of the passing down of culture between individuals and self-experience – identity also changes as the individual progresses along what is referred to as the 'life course'. The best way to understand what sociologists mean by the life course is to think about all the stages of life experienced by a human who lives a full life. The stages along this life course can be characterised as:

- Early infancy.
- Late infancy.
- Childhood.
- Youth.
- Young adulthood.
- Middle age.
- Old age.

The characteristics associated with each stage of the life course are defined by the culture of the society in question – and this culture determines how one comes to think about oneself. David Morgan (1996) uses the idea of the life course to illustrate how cultures perceive and define who individuals are in each passing stage. However Morgan points out that individuals themselves might use the idea of the life course in an active and reflexive fashion in order to think about their lives – past and future – and themselves.

Exercise 4.17

Our culture provides us with ideas about what each stage of the life course might be like. These symbols and images are important since they give us a basis for identity according to our age.

 Look back at the list of stages of the life course, then write a description of seven what our culture says a bout each of the stages.

Morgan notes that although the life course is in some senses biological as it is based on the aging of the human body, it is also cultural since it varies between societies. Also, humans are highly reflexive and creative in how they understand their lives and their place in the life course. This is a major source of identity formation. We do not simply move from one stage to the next and forget all that happened before. Rather we carry memories of our past actions and interactions and we have hopes and desires for our future. We can remember who we once were. We can reflect upon who we are with each new stage of the life course and we can try to influence who we become.

Exercise 4.18

 Over time, social definitions of age change. Choose any two stages of the life course and for each one write a paragraph on how our image of that stage has changed in recent times, compared with the image held in the past.

An interesting aspect of identity is that once people 'know who they are' they are sometimes dissatisfied with how they live their life. So what do individuals do to cope with the suffocating, mundane routines of everyday life? Cohen and Taylor (1992) argue that due to the routines and patterns of everyday life, interaction can become predictable and lose its interest to those who crave creativity, so individuals make what Cohen and Taylor call 'escape attempts':

> The life plan maps our existence. Ahead of us run the career lines of our jobs, our marriage, our leisure interests, our children and our economic fortunes. But sometimes when we scan these maps, traverse these routes, follow the signs, we become strangely disturbed by the predictability of the journey, the accuracy of the map, the knowledge that today's route will be much like yesterday's. . . . What we object to is the sense that we are sinking into a patterned way of existence . . . that they no longer appear to us as fresh and novel. They are becoming routinized. They no longer help us to constitute our identity (ibid.)

In this view, because the life course is mapped out in front of us, life is too predictable. We know what roles we will be required to take on and when. We can predict who others might want us to be. In order to continue to develop a sense of identity in an active and creative way, individuals might try to shape the direction of their lives and their future in special ways. Equally, they might try to use their time – especially their private or leisure time – to establish a stronger idea of who they wish to be, to mould their identities in new ways. Such individuals might turn to a number of different activities, such as:

- *'Activity enclaves'*, for example hobbies, games, gambling, sex and sexual fantasies.
- *'New landscapes'*, for example holidays, mass culture, art.
- *'Mindscaping'*, for example drugs, therapy.

These activities might help us to build a fresh, more interesting sense of identity and to escape the mundane routines of the life course.

Exercise 4.19

Gry to think of other examples that fit into the categories provided by Cohen and Taylor. For each of your examples explain, in a table espied from the one below, how they might help us to escape from our old routines and to build new identities.

Types of activity	Explain how your examples might help us to escape from old routines and to build new identities
Activity enclaves	
1.	
2.	
3.	

Types of activity	Explain how your examples might help us to escape from old routines and to build new identities
New landscapes	
1.	
2.	
3.	
Mindscaping	
1.	
2.	
3.	

Returning to the relationship between the individual and society

When trying to distinguish how different sociologists think about the role of humanity in society, Hollis (1977) identifies two main approaches. Structural sociologists (see Chapter 3) tend to see humans as victims of culture and structure. This is described as a 'plastic (wo)man' approach to thinking about the relationship between the individual and society since humans are seen as being shaped, moulded and manipulated by social forces. Action sociologists tend to see humans in the completely opposite way – not as plastic but as 'autonomous': totally able to make their own decisions and to control the course of their own lives. As Hollis notes, 'Where Plastic Man [sic] has his [sic] causes, Autonomous Man [sic] has his [sic] reasons' (ibid.)

Many contemporary sociologists find both these models too extreme – individuals are not the total puppets of culture, but without culture they would not become truly human! Therefore some sociologists have attempted to find a point somewhere in between the two approaches. We shall look here at the ideas of Pierre Bourdieu, who has been strongly influenced by action approaches even though he ultimately seeks a compromise between action and structure.

Pierre Bourdieu

Bourdieu (1990, 1993) is concerned with what people in society 'do' in their everyday lives – a common interactionist focus. He points out that social practices are more structured than simply the expression of free will, but are less controlled than a simple response to structural forces. Everyday life – or as he calls it, 'practice' – is characterised by four distinctive and important elements: time, space, unorchestration and improvisation.

All social practices take place according to the natural rhythms of time, although it is culture that makes these rhythms significant in our lives. Practice is also associated with a rhythm: different types of practice have different tempos, and they take different amounts of time to complete. Social practices also take place in cultural and physical locations – be it in the mind, or in an actual physical area. For example some activities that culture has established are acceptable in a private bathroom are not acceptable in a public street!

Social practices often appear to 'just happen' to those who live in society. The way we act is patterned, and some patterns are more common in some cultures than in others, but there is still an element of chance to the whole thing. In this sense it is sometimes unorchestrated. Finally, since social practices are not necessarily planned in advance by those who engage in them, they are fluid in nature. Practices are dynamic, constantly changing, and in order to 'get by' and to fit into society, we sometimes need to make them up as we go along. They are based on improvisation. We have to learn how to understand and cope with new situations and encounters.

According to Bourdieu, as we – the members of a culture – grow up we are instilled with some of the rules of the game of social interaction, which we experiment with and practise with others. At first these others are our immediate family group, later our peers, and later still, people of our own choosing. To become a competent social practitioner – to fit in – we have to develop the skills of interaction and we can only do this through interaction. Self-identity is important in becoming a competent actor in society. We need to have a sense of who we are and where we are in relation to the wider practices of those around us. Although we have to become familiar with the rules of practice through socialisation, there is a sense in which we can 'just get on with it' on a day-to-day basis, and do not have to question what we do within our culture. Bourdieu calls this 'doxa'.

Bourdieu rejects both the view that humans are free, and the opposite view that they are passive victims of culture. Instead he links these two views together through his idea of 'habitus'. This means that while we are never totally free, we do have choices – even though we are not always aware of making such choices or conscious that we will benefit from the choices we do make. How we act is based in part on creativity and in part on habit, on familiarity. We learn the rules but can bend and adapt them as we go along. Bourdieu likens the idea of 'habitus' to a living, thinking and learning computer program. It is self-correcting, not totally preprogrammed but certainly not free either. We have the general rules and the background experiences and we can apply them to specific situations:

> It can be understood by analogy with a computer program . . . but a self-correcting program. It is constituted from a systematic set of

simple and partially interchangeable principles, from which an infinity of solutions can be invented, solutions which cannot be directly deduced from its conditions of production (Bourdieu, 1993).

We learn to behave – to act with our bodies – in particular ways, out of habit and experience and requiring no conscious thought to put into practice in everyday life. Culture provides us with a routine – but one that has many possible outcomes, even if we are not aware of this at the time. Acting in society is partly determined by the culture of that society, which is beyond our control and our conscious intentions, desires and motivations. We also have a sense of everyday routine that we take for granted – that becomes a 'habit'. Finally, we all have a unique biography – all our past interactions stored in our memory – which we draw upon as a resource to help us to understand. Therefore how we act is, at one and the same time, regular, patterned and predictable, yet fluid, unique and unpredictable.

Conclusion

Along with Marx and Durkheim, Weber was a founder of sociology. However, with his work – and the ideas of Simmel – we have an alternative view to that espoused by the more structuralist sociologies of Marx and Durkheim. For Weber, culture and identity are underpinned by the active and creative role humans play in society. Culture and identity are the result of meaningful action. Humans are not passive 'robots' of either class forces or group solidarity.

The ideas of Weber and the 'action' tradition he represents have been very popular in Western sociology since the 1950s and 1960s and they represent an attempt to study the individual rather than to ignore the individual in favour of the group. Issues of meaning, agency and socialisation are still important in sociology today, as illustrated by the ideas of Bourdieu in this chapter and Giddens in the next.

Examination questions

Use the advice on pages 28–9 to answer the following questions:

(a) Assess the view that human society is built upon a social construction of reality.

(b) How useful do you find action sociological interpretations of the role of culture in society when compared with more macro sociological insights?

5 How much agency do individuals have in culture?

By the end of this chapter you should:

- understand the concept of 'agency';
- understand the importance of the concept of agency for action sociologies;
- be aware of the ideas of Goffman on the nature of humanity;
- be aware of the ideas of Giddens and Beck on 'reflexive modernity';
- be aware of the contribution made by Habermas to the study of the relationship of the individual to society.

Introduction

So far we have established that a dominant theme running throughout sociological thought is the relationship of the individual to society. Since sociologists have conceived this relationship in different ways, a variety of theories, theoretical perspectives and world views have been developed to help social theorists to establish frameworks with which to understand why social life is as it is.

Exercise 5.1

 This chapter focuses on the idea of free will – the freedom individuals may or may not have to create culture and shape their own identities. As a reminder of the ideas presented so far in this book, write a couple of sentences on the freedom that each of the following thinkers claim that humans have to create their own culture and identity, that is, these thinkers' views on the existence of free will.

- Durkheim   • Parsons   • Marx   • Simmel   • Weber   • Bourdieu

An important theme we have touched on in other chapters is the notion of 'agency', which in a very limited sense means freedom to act, or having free will. However for many sociologists the concept has a more precise meaning. Consider the following definition by Anthony Giddens (1993):

Agency refers not to the intentions people have in doing things but to their capability of doing those things in the first place. . . . Agency concerns events of which an individual is the perpetrator, in the sense that the individual could, at any phase in a given sequence of conduct, have acted differently. Whatever happened would not have happened if that individual had not intervened. Action is a continuous process, a flow, in which the reflexive monitoring which the individual maintains is fundamental to the control of the body that actors ordinarily sustain throughout their day-to-day lives.

In this view agency is about choice and the freedom to exercise that choice. It is about the ability of an individual to imagine the outcome of a social encounter and to act in such a way as to achieve that outcome. Central to this notion of agency is the idea of reflexivity, which is people's ability to think about themselves and others around them. People are the product of their experiences, but they can try to shape and mould these experiences. Whereas structural sociologists (see Chapters 2, 3 and 4) may deny that individuals have agency in society, it is a key concept in many versions of the action approach, as it is for those who have attempted to bridge the divide between structure and action sociologies.

The anthropologist Anthony Cohen (1994) stresses that when thinking about agency we must not totally separate the individual from wider society. To do so would be to ignore the fact that humans are social beings who live within a culture. To see humans as creative and totally free in everything they do would be to ignore power and the importance of the group. It overstates the amount of freedom we have 'to be who we wish'. Cohen suggests that we should see humans as having a 'creative self', but they have been given the ability and power to be creative because of culture, not despite it, or because of its absence.

According to Cohen, 'Culture requires us to think, gives us forms – metaphors, dogmas, names, "facts" – to think with, but does not tell us *what* to think: that is the self's work' (ibid.) In other words, culture offers us a range of choices to choose from in a creative fashion. Culture provides us with the possibilities for action, but we take responsibility – through our possession of agency – for what we actually do. Such a view would come under criticism from many feminist and Marxist sociologists, who would argue that the possibilities provided to us are extremely limited and are the outcome of power struggles in society. In this view we only have the freedom to choose between a number of situations of inequality – not much freedom of choice at all!

Link exercise 5.1

 Copy out and complete an extended version of the following table to summarise the Marxist and feminist views on culture, identity and socialisation discussed in Chapters 2, 3 and 11.

	Views on the role of culture in society	Views on how identity is created	Views on the role played by socialisation in society
Marxism			
Feminism			

Link exercise 5.2

ku Refer to the previous chapters (and the index at the back of the book) and remind yourself of the following key concepts by defining each one:

- Structure
- Action
- Social control
- Voluntarism
- Determinism
- Habitus
- Nature
- Nurture

Thinking using culture: the creative self

In this chapter we shall look at the contribution made by three key thinkers to the understanding of how much freedom individuals to create their own identity: Erving Goffman, Anthony Giddens and Jürgen Habermas.

Erving Goffman

Writing from the symbolic interactionist tradition (see Chapter 4), American thinker Erving Goffman (1968, 1971a, 1971b) presents us with a version of looking at 'thinking, creative and self-aware individuals' that he calls 'dramaturgical analogy'. In *The Presentation of Self in Everyday Life*, Goffman (1971b) states:

> The perspective employed in this report is that of the theatrical performance; the principles derived are dramaturgical ones. I shall consider the way in which the individual in ordinary work situations presents himself and his activity to others, the ways in which he guides and controls the impression they form of him, and the kinds of things he may and may not do while sustaining his performance before them.

For Goffman, humans are creative in the sense that they think about the interactions they have and the contexts in which these interactions take place, and about their and others' motives for action. In doing this, they seek to take control of the situation for their own ends by presenting a mask or impression. Goffman sees the purpose of inter-action as being about control of the definition of the social situation. Goffman's 'dramaturgical analogy' is so called because he compares social life to the theatre:

- Humans play many different roles.
- They follow certain scripts that are relevant in some situations but not in others.
- Individuals give 'front stage' and 'back stage' performances.
- Interaction – since it is social by nature – is a performance to an audience.

In developing the conceptual framework employed in this report, some language of the stage was used. I spoke of performers and audiences; of routines and parts; of performances coming off or falling flat; of cues, stage settings and backstage; of dramaturgical needs, dramaturgical skills, and dramaturgical strategies (ibid.)

This means that the public identity we convey may be no more than a mask or a performance, designed to create a specific and calculated impression in order to take control of the definition of the situation or public encounter. The implication of these ideas for self-identity is that when we are in public we wear many different masks of our self. In a calculating way we adopt many different roles, many differ-ent identities, in order to get what we want from an interaction. Goffman refers to the techniques we use in day-to-day life to convey the impression we wish as 'impression management'. We use these techniques to shape, mould and direct how we behave towards others, and how we wish others to behave towards us.

Exercise 5.2

Reread the above discussion and provide examples of Goffman's key ideas in a copy of the following table.

Give four examples of scripts we act out in society	1. 2. 3. 4.
Give two examples each of back- and front-stage activities	Back stage: 1. 2. Front stage: 1. 2.
Give five examples of social situations in which you might wish to manage the impression others have of you, such as a job interview	1. 2. 3. 4. 5.

Evaluating the ideas of Goffman

Goffman's ideas have proven very influential, but some writers argue that his work is unclear about the nature of 'true' self-identity. Goffman's strengths are as follows:

- He sees humans as active and creative.
- He has conducted a variety of studies based on participant observation to back up his claims.
- The 'dramaturgical analogy' is a useful tool for thinking about everyday life.
- Goffman relates human interaction to structures of a sort. He notes in his study on life in asylums (1968) and elsewhere that interaction can be patterned and routinised by institutions (which can have power inequalities). He even thinks that people within these institutions can calculate their actions.

With regard to weaknesses, it is unclear what the precise relationship is between front-stage and back-stage performances. This confusion begs questions about identity that Goffman never clearly answers:

- Do we act in a manipulative and calculating way, yet really 'know who we are'?
- When alone, or with those with whom we are familiar, does our 'real self' come out?
- Do humans have a 'real self' or are we just a collection of masks?

Exercise 5.3

Answer the following questions (try to write a couple of paragraphs on each). Use ideas presented in previous chapters to help you and give reasons for your views.

1. Do you ever act in a manipulative and calculating way?

2. When alone, or with those with whom you are familiar, does your 'real self' come out?

3. Do you have a 'real self', or are you just a collection of masks?

By ignoring structure altogether, some action sociologies give us a blinkered view of human identity. When we act in society, we might choose a particular type of performance for self-serving reasons, but the scripts and roles that we follow were constructed for us by others before our birth. They are a 'structure' of sorts. This observation has led some commentators to think again about the relationship between agency and structure – as seen in the work of Anthony Giddens.

Anthony Giddens

In order to understand how Giddens sees the relationship between the individual and society – between structure and action – we shall consider the following quotations from his book *The Constitution of Society* (1984, pp. 25–6):

- 'Structure is not "external" to individuals . . . it is in a certain sense more "internal" than exterior.'
- 'Structure is not to be equated with constraint but is always both constraining and enabling.'
- 'Structure has no existence independent of the knowledge that agents have about what they do in their day-to-day activity.'

From these three quotations we can sense an attempt to unite structure and agency/action – to see them as a 'two-way street' or as being in what is known as a 'symbiotic relationship'. This means that they feed off each other, rather than one being the outcome of the other. Structure cannot exist without the humans who create it through their actions and meanings. Equally, young humans are born into the structures of others. These unchosen structures do not simply control, they also enable action to take place. For example, although the structure of language controls us from birth, without it we would not be able to act in a creative way. We may have a great deal of choice about the language we do use, but this choice lies within a set of rules we do not decide. Humans are seen as being able to think about their position within structures and to think about their actions – they have 'knowledgeability' of themselves and their place. Equally, knowledgeable actors can change structures through their actions over time.

Structures cannot exist without agents (humans), and agents cannot have agency without structures. When thinking about the relationship between structure and action in this way, Giddens formulated what he calls 'structurational sociology'. The aims of this type of sociology are indicated by the word used to describe it. Not just 'structure', or just 'action', but 'structure-action', or, if we combine these words – 'structuration'. In the *New Rules of Sociological Method*, Giddens (1976) lists a number of new rules that he would like to see taken up by sociology, and that eventually formed for him the basis of structurational sociology. He argues that humans must be seen as skilled performers. They have a great deal of knowledge about the rules of society, and when using these rules they are sensitive to variations in old situations and the problems of new encounters. Although humans have agency since they can make choices, Giddens stresses that humans are still in some ways controlled: 'The realm of human agency is bounded. Men produce society, but they do so as historically located actors, and not under conditions of their own choosing' (ibid.) Giddens refers to these structures as both 'enabling' and 'constraining'. There are still power differences in society, yet we can work within the structures to change them over time.

Exercise 5.4

1. How realistic do you find Giddens' claims about the interrelationship between structure and action?

2. Has this view helped to resolve previous sociologists' debates on structure and action?

Answer both these questions in detail (approximately 150 words each).

Exercise 5.5

Identify two strengths of Giddens' arguments and explain why they should be seen as strengths.

Two criticisms of Giddens

First, Archer (1982, 1995, 1996) (see Chapter 2) argues that, contrary to Giddens' claims, Giddens emphasises the role of agents more than he does structures. What this indicates is that although his intention is to bridge the gap between structure and action, ultimately he comes down on one side – the side of action. A consequence of this is that he exaggerates the degree of choice that individuals have over their own lives, and plays down the fact that often our lives are not of our own choosing.

Second, Caroline New (1993) offers a somewhat opposite but complementary criticism. She suggests that Giddens ignores the fact that some individuals have more agency than others in society, since they have more power. Some people cannot be the authors of their own lives, but have to put up with lives that others have control over. Structures tend to control some people more than they do others. For example, 'If Giddens has taken the prison bars from structure, by the same token he has taken the bite from agency. . . . Giddens does not address the question of who can transform what aspects of social structure and how' (ibid.)

Exercise 5.6

Giddens' work on structurational sociology is a popular topic in sociological debates and he is not without his critics. In your own words, rewrite the above criticisms by Archer and New to show that you understand them.

Exercise 5.7

In your opinion, how would Giddens himself evaluate/criticise the ideas of (1) functionalism, (2) Marxism and (3) interactionism, as discussed earlier? Give reasons for your answers.

Jürgen Habermas

The German thinker Jürgen Habermas (1981) is often regarded as a 'second generation' member of the Frankfurt School (see Chapters 2, 3 and 7), and as such he has continued the project known as 'critical theory', established by the original members of the Frankfurt School before the Second World War. Critical theory is an interdisciplinary approach to social theory that draws its inspiration from many intellectual sources, including the works of Marx, Freud and Weber. To this intellectual melting pot Habermas adds influences from the work of Durkheim and Parsons (see Chapter 3) and the more action-oriented approach found in the work of G. H. Mead (Chapter 4).

Habermas is interested in how and why people act as they do, and in particular the role played by language, or rather by communication in social relations. In *The Theory of Communicative Action* Habermas (1981) draws an important distinction between two types of action: instrumental action and rational action. Whereas instrumental action is based on goals, rational action allows a more critical way of thinking that can aid the understanding of oneself and others. Habermas explains how rational thought is used by ordinary social actors to help them to engage in rational action, especially when they communicate with others. This rational action can be used to break what Habermas sees as the exploitative chains of capitalist society.

Critiques of capitalism and ideology

Under capitalism the masses are constrained by economic structures and therefore have no power. In order for people to break free from capitalism they have to be able to judge in a rational way their social situation and that of the wider society. They need to think about the world, and to reach agreement with others about what should be done, and how they should act. This agreement would be rational, not based on power inequalities, and it would be a way for individuals to get at the 'truth' of their society. In continuing the Marxist project, Habermas (1987) takes up the concept of ideology (see Chapter 3) in his book *Toward a Rational Society*. Habermas seeks a society in which unrestricted communication can occur, a society free from domination, free from the constraints of ideology. The existence of ideology is seen to lead to:

- Falsehoods.
- A lack of critical thinking.
- Inequalities of power during communication.
- Passive acceptance of society as it is.

The above are seen by Habermas as characteristic of what previous Marxists referred to as 'false consciousness'. In making this critique of the role of false ideas in capitalism, Habermas's ideas link directly to those of the original members of the Frankfurt School, who were concerned with the part played by mass culture in denying critical thought to the masses (see Chapter 7). Central to Habermas's notion of the emancipation of humankind is the achievement of a truly 'ideal speech situation', where individuals are able to communicate in an active and free fashion, without the constraints of power, structure and ideology. This means that people become 'critical' in order to become free – hence the label given to the theorising conducted by the Frankfurt School: 'critical theory'. This is a notion of agency, but by another name.

Exercise 5.8

 Think about how Habermas's ideas relate to discussions of culture and identity and how they are both formed in a capitalist society. Copy out and complete the following table, focusing on the four observations by Habermas that are listed in the text above.

Features of ideology in a capitalist society	What consequences might these have for the formation of culture and identity in an unequal, class-based society?
Falsehood	
A lack of critical thinking	
Inequalities of power during communication	
Passive acceptance of society as it is	

Exercise 5.9

 Suggest two strengths and two weaknesses of Habermas's ideas.

Conclusion

The ideas of action sociology have been highly influential in contemporary sociology, and they have led to a number of similar yet different ways of thinking about the role of human agency in shaping the society we live in. The concern with meaning can be dated back to Weber and Simmel (Chapter 4) and has its contemporary expression in the very influential ideas of Bourdieu (Chapter 4), Giddens and Habermas.

What Giddens and Habermas have in common is a concern to continue the 'modernist' project (see Chapters 3 and 6) that characterised the birth of sociology: to unearth the truth about social life, and to understand how individuals can improve their lives. However postmodernists claim that since there is no longer a way of understanding truth because everything has become relativistic, then sociology has no more hope of providing a better understanding of social life than anything else. In the postmodern world, all claims to truth are as truthful as each other. Both Habermas and Giddens want to rescue sociology from what they see as the excesses of postmodern ideas, and it is to these ideas that we shall turn in the next chapter.

Examination questions

Use the advice on pages 28–9 to answer the following questions:

(a) Assess the contribution made by Giddens to debates on culture and identity.

(b) Evaluate the idea that the individual has choice in the creation of her or his own identity.

6 The 'new sociology' of culture and identity: modernity and postmodernity

By the end of this chapter you should:

- be able to compare and contrast modernist theories and post-modernist theories;
- have an understanding of the arguments raised by different branches of postmodern thinking;
- understand the postmodern view of culture and identity;
- be able to evaluate postmodern ideas;
- understand alternatives to postmodern thinking, in particular the idea of 'reflexive modernity'.

Introduction

For many commentators, sociology in particular and social theory in general are undergoing profound change due to the development of ideas referred to as 'postmodern'. Postmodern*ism* (the theory) is based on the attempt to understand postmodern*ity* (the time period). Although opinions vary, this change in society – and particularly in culture and identity – is said to have been taking place since the Second World War, and especially since the 1970s. Postmodernist views vary and are often complicated, uncertain, confusing and ambiguous. This is sometimes the result of a deliberate attempt to play with language, style and meaning since this sense of 'uncertainty' is an important part of 'the postmodern condition'. In terms of actual changes in society and the way in which we live our lives, there are three main attitudes towards the existence of postmodernity:

- Postmodernity *has* occured.
- Postmodernity *is* occuring in society at present.
- Postmodernity *will* occur.

Added to this is concern about the usefulness of the idea of post-modernity. For some it should happen, for others it should not, and for others it will not happen and the theory should be replaced by other ideas. As Mike Featherstone (1994) comments:

Any reference to the term 'postmodernism' immediately exposes one to the risk of being accused of jumping on a bandwagon, of perpetuating a rather shallow and meaningless intellectual fad. One of the problems is that the term is at once fashionable yet irritatingly elusive to define.

Another point of confusion is whether postmodernity (the time period) represents a dramatic, sudden break with the past, or whether it is a more gradual extension of what came before. As the prefix 'post' indicates, whatever it is, postmodernity occurred, is occurring or will occur after the era of 'modernity' (see Chapter 3) and it is this idea that we must examine first.

What is modernity?

Although it is difficult to pinpoint exactly, what we call 'modernity' is usually associated with the era of industrialisation and the time when sociology was developed by its founders (see Chapter 3). Modernity – the period of the modern – comes from the Latin word *modo*, meaning 'just now', and this is a key feature in the modernist spirit: the founders' idea that life and society had changed. Their times – their 'just now' – were totally different from those of the traditional preindustrial societies of the past.

Exercise 6.1

The work of the founders of sociology is often seen as the starting point for the discussion of all sociological topics in all syllabus areas. Given the importance of the founders' ideas, brainstorm all that you can remember about them from your studies so far, before continuing with the rest of this chapter.

Taking place in a time of rapid and massive change, modernity was characterised by the following elements:

- Industrialisation.
- Urbanisation.
- A rise in the importance of science.
- The growth of the manufacturing industry.
- Secularisation (the decline of religion).
- The invention of more advanced technology.
- Rationalisation.

This was the age of science, based on the belief that humans could understand and control everything. The world of nature was the slave and humans were now in charge. The goals of these scientists – sociologists included – was to:

- Find the absolute truth.
- Develop universal general laws.
- Control the present.
- Predict the future.
- Control the shape and direction of the future.

Exercise 6.2

in id a e

Do you think that the founders got it right with their view of modernity, or has it become out of date? Copy out and complete the following table.

Feature of modernity as described by the founders	To what extent has sociology met these goals?	Is this view dated or not? Explain your answer
To find the absolute truth		
To develop universal general laws		
To control the present		
To predict the future		
To control the shape and direction of the future		

At its inception, modernity was based on what is called the spirit of the 'Enlightenment' – the eighteenth-century philosophical movement that stressed the importance of reason and the replacement of religion and superstition with science and rationality. An excellent illustration of the modernists' preoccupation with rationalisation is the work of Max Weber, and in particular his 'sociology of music' (1968, originally written in 1910–11). Weber saw the historical development of society as the development of rationality in all spheres of social life and social organisation. In this context 'rationalisation' means the breaking down of an object of study into its constituent parts in order better to understand the whole. Rationality is thus seen as a fundamental part of the rise of both science and technology in the industrial era, and as providing the momentum for industrialisation itself – a highly modernist image of social change.

Weber illustrated the historical development of rationality with reference to musical notation. For example in preindustrial 'traditional' society, music was passed down the generations as part of 'folk culture'. Songs were passed down by word of mouth and instrument making was the task of skilled individuals. With the onset of rationalisation there developed a concern to analyse what music actually was – to break it down in order better to control it. Hence the creation of a universal system of notation, scales and so on. Likewise the making of instruments became a matter of mass production. The rationalisation process was seen as aiding humans to control the world around them: to seek out absolute truth and to make order out of the chaos of nature.

Exercise 6.3

In a copy of the table below, list the aspects of society that you think have become more 'rational' over time, as in Weber's example of music. For example knowledge can now be 'broken down' and analysed (rationality) due to the growth of computer technology.

Area of social life that has become rational	How and why has this happened?
1. The role of knowledge in society	Advances in computer technology mean that knowledge can be collected more easily and swapped between groups of people.
2.	
3.	
4.	
5.	

This process of rationalisation can also be seen as responsible for the creation of sociology itself since its aim was to develop a 'truthful' account of the social world. This modernist sociology project – the search for truth, absolute certainty and progression in society – is now under challenge from writers who suggest that society has moved away from and beyond this. We no longer live in modernity, but in postmodernity.

Exercise 6.4

Although the founders of sociology were all theorists of the impact of industrialisation on society, they each interpreted the process of modernity slightly differently, paying more attention to some aspects of it than others. Match each of the aspects listed below to the classical sociologist most associated with it. To do this you may need to refer back to the previous chapters.

Contribution to sociology

1. The role of class forces in society.

2. The dark side of the city for social identity.

3. The process of rationalisation.

4. How solidarity changes with industrialisation.

5. The decline of religion in society.

6. The decline of community with urbanisation.

7. The importance of science for society and sociology.

8. The growth of an iron cage of bureaucracy.

9. How the group deals with the problems of individuality.

Classical sociologists

- Marx - Durkheim - Weber - Tonnies - Simmel - Comte - Spencer

What is postmodernity?

Postmodernity is that which comes after modernity. For many post-modernists this era is characterised by a shift away from production and towards an economy, culture, identities and life-styles based on consumption. Postmodernity has brought the aims and spirit of modernity crashing down, especially the Enlightenment preoccupation with absolute truth and certainty.

As Anderson (1996, p. 6) notes, 'We are living in a new world, a world that does not know how to define itself by what it is, but only by what it has just-now ceased to be.' In this view the world has changed rapidly, so rapidly that confusion has taken over from certainty. The modernist world was fixed – it had a definite character. The postmodern world is based on the collapse of all that modernity held to be true and fixed. In postmodernity truth, certainty and reality are provisional and relativistic. There are no more absolutes – no more definite standards. This is the case not just for morality but also for the knowledge we have about the world around us. There are too many choices on offer, all claiming to be the 'real' version of the 'truth'. Religion, politics, the sciences and so on all claim special access to the truth, but how can we tell which is correct? Knowledge has become a commodity and a form of power, rather than an absolute, a truth. Just as truth fragments into a plurality of truths, so the traditional means of identity formation based on class, gender, ethnicity and so on has been replaced by a plurality of sources of identity. In this way, dominant cultural meaning has been replaced by an individual search for meaning, and life-style has becomes a matter of choice. Ultimately, uncertainty, confusion, ambiguity and plurality will be all that is left.

Exercise 6.5

Consider the above characteristics of the postmodern world. Do they all apply to present-day society? Taking each of the six points in turn, in a copy of the following table write a couple sentences on whether or not you think it is a realistic description of the times in which we live. Provide an example of each one.

Feature of postmodernity	Is this true of present-day society?	Example
The world has changed so rapidly that confusion has taken over from certainty		
In postmodernity truth, certainty and reality have become provisional and relativistic. There are no more absolutes, no more definite standards		
There are too many choices on offer – religion, politics, the sciences and so on all claim special access to the truth, but how can we tell which is correct?		
Knowledge has become a commodity and a form of power, rather than an absolute, a truth		
The traditional means of identity formation, based on class, gender, ethnicity and so on, have been replaced by a plurality of sources of identity		
Dominant cultural meaning has been replaced by an individual search for meaning, and lifestyle has become a matter of choice		

As Featherstone (1992, p. 265) observes: 'Despite the oft-remarked looseness and imprecision of the term postmodernism, it does have the merit of directing our attention towards the nature of contemporary cultural change.'

Modernity is seen by postmodernists, as a mistaken project. Investment in it is shown to have been illusory. No absolutes are possible in an age when 'anything goes'.

According to Anderson (1996), postmodernity has occurred in four key areas of social life:

- Our self-concepts have become more mouldable – we are able to be who we want to be and there are innumerable choices on offer.
- Morality has disolved – there are no fixed and absolute moral standards.
- As there are no rules or set ways to behave, in art and culture there is no way of telling if one tradition or style is 'better' than any other. The distinction between 'high' and 'low' culture is no more (see Chapter 7). All there is left to do is to play with styles – to mix and match.
- The process of globalisation has had a dramatic effect on the world. The world appears a much smaller place due to global communications, world travel and tourism and the spread of ideas across the globe.

Postmodernity, then, is the age of over-exposure to otherness – because, in travelling, you put yourself into a different reality; because, as a result of immigration, a different reality comes to you; because, with no physical movement at all, only the relentless and ever-increasing flow of information, cultures interpenetrate (ibid., p. 6).

This means that what we once thought was true is now exposed as simply one truth among many. The more contact we have with other peoples and once distant cultures the more we question the way we are. Space and time have changed – we can contact people on the other side of the world in an instant via the phone, the Internet or video-conferencing. We can travel to any where we wish and can experience and appreciate other cultures, art forms and music.

Exercise 6.6

Consider the four aspects of postmodernity identified by Anderson, then in your own words explain what each means and list as many examples of it as you can:

1. We can be who we wish to be.

2. Moral standards are no longer fixed.

3. The distinction between high and low culture has dissolved.

4. Globalisation has made the world feel smaller.

Varieties of postmodernism

Postmodernists themselves disagree about how the condition of postmodernity can and should be interpreted. Some suggest that the fragmentation of truth and the rapid growth of possibilities will cause chaos and ambiguity and are a threat to civilisation as we know it, while others suggest that the collapse of absolutes is liberating – providing freedom and allowing us to be who we want to be.

Exercise 6.7

In what respect might some postmodernists be correct when they claim that self-identity is now freer and more liberating than ever before. Give examples of all the sources of personal identity currently available to the individual, for example sexuality, class and so on.

The french thinker Jean-François Lyotard, in his book *The Postmodern Condition* (1984, p. xxiv), defines 'postmodern' as 'incredulity toward metanarratives'. What he means by this is that in the postmodern age knowledge has become provisional and as humans we see the old claims to truth for what they really are – fictions, stories or 'narratives'. Knowledge itself has undergone a profound change, and we have changed our uses of it and response towards it. Lyotard suggests that science and scientific knowledge have been exposed for what they are – once powerful illusions that are powerful no longer. Hope can no longer be placed on the highly modernist notions of progress or reason since what accounts for 'knowledge' depends on where one is, and how one chooses to see what is around one. There is no such thing as a single truth, only a multiplicity of truths, and knowledge – which was once thought to give us access to the truth – is nothing more than a commodity. Knowledge can be bought and sold, and in the age of the computer those who have the most knowledge have the most power.

Exercise 6.8

Lyotard suggests that in the postmodern age knowledge is no longer about the search for 'truth', but is instead a form of power. Copy out and complete the following table, basing your answers on this claim by Lyotard. A few examples are provided to start you off.

Organisation that might hold information (knowledge) about you	What sorts of information might they have about your life?	How might this situation lead to inequality of power?
1. Your bank		
2. The supermarket		
3. The local council		
4.		
5.		
6.		
7.		
8.		

According to another French postmodernist thinker, Jean Baudrillard (1981, 1988), under postmodernity the nature of consumption has fundamentally changed (see Chapters 7, 9 and 10). When we buy objects and products – commodities – we no longer consume them as 'objects' but as 'signs' or 'symbols'. In other words, when we consume it is not the actual physical 'thing' – the material object – that matters, but what the object stands for in our culture. In other words, for most people buying a pair of Nike trainers says less about the physical activity they will be involved in, and more about the image they wish to project to others. The consumption of signs in this way is considered by Baudrillard to be the basis of identity formation and life-style construction.

Exercise 6.9

in *id* *a*

Baudrillard claims that when buying a product, one is really consuming the image or sign that the product stands for, which in turn leads to identity and life-style formation. Draw up and complete a more spacious version of the table below.

Choose any four designer logos from clothing companies and draw them below	When we see this logo, what images come to mind?	What might people be trying to say about themselves by wearing this logo?
1.		
2.		
3.		
4.		

Baudrillard goes further still and suggests that the signs and symbols used by the media – their 'simulations of reality' – have become so powerful in postmodern society that the audience has come to depend on and use these media-generated symbols more than their sensory experiences. This makes the media 'more real than real' – or 'hyper-real'.

Postmodernity and truth

A great deal of postmodern thinking is characterised by a belief in what is called 'relativism': the view that there are no absolute standards of truth, correctness, reality or morality. Instead everything comes down to a matter of choice. This claim is in direct opposition to the modernist thinking discussed at the start of this chapter (see also Chapter 3). The founders believed in progress, development and objectivity, but these are seen by many postmodernists as nothing but games we once played – nothing but stories, which in their time were powerful and shaped our thinking, but do so no longer.

Richard Rorty (1989, 1996), a postmodern philosopher, suggests that what we see as 'truth' is created rather than found. It is not 'just there', rather it is the result of how we see what is around us, and who it is that is doing the seeing. Rorty distinguishes between two groups' response to 'the truth' – one is essentially modernist, the other postmodernist:

- *Metaphysicians*. These people base how they see the world on common-sense thought. They believe that there are ultimate truths – absolutes – and that their own approach to understanding the world is true, correct, right and just. This is highly modernist since it does not see that truth is a matter of where you happen to stand. These people are convinced – know – they are right.
- *Ironicists*. Postmodern people accept that truth and reality are relative, and that any claim to truth is as good as another. Since

there are only variations, these people accept that all one can do is to play with the variety of truth claims on offer.

Postmodern identities

Due to the emphasis on plurality, divergence and freedom in some versions of postmodernism, it makes more sense to talk about the rapid expansion of identities rather than a single postmodern identity. Postmodern identities are often described as 'fragmented' or 'fractured' – meaning that the dominant, absolute and rigid traditional sources of identity have been replaced by new sources. In other words the modernist sources of identity such as class, gender and ethnicity have become much looser, much freer – able to be manipulated and played with as never before.

Crook *et al.* (1992) suggest that with the decline of modernist sources of identity the media is often turned to since it allows us to see, understand and perhaps copy a whole range of new identities. They refer to the media as providing 'symbolic communities' that, if we so desire, we can incorporate into our own sense of self. Douglas Kellner (1992) characterises postmodern identities as:

- Accelerated.
- Extended.
- Unstable.
- Disintegrated.
- Fragile.
- Superficial.
- Illusory.

Exercise 6.10

This exercise requires you to think about the characteristics identified by Kellner regarding the nature of postmodern identities. For each of the characteristics listed above this exercise, define the word and suggest an example that might fit this category.

In the postmodern age identity is both a problem and a 'project'. Our sense of who we are is not given to us, handed-down in a fixed and stable form – it is up to us to construct or create it. Postmodernists claim that it is through the consumption of popular culture, especially media products, that we are able to construct a sense of identity (see Chapters 7 and 8). However Kellner rejects this particular version of postmodernism as it is too different from and opposed to the modernity that came before it. Kellner objects to the simplistic division between:

- *Modernist identity*: fixed, passive, stable, certain.
- *Postmodernist identities*: open, active/creative, fragmented, illusory.

Kellner argues that this differentiation between modernity and post-modernity ignores the fact that identity was/is also a problem in modernity. He argues that ever since preindustrial 'traditional' society identity has been expanding with the opening up of new possibilities, requiring choices to be made and therefore causing anxiety and uncertainity. Kellner suggests that it is a mistake to see these as exclusively new aspects of a new era. In this view postmodernity is an extension of modernity, not a complete challenge to it and change from it. Post-modernity starts where modernity left off, leading to even more uncertainty and fragmentation – but this was a condition of late modernity in the first place.

Evaluating the politics of postmodern identities

Kobena Mercer (1990) is concerned about the effects on identity formation in a postmodern age where the subject has been 'decentred'. In other words, if there are no more absolutes, no more dominant meanings, this might set us free to be who we want to be (we have control over our own 'centre'), but it is also a form of enslavement – enslavement to darkness and chaos:

> Like 'identity', difference, diversity and fragmentation are keywords in the postmodern vocabulary where they are saturated with groovy connotations. But it should be clear that there is nothing particularly groovy about the postmodern condition at all. As a bestseller ideology in artistic and intellectual circles the postmodern paradigm has been and gone, but as a pervasive sensibility in everyday life its smelly ideological effect lingers on (ibid.)

We can make more choices about our lives and life-styles than ever before. We can decide what sort of people we want to be and build the sort of lives we wish. We can change and remould ourselves over time. If there are no absolute standards then no one is able to say that who we are and how we behave is wrong. This is a tremendous amount of freedom. For example many postmodernists claim that class is no longer the basis of individual or group identity. It was a key feature of modernity, but with the shift from production to consumption 'who we think we are' is based not on what we do or make, but on what we buy and use, and how we use it. However, with no standards to turn to there is much more uncertainty. How can we tell if we really are who we think we are? How can we tell if how we are behaving is really the best way for us?

Those who are critical of the postmodern proclamation of the 'death of class', such as Mercer (1990) and Hall (1988), note that the concern with freedom through consumption echoes a great deal of the New Right thinking of the Thatcher governments during the 1980s. It is not so much that everyone is free, but that some people can afford to be freer than others. The result is that the state is freed from its traditional responsibility to provide welfare support for those in need. From a political viewpoint, if 'anything goes' in the postmodern era and there are no rational grounds upon which to establish truth, reality, morality and identity, then it is hard to make the sort of absolute moral judgements upon which anti-racism and anti-sexism are based.

Mercer (1990) notes that postmodernity's emphasis on the immediate, the illusory, the meaningless and the ambiguous not only denies the existence of a 'truth', but also encourages us to forget our pasts. If we can be who we want to be, we might as well forget who we once were! Politically this 'active forgetting' of the past can be dangerous, since it tends to lead to some aspects of our past history being ignored while others are redefined and brought back. For example class conflict is but a distant memory, and a hazy one at that, but both the New Right and New Labour are asking us to return to the basics and to embrace 'traditional values'. Hence it seems that we are not moving away from traditional absolutes altogether, merely leaving behind those which do not fit in with the dominant values and world view of dominant groups.

Evaluation of postmodernism

While many have embraced postmodern ideas, others have rejected them. The critics of postmodernism are particularly concerned about the implications of these ideas for the future of sociology itself. If there is no such thing as truth, then what is the point of sociology trying to determine what the world is like?

The strengths of postmodernism are:

- It allows us to update the sociology of the founders and to reassess their image of the future – our present.
- It allows us to consider the importance of globalisation for culture and identity in society.
- Since postmodernism sees identity as pluralistic, we can think about how people try to define themselves in the present age.
- The observation that society has moved from production to consumption allows us to think about the nature of work and of class formation (see Chapter 10).
- It gives a central place to the role of the mass media and popular culture in society.

However there are four main and powerful criticisms of postmodern ideas. First, Norris (1992, 1993) considers that postmodernism is far too sceptical and relativistic to be of any use. Norris (1992) quotes an observation made by Tony Bennett:

> if narratives are all that we can have and if all narratives are, in principle, of equal value – as it seems they must be if there is no touchstone of 'reality' to which they can be referred for the adjudication of their truth-claims – then rational debate would seem to be pointless.

Second, Giddens (1990, 1991) notes with some concern that postmodernism does not give sociology a future. In fact it denies the very Enlightenment spirit that led to the creation of sociology in the first place. For Giddens the postmodern denial of truth and reason leaves us with nothing upon which to build knowledge about the world, knowledge that in time may help inform our lives – personally and at the level of social policy.

Third, many Marxists point out that postmodernism may preach about the individual's liberation from the past, but this freedom is an illusion since it is based on consumption. Given that consumption costs money, then surely some people are going to be more free than others? Postmodernism is said to provide a thinly veiled justification for the false needs created by the capitalist economy – these simply provide more profits for the capitalists themselves and thus ensure the perpetuation of an exploitative and unequal society.

Finally, if in terms of morality 'anything goes' – everything is relative – then this leaves us with no means of challenging, discrimination and prejudice in society.

Exercise 6.11

Copy out and complete the following table as a summary of the ideas of modernity and postmodernity.

	Modernity	Postmodernity
Key thinkers		
Basic characteristics of this sort of society		
Possible evidence		
Possible criticisms		

Conclusion

Postmodernism has provided sociology with many important and influential ideas but it has also provoked controversy and criticism.

Taken to its logical conclusion, postmodernism attacks the very origins of sociology. It denies absolute knowledge and instead suggests a reality based on fragmentation, relativism and plurality. Postmodernism has, however, allowed previously 'invisible' groups within sociology and society to have their say. It has illustrated the relationship between power and knowledge, and it has embraced plurality – 'anything goes'. Some see this as liberating, but for others the result can only be chaos.

Exercise 6.12

Do you think the ideas of modernity or of postmodernity best describe the society we live in at the moment? Answer this question in approximately 150 words and provide examples.

When rejecting the claims of postmodernism some authors have adopted the terms 'high modernism' or 'late modernism' to suggest that fundamental change has taken place in contemporary society, but that this change has extended the features developed under modernity, rather than replaced them. Giddens (1990, 1991) describes society as being in a period of 'reflexive modernity', where culture and identity are based on individuals' awareness that decisions about life are more unrestricted than ever before. Therefore we must become 'reflexive' about who we are, what we want and how we want to live.

A similar approach to the idea of 'reflexive modernity' is contained in the book *Risk Society* by German sociologist Ulrich Beck (1992). Beck claims that the current era of 'late' or 'high' modernity is characterised by the development of what he sees as a 'risk society', where life-style and identity are based on assessment of the risks of everyday life and their avoidance through careful action. These life-styles and identities are rational and active responses to the dangerous challenges of the age, such as AIDS, skin cancer, pollution and so on. Risk avoidance can be seen as a political act that enables individuals to think about who they are and what sort of world they live in.

The idea of reflexive modernity will be addressed further in Chapters 10 and 13.

Examination questions

Use the advice on pages 28–9 to answer the following questions:

(a) To what extent are the ideas of a postmodern identity useful when thinking about modernday society?

(b) Critically evaluate the idea that we can choose who we want to be.

7 Mass culture and popular culture

By the end of this chapter you should:

- understand the differences between the key concepts of mass culture, mass society, high culture, low culture and popular culture;
- understand Marxist and neo-Marxist discussions of popular culture in modern society;
- be able to evaluate Marxist ideas on popular culture using the perspectives of interactionism, pluralism and postmodernism.

Introduction

Consider the amount and type of media that you encounter in an average day. Perhaps as you wake up you turn on the radio, or you may even wake up to the radio alarm clock. Do you watch breakfast television before leaving home? Do you read a book, magazine or newspaper during the course of your journey to work or school – perhaps on a bus or train? In the evening, is the TV playing 'to itself' in a corner of the room while you eat your evening meal, is it switched off, or is your meal eaten in front of the TV? Do you reject conversation with those in your home in favour of watching TV? When you work at home, do you have music playing in the background? Do you listen to music when you dress to to go out for the evening?

Exercise 7.1

Think about the questions on media usage in the above paragraph. Write a list of all the media products you watch/read/listen to in an average day. Write a paragraph explaining why you consume these products as you do. You could present your observations in a table like the one.

	What did you watch/read/listen to?	For how much time?	What were your reasons for doing so?
Monday			
Tuesday			
Wednesday			
Thursday			
Friday			
Saturday			
Sunday			

Although in sociology we favour actual research over generalisations based on personal experience, which tends to be limited, it does seem that the mass media dominate our lives. They are an ever-present feature of most people's day-to-day routine. This observation has led many cultural commentators to suggest that modern life is 'media saturated' – that every aspect of our lives is swamped with flickering TV and video images, the audio output from tapes, CDs and so on.

Given the wide reach of all these media – a reflection of the extensive technological developments of our time – it is important that, as sociologists, we look very carefully at the media we use and ask ourselves the following questions:

- Exactly what is it that we are consuming?
- Why are we doing so?
- What are the consequences of this consumption – what might it do to us?

Sociologists seem to fall into two 'camps' when thinking about the value and role of the media in society. This is also true of other popular cultural products, including clothes, food, popular forms of technology and so on.

First, the *pessimistic view* is to see the products of popular culture as a problem for society, that they are cheap, unintellectual and have no 'artistic' value. The consumption of these products is seen as damaging to those who do so, holding them back from thinking for themselves, denying them the pleasure to be had from looking at/reading 'great art'. In this view popular culture has little or no value at all.

Second, the *optimistic view* is that there is nothing wrong with, and sometimes there is great value to be had from, the consumption of popular culture. Simply because something is mass produced for profit does not necessarily mean that it is unintellectual or worthless. In this view the media audience can use popular culture in highly creative ways.

Basic definitions

In order to discuss the two views above – and the many arguments that rest in between these two extremes – we must first be clear about the key terms used in what is known as 'the mass culture debate': 'culture', 'mass culture/popular culture' and 'high/low cultures'.

Culture

Although the concept of 'culture' can be thought about in many different ways (see Chapter 2), a basic distinction is drawn between 'social culture' and 'artistic culture':

- 'Culture' can refer to the 'way of life of a social group', including their values, norms, behavioural patterns, customs and rituals, and even material objects.
- The 'artistic' definition of 'culture' refers to the highest and greatest artistic and intellectual creations of an age, as defined by the society of the time. For example we might say that a person is 'cultured' if he or she listens to opera, reads the novels of Charles Dickens or frequently visits the theatre.

While these are quite different uses of the same word, they are related. The 'artistic and intellectual' products of great worth and merit in the second definition are produced by a society and can therefore be seen as the 'material objects' of the first definition. Judgement of what is or is not 'great art' only can happen within a wider culture – a wider 'way of life', with all its norms, values, customs and so on. In terms of the mass culture debate we are more interested in the second definition, the 'artistic' one.

Mass culture/popular culture

This relates to cultural products (often but not exclusively produced by the media) that everyone has access to, and that the vast majority of the population consume. These products are often associated with the 'common person', and are easy to understand and consume.

High/low cultures

A distinction is often made between:

- 'high culture' – products that are intellectual, artistic, difficult to understand, expensive, and aimed at those with an exclusive taste not shared by 'ordinary people',
- and 'low culture' (frequently equated with popular or mass culture) – products that are easy to understand, cheap, throwaway, common and so on.

Exercise 7.3

 Explain in your own words what 'high culture' and 'low culture' mean, and provide about eight examples of each.

Questions concerning mass culture

The 'mass culture debate' involves the following questions:

- Are modern cultural creations less artistic and intellectual than those of the past?
- If a cultural product is 'popular', does this mean it has less value than something that is only experienced by an elite few?
- If a cultural product is mass produced for financial gain, is it necessarily less artistic or intellectual than one produced by the 'lone artist' simply for pleasure?
- Does popular culture encourage critical thought about society, or hamper it?

Exercise 7.4

 Provide a detailed answer to the above questions for each of three categories: (1) paintings (fine art), (2) television and (3) cinema. Justify your answers.

The poet T. S. Eliot (1948) saw 'high culture' as the concern and product of an educated, sophisticated, artistic and elite class grouping. The culture of the masses was seen by Eliot as less 'worthy', as having less 'value' than that of their educated 'betters'. Marxist sociologists see this highly conservative view of the popular/mass culture of the working classes as providing intellectual justification for the continuation of the class system in society, that the working classes need the ruling class to help them 'better themselves' through ruling-class cultural products, yet at the same time only the ruling classes are able truly to appreciate such products, or deserve to have them!

The 'mass society thesis'

This pessimistic criticque of mass/popular culture is often based on left-of-centre sociological theories such as Marxism. It suggests that popular culture prevents critical and revolutionary thought. It is ideological and leads to false consciousness. In this view, popular culture creates a 'mass society', that is, a society where:

- individuals lose their sense of community;
- lose their individuality;
- and come to rely on strong authority from above.

This is seen as dangerous since if the masses cannot think for themselves, then those who rule society can dominate the masses as they wish, for their own gain. Many mass society arguments owe a great deal to the ideas of traditional Marxism on commodification and commodity fetishism (see Chapters 3 and 10). Marx himself was concerned with the trend in capitalism towards the creation of cultural products as 'commodities' – things to be bought and sold. This process of commodification is seen as devaluing such products because their value is reduced to price, rather than reflecting their cultural, artistic and/or intellectual merit.

The process of commodification is also seen as creating false needs – making people purchase objects/products they do not really need in order to provide capitalists with profits. These false needs give rise to 'commodity fetishism' since people come to worship products and seek ownership of them, and in doing so they see the economic system as valuable since it produces such commodities. Since capitalism 'delivers the goods' and satisfies people's desires it goes unquestioned.

Exercise 7.5

 List three strengths and three weaknesses of the traditional Marxist view of popular culture.

The Frankfurt School

Perhaps the most well known and influential version of the Marxist interpretation of mass culture and commodification was provided by Marcuse, Adorno and Horkheimer of the Frankfurt School in Germany during the lead-up to the Second World War (see Chapters 2 and 3). Adorno and Horkheimer (1979, 1993) argued that advertising in capitalism creates and subsequently manipulates false needs and desires that are fulfilled by consumption. However this fulfilment is only achieved by consuming the latest, newest and 'best' products available over and over again. The consumption of cultural products – commodities – under a capitalist economy creates fetishism, which in turn safeguards the dominance of the ruling group. In this respect consumerism is ideological.

For Marcuse (1964) commodity fetishism, this worshipping of objects through consumption, cheapens these products. Popular culture becomes only as valuable as the price paid for it. This low culture is therefore cheap, crass, vulgar and used to dominate the masses – to stop revolutionary thinking. In this way the mass consumption of mass-produced popular cultural products leads to the creation of a mass society. Free intellectual and critical thought is lost and the masses become passive victims of ideology. Marcuse referred to the masses as 'one-dimensional' since they are only able to be socialised into the dominant culture through the media. This results in a 'paralysis of criticism'.

Adorno and Horkheimer (1979; Adorno, 1991) described the media as a 'culture industry' since it does not attempt to create great pieces of art, but is simply a business – an industry – and like any other business it is only concerned with making a profit. When making this claim they had in mind the early Hollywood film industry. The Frankfurt School proposed a 'hypodermic syringe' model of the effects of popular culture: the masses, living in a mass society, are passive victims of capitalist ideology – injected with false needs by the media and unable to fight, resist or think for themselves.

Evaluation of the Frankfurt School

- The Frankfurt School saw the masses as highly passive victims of ideology.
- In their discussion of commodification, they ignored the creative practices and uses to which people can put popular culture.
- They saw people as controlled by ideology rather than as being able to manipulate and redefine it in revolutionary ways (see Chapter 8).

Exercise 7.6

 List three strengths of the Frankfurt School's views on popular culture.

Although criticised by some, the arguments raised by the Frankfurt School have been influential. For example the German thinker Walter Benjamin, writing at the same time as the members of the Frankfurt School, presented a slightly different but complementary image of the mass production of popular culture. In an essay entitled '*The Work of Art in the Age of Mechanical Reproduction*', Benjamin (1970) divided the consequences of mass production and distribution into two contradictory elements:

- Mass production is in some senses anti-elitist in nature since technology enables elite-only 'high' cultural artifacts to be copied for the masses to see and gain pleasure from.

- However at the same time mass production leads to consumerism, which in turn leads to the problems of commodification suggested by Marx.

Hence mass production is both liberating and dominating at the same time.

The pluralist perspective

The strongest criticisms of the Frankfurt School have come from the advocates of pluralism. This approach to sociological theorising owes a great deal to the interactionists' concern with the active nature of humans. It is referred to as pluralism because its exponents argue that:

- Different people perceive the media in different ways.
- Since there is a large plurality of cultural products, individuals have considerable choice over what they do and do not consume.
- By exercising their choice of what to consume, power is distributed among many different groups in society.
- Humans are active, and as many different choices are made by these creative beings as there are creative beings themselves.

For example Gans (1974) suggests that the mass production of popular culture does not devalue its worth, but instead offers a free and democratic choice to consumers. However Alan Swingewood (1977) argues that the whole idea of a 'mass culture' is a myth (see Chapter 2). Instead it is an elitist value judgement used by some to devalue the interests, activities and pleasures of others in favour of their own.

Exercise 7.7

Obtain a weekly TV guide and select one day only. How much television output is high culture and how much is low? In light of your observations, which of the above views – pluralism or Marxism – appears to be correct about the nature of popular media content? Record your thoughts in a larger version of the table below.

Channel	Day and date:Describe the content of each channel's broadcasting on this day	How much is 'high' and how much is 'low' culture?	What type of programmes are shown at prime time viewing?	When are the more intellectual or critical programmes likely to be shown, if at all?	Which theory – Marxism or pluralism – appears correct on the basis of your evidence?
BBC 1					
BBC 2					
ITV					
C 4					
C 5					
Sky One					

Exercise 7.8

Summarise the Marxist and pluralist positions on mass culture in a table copied from the one below.

	Marxism	Pluralism
Key thinkers		
Key concepts		
Views on popular culture		
How do they see the consumer/audience?		

Exercise 7.9

Write a paragraph as though you were a Marxist criticising the pluralist view, and then the opposite – as though you were a pluralist criticising the Marxist view.

Who exactly are the masses?

The mass culture debate is based on the assumption that the audience, consumers and users of popular culture are a massive 'lump' of individuals – a 'mass' – without free thought or critical awareness. This is a very difficult argument to uphold and it is insulting and elitist. It seems to suggest that some sociologists can see popular culture for the 'intellectual wasteland' it is, but that everyone else – 'ordinary people' – are tricked, fooled and controlled by it.

Ien Ang (1991) suggests that it is very difficult truly to know how people engage with the media and popular culture since a great deal of their use occurs in the home behind closed doors or in the individual mind, and is therefore difficult to observe. Defining the audience/consumers as simply a 'mass' is unrealistic and gets in the way of true understanding. She notes that despite the fact that television has become a significant aspect of society and of people's daily lives, we know little about the actual audiences of the media in general and of TV in particular. So much so that the views of 'ordinary viewers' are often ignored by TV producers, or viewers are categorised into large masses and are seen as unthinking or fickle. This idea that the masses are 'out there' watching TV is little more than an abstraction and a gross generalisation. It is not based on any real understanding of how people view TV and how they understand it.

Raising a similar argument to that of Ang, Raymond Williams (1963) writes:

The masses are always the others, whom we don't know, and can't know. . . . They are here, and we are here with them. And that we are with them is of course the whole point. To other people, we are also masses. Masses are other people. . . . There are in fact no masses; there are only ways of seeing people as masses.

Williams is highly critical of those Marxist sociologists – such as the members of the Frankfurt School – who condemn popular culture as uncritical and therefore unworthy. To make such a claim is to devalue the culture of the working classes themselves – something that Marxists especially should not do given their emphasis on the need to help the working classes to break free from capitalism.

How does the audience use popular culture?

A great deal of present-day discussion on popular culture is less concerned with what it might do *to* the audience and more with audiences *do with it*. This notion that audiences have power, freedom, creativity and choice can be associated with a whole range of perspectives, including interactionism, postmodernism and some versions of neo-Marxism. Added to the image of the audience as creative and active is the idea that the definition of 'high' and 'low' culture is a matter of taste and value judgement. This position is sometimes referred to as 'cultural relativism' (see Chapter 2). In this view all cultural products are as valuable as each other and value is ultimately in the eye of the consumer.

Some Sociologists have suggested that the culture of working-class people – often based on the consumption of popular culture – is just as worthy as that of the middle and ruling classes. To argue otherwise would be to adopt a position of 'cultural elitism' or 'cultural absolutism', suggesting that there exists some absolute value of artistic worth to which all products can be compared in an objective and value-free way.

The 'excorporation' of popular culture

John Fiske (1989) suggests that popular culture can be used by audiences in an active and highly critical fashion. He argues that popular culture is used by subordinate subcultural groups (see Chapter 8) to resist and fight against the dominant ideology of ruling groups. This resistance by subordinate groups – including the working classes and youth subcultures – is based on a process of 'excorporation'. What this means is that the symbols and dominant meanings of a dominant culture can be changed, challenged, turned around and redefined to mean something quite different. These new meanings can then be used to create an alternative world-view to that which dominates society, an alternative way of thinking that uses popular culture in an active rather than a passive way. In this view the audience are not passive, unthinking victims of ideology in popular culture, but highly creative actors with 'agency' (see Chapter 5).

In *Common Culture* Willis *et al.* (1993) suggest that the culture of 'ordinary people' is by no means a reflection of passive acceptance of an uncritical low culture, but is highly creative. Willis writes of the 'symbolic creativity' of subcultures – especially of youth subcultures (see Chapter 8) – whereby popular cultural products, images and signs are actively manipulated. Willis notes that a massive amount of 'cultural work' is undertaken by young people in their everyday lives.

Exercise 7.10

 Design a questionnaire to research the ways in which people at your school/college use popular culture in creative ways.

Willis dismisses the notion that high culture is somehow better than low culture. He argues that the merit of cultural products lies not in what they are, but in how they are used. Since the use to which cultural products are put is not necessarily that which was originally intended, in order to understand the true nature of cultural consumption we need to look at what people actually do. Willis suggests that consumption cannot take place without a massive amount of symbolic action, creativity and interpretation by consumers. Consumption is not passive – it is based on decoding and reading the signs and symbols of cultural products. Even cultural products that might be deemed 'throw-away' or 'profane' (unartistic) may still offer consumers pleasure, new interpretations and possibilities for free thought. In this view there is no such thing as high or low cultures – only degrees of creativity to which all cultural products can be put, be they popular or not.

Models of the audience

To suggest that popular culture can be used in an active fashion to create identity and new cultural meanings is to give humans a degree of agency that was denied to them by the Frankfurt School. They saw the audience of the culture industry as passive victims of media that operate like 'hypodermic syringes'. We turn here to some alternative ways of thinking about the media audience that focus on people's active attempts to construct identity and use popular culture, rather than be used by it.

Barwise and Ehrenberg (1988) describe television as 'low involvement', in other words, the audience does not have to do much in order to consume the product. They provide two examples of this low involvement:

- Little effort need be made by a viewer, and she or he views TV in the same way as every other member of the wider audience.
- People often watch TV while waiting for something else to happen: it is used to fill up 'dead time'.

Barwise and Ehrenberg therefore see the viewing of popular TV programmes as a passive activity, and not one that allows or encourages the creative cultural manipulation spoken about by writers such as Willis. On the other hand, two models suggest that popular viewing *is* highly active and creative:

The first model, known as the 'uses–gratifications approach', is explored in *The Uses of Mass Communication* by Jay Blumler and Elihu Katz (1974). According to this model the audience of popular culture – in this case popular TV – are able to use the media for specific purposes. Thus if one needs background noise, the TV is used in a different way than if one is looking out for a particular item in a news broadcast – the audience have needs that they fulfil, or gratify, through active and selective TV use.

Some sociologists use a model of the audience that is aimed at identifying how people 'decode' (make sense of) what they see. David Morley (1980) was concerned to establish how and why audiences use TV. He chose to focus on a programme called *Nationwide* – a magazine-style programme on current affairs and news. Morley suggests that the audience members in his study used and interpreted the programme in different ways, depending on who they were and the backgrounds they came from. For example he suggests that class, gender, ethnicity, age, cultural identity, political views and personal experience served to 'filter' the messages contained in the programme.

Morley identifies three types of 'decoding' that are performed by audience members – that is, individual audience members 'read', interpret or pull apart (decode) the messages and images they see in different ways, with their backgrounds operating as filters through which this happens:

- *Oppositional.* Some audience members reject what they see and replace the intended meaning with a new one that diverges from the message intended by those who made the product.
- *Negotiated.* Some audience members twist the intended meaning to make it fit in with their own views of the world, and bits of each are fitted together for future use.
- *Dominant.* Some audience members fully accept the dominant or intended meaning of the product and go along with it.

Hence Morley suggests that popular culture produces a wide variety of responses, not just the intended or dominant ones. This idea is reflected in a study by a member of the Glasgow University Media Group (GUMG), Greg Philo (1990). Philo adopts a neo-Marxist stance, but he takes up Morley's idea that the consumers of popular culture interpret the messages of the products in different ways. He suggests that whereas some audience members are affected by ruling-class ideology (what he calls 'hegemony' – see Chapter 8), other members respond to the popular media in a more oppositional and reflexive fashion – seeing ideology for what it is and rejecting it.

Like Morley, Philo argues that our unique personal biographies, experiences and life histories act as a filter and influence our view of popular media products. The users of popular culture are seen as sophisticated, thinking beings, not necessarily taken in by dominant ideology or unable to think critically about the world because of the influence of mass culture.

Exercise 7.11

 List all the aspects of people's backgrounds that might influence what they consume and how they interpret it, for example class and gender.

Postmodernity and popular culture

Postmodernity and popular culture can be seen as fundamentally interlinked. Jameson (1983) locates the emergence of postmodernity in a change in the organisation of the economy. Whereas modernity was characterised by the manufacture of products and the use of raw materials, postmodernity – seen as the 'late industrial era' – is based on consumption rather than production. Given this, postmodernity is characterised by an unprecedentedly rapid expansion in the consumption of popular culture.

Mike Featherstone (1991) points out that in postmodernity, lifestyle construction and the creation/establishment of self-identity are based on the type of popular cultural products we consume, and the creative uses to which we put these products or commodities. The early development of 'modernist' mass consumerism in the West, especially America, after the Second World War is seen as limited in comparison with the postmodern consumerism of today. For example Henry Ford, the creator of the Ford motor car, is famous for his declaration that the purchasers of Fords could 'have any colour they wanted as long as it was black'. The products of mass production in the modernist era were therefore very different from the range on offer today – an almost bewildering array in terms of choice and flexibility.

The wide variety of postmodernist views on popular culture (see also Chapter 6) fall either side of the optimistic–pessimistic divide discussed at the beginning of this chapter. For the 'postmodern optimists', popular culture has become sufficiently widespread for it to be used in many different ways – people create so many different meanings that the traditional difference between high and low cultures has been broken down. The consumption of popular culture is seen as truly liberating – offering the individual a wide choice from which to construct meaning. This optimistic postmodern interpretation is summed up well by Walter Anderson (1996):

> No style dominates. Instead we have endless improvisations and variations on themes; parody and playfulness. Postmodern architects are unabashedly eclectic and call attention to it. People everywhere similarly combine traditions, borrow rituals and myths. All the world's cultural symbols are now in the public domain.

Popular culture is therefore seen as a vast and complex, postmodern playground where we are free to play whatever games of meaning and identity we wish.

However writers such as Jean Baudrillard paint an altogether different, 'darker', pessimistic and sinister picture of the playground of popular culture, one where meaning has collapsed, identity has crumbled and chaos reigns. When discussing the collapse of truth, certainty and meaning, Baudrillard (1993) says:

> It has all been done. The extreme limit of these possibilities has been reached. It has destroyed itself. . . . All that remains to be done is to play with the pieces . . . postmodernity is the attempt – perhaps its desperate, I don't know – to reach a point where one can live with what is left.

For Baudrillard all idea of what is 'real' has come to an end. There is no more certainty, no more means by which to decide what is 'truth'. He describes the experience of watching TV and the signs and images used on TV as 'hyper-real' – 'more real than real'. What he means by this is that since there is no means by which to judge the truth, individuals can turn to whatever source of knowledge they wish. No one can say what is right or wrong. Actual lived experience is no more or less 'true' than the 'truth' offered to audiences by TV programmes. In fact TV images may even appear to be 'more real' than one's own life. It must be noted here that such is the ambiguity in Baudrillard's work – deliberately so, since this is also part of the 'postmodern game' – he seems to find this collapse of meaning exciting and at times even humorous!

In an even more pessimistic tone, Baudrillard (1983) warns against the rise of the 'silent majority'. He paints a picture of a postmodern future where populations return to the sort of mass society written about by the Frankfurt School. The masses become unable to be interested in, or represented by political ideas, religion, science or any other modernist view of a single absolute truth. Instead, all there is left is popular culture, which is consumed in an attempt to try to put some sort of order back into the world, but which in time becomes 'hyper-real' – more real than real. Popular culture alone remains for this silent majority to use/enjoy/think through. They turn to the flickering images on TV screens, unable to divorce the media from their 'real' world of sensation.

Exercise 7.12

 Identify two strengths and two weaknesses of the postmodern view on popular culture.

Conclusion

The role of the media in society and of popular culture in general is certainly a major concern of a number of academic disciplines: sociology, media studies and cultural studies. Given that the forms and styles of popular culture vary greatly and change rapidly, it is an important area of sociological investigation. Everyone in British society is a consumer and virtually everyone is a part of a wider media audience. Within sociological thought we have seen a move away from alarmist and pessimistic 'doomsday scenarios' of the power of the media towards a much more considered approach that looks at the content of popular culture, its producers and its audience. The audience, or consumer, is seen by many thinkers as active and creative. This is not to say that ideology does not exist, but rather that the process of 'decoding' and 'reading' is too complicated for people to be seen as 'cultural robots'. The idea of a 'decoding' individual and a creative group that uses popular culture in an active fashion will be taken up in Chapters 8 and 9.

Examination questions

Use the advice on pages 28–9 to answer the following questions:

(a) Evaluate the idea that popular culture has limited value.

(b) Assess the claim that the media help us to create an identity.

8 Youth culture and subculture

By the end of this chapter you should:

- be able to define the concept of 'subculture';
- have an understanding of various theoretical approaches to the study of youth culture and subcultures;
- have an understanding of how theories interpret contemporary examples of youth subcultures;
- understand the role played by class, capitalism and hegemony in the creation of subcultures;
- be able to evaluate key theoretical interpretations of youth subcultures.

Introduction

Many contemporary sociologists, especially postmodernists, are interested in the role played by popular culture in the creation of identity (see Chapters 6 and 7). 'Popular culture' – or sometimes 'mass culture' – is usually defined as media and other cultural products that are readily available, often cheap to consume and have a popular or mass appeal. Popular culture – especially fashion and music – is also seen to be a major feature of youth subcultures.

Youth subcultures, which are often perceived as 'deviant' (against the norms of society) make good 'copy' for British newspapers. We often hear of the dangers of certain 'deviant' groups of young people who are characterised as drug-taking, wild, often violent, partying all night, having casual sex, listening to unacceptable music and not facing up to the responsibilities of early adulthood. We see, hear and read about politicians criticising single-parent families, poor discipline in schools and a decline in religious morality, and speaking of a rising tide of apathy, fatalism and hedonism among the young. We are told by the tabloids that young people are behaving worse than ever before and that this represents some sort of crisis that must be stopped.

Interestingly, such fears about young people have existed in Britain and elsewhere for a very long time. For example Geoffrey Pearson (1983) notes that the idea of 'young hooligans' roaming city streets and unable to be controlled by the police can be dated as far back as 1898! Not such a modern phenomenon after all! It seems that each generation fears, blames and wishes to protect its youth in equal measure, and each older generation looks back to a time, a 'golden age', when they themselves were young and when young people respected the law and their parents – unlike today! This sensationalism over the activities of the young might be described as a 'moral panic' – an exaggerated, media-provoked fear that causes the members of society to perceive that a problem is much greater than it is. In some cases a problem might not exist at all until it is defined as such by the media. Such moral panics about the young have often featured in political ideologies, especially that of the New Right, who see young people as presenting a hazard to the smooth-running of society if they are not disciplined enough.

Exercise 8.1

Write a list of recent moral panics involving young people. For each one state why you think it occurred. Present your answer in a three-column table with the following headings: 'What groups were targeted as a "problem"?', 'What was it about the behaviour of these groups that made them a problem?', 'Why did they come to public/media attention?'.

The young – and especially teenagers and twenty-somethings – are not, however, solely targeted by the media as a 'problem'. They are also targeted as active and discerning consumers. In other words youth culture is big business for the 'culture industry':

- More than ever before, young people consume cultural goods, especially music and clothes.
- Youth subcultural identities are often associated with specific styles of music and/or bands.
- The life-styles of youth subcultures make interesting subjects for films, docusoaps, musicvideos and TV commercials.

Sociologists are interested in going beyond the ways in which the media characterise youth groups, and to study these people and their life-style choices. They want to explore what subcultures mean for those involved in their creation, and what this in turn means for wider structural forces.

Exercise 8.2

Consider the following examples of youth cultural style. For each one, describe the 'look' that the members of the group have, and what values are most associated with each culture.

- Hip hop　　　● Nu-Metal　　　● Indie kids　　　● Punk　　　● Rave

Before we can discuss the phenomenon of youth subcultures in detail, we need to define the main terms and briefly look at the historical development of the sociological study of youth subcultures. There is an important distinction between the following key concepts:

- *Culture.* This usually refers to the 'way of life' of a larger group and includes the ideas, values, behaviour, ritual practices and material goods of the group.
- *Subculture.* This usually refers to a group that has broken away from the wider, dominant culture: a culture within a culture that has its own specialist norms and values – its own way of life, shared by a smaller proportion of a population.
- *Deviant subculture.* While some subcultures conform for most of part to the broader norms and values of the dominant culture, other groups seek to reject these norms and values and are therefore be considered as a 'deviant subcultures'.

According to these classifications, a group of young people might be seen as members of a subculture if, for example, they all dress similarly and follow a particular type of music; while a group of young people whose central value is committing criminal acts could be seen as members of a deviant youth subculture.

The historical development of subcultural study

Robert K. Merton

An early and influential attempt to define the relationship between culture and subculture was made in the mid 1930s by Merton (1989). Merton's functionalist ideas are sometimes referred to as 'strain theory' since he identified a strain or tension between what he referred to as the 'instititionalised means' and the 'culture goals' of a dominant culture:

- The 'cultural goals' of a society are the main goals that the members of the society are expected to achieve. For example in our culture these are usually seen as getting a good job, being successful at a career, having money, owning a nice house and car, and so on.
- 'Institutionalised means' refers to the legitimate ways in which people seek to reach the goals of the dominant culture. For example, in order to the achieve the dominant goals of Western culture we need to work hard at school, obtain good qualifications and work hard at a career.

Merton noted that the socialisation of culture into the members of society might not lead to everyone being bonded into a state of harmony and consensus, as believed by other functionalists such as Talcott Parsons (see Chapter 3). Instead, Merton suggested that only some people will be able to achieve society's cultural goals. Many others will aspire to the goals but lack the means to achieve them. According to Merton there is a tension between the values or goals that one might have, and the structural position one might hold. Those who are white, middle class and male usually enjoy more advantages in society than those who are not. Equally, in another form of prejudice, the able-bodied are often given more opportunities than the disabled.

Merton saw this tension between structural position and dominant cultural goals as a huge problem for society and one that might provoke a range of subcultural responses. Eventually this could lead to 'anomie' or 'normlessness' since great numbers of people would end up with a wide range of different subcultural values. They would not be bonded together since they would be following different norms, and the possibility of conflict and social breakdown would increase.

Merton identified the following solutions to the structural problems of having a tension/strain between the goals and means in society developed by individuals who join subcultural groups:

- *Conformity.* Strictly speaking this response is not 'deviant' or 'subcultural', since if one conforms one is following the dominant culture. However all other responses are 'deviant' and 'subcultural' since they are not the norm. Many of the latter responses might be made by groups of young people.
- *Innovation.* This means that one accepts and pursues the goals of society, but the legitimate means of reaching them are replaced by illegitimate means – such as delinquency and crime.
- *Ritualism.* This response involves 'going through the motions' by following the means, but never achieving success. The goals are lost sight of.
- *Retreatism.* Here individuals 'retreat' from the wider cultural means and goals and drop out of society, giving up on any form of success, be it deviant or otherwise.
- *Rebellion.* Here the goals and means of the dominant culture are totally replaced by new goals and means.

Exercise 8.3

u in id Consider Merton's classification of deviant responses. In your own words, describe what he means by 'innovation', 'ritualism', 'retreatism' and 'rebellion', and for each one identity a subcultural group that could be classified in this way.

The Chicago School

The ideas of Merton, although based on a functionalist perspective, proved influential in American sociology. The Chicago School shared a number of common concerns with Merton, but developed their ideas differently. The Chicago School is best known for adopting the 'symbolic interactionist' approach to interpretive sociology (see Chapter 4). Robert Park (1929; Park and Burgess, 1925), a one-time student at Chicago University and by the end of his career the head of the Chicago School itself, came up with the idea of 'urban ecology', an idea that was related to the more popular 'symbolic interactionism'.

With 'urban ecology' the city and its organisation are depicted as a series of concentric circles, at the middle of which lies a central business district – the inner core of the city. Next to this central area is a zone referred to as a 'zone of transition' since it has a high migration rate and consequently an unsettled culture. Life in this zone mirrors, in many respects, the idea of the functionalist concept of 'anomie' or normlessness, since with so many groups, many different subcultures emerge. All of these have their own goals and often do not share similar values.

Theoretically speaking, Park's ideas represent the joining together of what are often seen as contradictory theoretical positions. Urban ecology incorporates the functionalist idea of the city as an organic system, but we can also see the development of symbolic interactionist sociology. Edwin Sutherland (1924) noted that individuals can more easily learn the ways of deviant or criminal subcultures in the zone of transition, since they are more exposed to such subcultures in this area. These early ideas on the development of subcultures in the city are still relevant to present-day sociology, and the chaotic life of the city is often a preoccupation of postmodern writers (see Chapters 4 and 6).

Howard Becker

Howard Becker – like Erving Goffman (see Chapter 5) – is a key interactionist figure. Becker applies the ideas of 'self' and 'self-identity' to study how deviant subcultures develop in opposition to the dominant culture. Becker's work is referred to as a 'labelling approach' since he suggests that being seen as deviant is not so much a question of what you actually do, but more a matter of how you are 'labelled' by others. Others have the power to change your self-image. According to Becker (1973):

> social groups create deviance by making the rules whose infraction constituties deviance, and by applying those rules to particular people and labelling them as outsiders ... the deviant is one to whom that label has successfully been applied.

Hence for Becker it is not an individual's actions but the social reaction to them that creates deviance. Becker's ideas are important for the sociological study of subcultures since they show that membership of a subculture defined by others as deviant, marks or labels the individual members as deviant. This shows that subcultural identity can be the result of what others think about you, rather than what you think about yourself.

Exercise 8.4

Evaluation is one of the most important skills to develop as a sociology student. It involves being able to identity both the strengths and the weaknesses of a given idea. Evaluate Becker's ideas by drawing up two lists – one consisting of what you see as the weaknesses of his ideas and the other describing the aspects of his work that you find convincing. Explain each item on both lists, using the ideas of other sociologists either to support or to critique what Becker says.

Subcultural solutions to the problems of society

Becker's ideas are reflected in the work of Stanley Cohen. In his classic text *Folk Devils and Moral Panics*, in order to understand how and why youth subcultural movements emerge and how they might become labelled as 'deviant' by wider society and its dominant culture. Cohen (1987) attempts to unite four factors:

- Labelling.
- Subcultural membership.
- Structural forces.
- Action.

Cohen distinguishes between the concepts of structure and culture:

- *Structure*. This refers to those aspects of society that are beyond the control of and bear down on the individual. Cohen points to the existence of the class system in capitalism as a major structure that controls the life of groups in society.
- *Culture*. This refers to a collective response to the structures that control us. In this sense 'culture' is meaningful to those involved in its creation and helps them to 'act out' their lives. It helps people to make sense of the world around them and is created by people themselves. It is not an impersonal structure or force that turns people into puppets.

Cohen argues that whereas structure creates problems, culture offers individuals potential solutions to these problems. The example that

Cohen uses is the problem of being a young working-class member of a capitalist society. Such a person's life is likely, due to structural forces, to be characterised by:

- Alienation.
- A poor education and few qualifications.
- Low-paid, low-skilled employment or even unemployment.
- Routine and repressive working conditions.
- Poverty.

Given these problems, many working-class adolescents try to act in ways that help them to 'make their own history' – to fight against structural forces through membership of a subculture that offers them the chance to gain ownership of their lives. In this respect the term 'subculture' relates to the ways in which subordinate groups attempt to create a meaningful world to live in, by challenging their problems in a conscious way. Cohen notes that youth subcultures – since they offer resistance to wider structural forces – are frequently labelled as deviant by capitalist society, and are the subject of moral panics in the media. They represent a threat to the dominant culture of capitalism, and therefore need to be controlled.

Exercise 8.5

List the reasons why and how the values and actions of each of the following youth culture groups might threaten the dominant values of capitalist society:

- Hippies
- Skin heads
- Hip hop
- Indie kids
- Ravers
- Nu-Metal

In Cohen's work we can see the unification of two very different types of sociological theory: interactionism and Marxism. The synthesis of these ideas also characterises the work conducted at the *Centre for Contemporary Cultural Studies* (CCCS), based at Birmingham University. The theoretical position held by the members of the CCCS is a version of neo-Marxism and is characterised by the following central beliefs:

- Both structure and action need to be studied.
- Capitalism is exploitative and creates problems for the working classes.
- Subcultures are meaningful attempts to resist the dominant capitalist culture.
- Behind their surface 'style', youth cultures contain hidden meanings that are symbolic and enable those who follow them to evaluate society and respond to the structures they are born into.

Subculture and resistance

A central theme of the CCCS is the idea of youth subcultures as a form of 'resistance'; that is, that all subcultures offer a challenge to the structural forces that cause problems for their members. Cohen (1987) identifies two further aspects of the notion of resistance:

- Subcultures are always fighting against a dominant culture and therefore develop only amongst the subordinate.
- The resistance offered by these subcultural groups is often not very successful. This is referred to as a 'magical' form of resistance: it does not achieve what it sets out to achieve, and it contributes further to the problems of the group.

For example working-class youths might reject education as a protest against a society that has denied them the opportunity to do well. But by giving up before obtaining qualifications their lives are even more likely be characterised by poverty and inequality. Cohen notes that many protests by youth subcultures against the dominant culture are concerned with 'winning space'. In other words they are trying to claim or reclaim their communities, bodies, identities, life-styles and so on by winning both the personal and the symbolic spaces needed to live a life without the problems of structure.

Popular culture as a symbolic 'battleground'

In *Reading the Popular*, John Fiske (1989) develops the idea that battles over class inequality are fought through the life-styles of youth subcultures just as much as by more traditional working-class means, such as trade unions, strikes and demonstrations. The key idea behind the notion that subcultures can fight and resist is the concept of 'excorporation'. What this means is that the cultural products, images, styles, life-styles, behavioural patterns and so on of the dominant culture are taken over by a subculture in order to challenge and change the meanings that the dominant culture has given them. This fight is therefore symbolic in nature since it is an attempt to take a dominant meaning of a symbol and change it to something else. Fiske suggests that popular culture – far from being a mass of cheap, unintellectual, throwaway and ideological media products that lack critical content – can actually contain the seeds of revolutionary struggle:

> Popular culture is made by subordinate peoples in their own interests. . . . Popular culture is made from within and below, not imposed from without or above. . . . Popular culture is always a culture of conflict, it always involves the struggle to make social meanings that are in the interests of the subordinate and that are not those preferred by the dominant ideology (ibid.)

Paul Willis's ideas on the interplay between structure, action and subculture have proven highly influential both within neo-Marxism and among non-Marxist sociologists. For example, by stressing the fact that individuals are born into structures not of their own making, and within these they create their own meaningful action, some of Willis's ideas reflect the 'structurational' sociology developed by Anthony Giddens (1984) – and this similarity is recognised by Giddens himself (see Chapter 5).

In *Learning to Labour*, Willis (1977) argues that the educational experience of working-class youths is shaped by the structure of capitalism. By this he means that schools are largely middle-class institutions that teach middle-class knowledge, are based on middle-class cultural experiences and are largely run by middle-class people – teachers. Within this environment, working-class youths often feel unvalued, alienated, bored and 'picked on' by teachers. Willis argues (as do Bowles and Gintis – see Chapter 3) that this disheartening educational experience instils in working-class youths the characteristics they will need to cope with working in factories and other routine and manual occupations. Through their boredom, they 'learn to labour'.

Willis notes, however, that many working-class youths are not passive in this process, nor are they unconscious of it, rather they are fighting against the unequal class-based structures of capitalist society. Through the creation of a subculture based on 'having a laugh' they frequently 'bunk off' lessons, give up on homework, do not take examinations seriously and ridicule middle-class children for being 'swots' or, in Willis's study 'ear 'oles'. They refuse to be taken in by the education system – they resist.

Exercise 8.6

Think about Willis's example of schooling, then write a detailed list of the ways in which young people might fight against the school system (for example they might pass notes around the classroom in secret). For each example on your list, state why and how this might help them to define themselves as a person/individual (for example, passing notes around enables them to discuss what they wish and deny the authority of the teacher).

However this is 'magical resistance'. It is largely ritualistic, since not only does it not get them very far, but not having qualifications further reduces their power to fight against the class-based structural forces later in life. Through their subcultural actions their worst fears about their future lives are realised!

Rethinking our definitions

Willis's ideas lead us to reconsider terms such as 'culture' and 'subculture'. Willis (1993) makes an important distinction between the following concepts:

- *Dominant/hegemonic culture.* Western societies have a dominant culture that is based on the values of the class that rules – the capitalist class. This observation reflects the traditional or classical Marxist notion that a 'dominant ideology' (see Chapter 3) is used by one group to benefit themselves and reinforce their position of power.
- *Parent culture.* Within a dominant culture, individuals' life-styles are largely based on their social class. Thus everyone has what is called a 'parent culture' – a class-based culture from which different groups are given limited choices within the structural forces that control society. These are not 'subcultures' since this term is reserved specifically for a culture of resistance to wider dominant forces.
- *Common culture.* Whereas the dominant culture – based on the values of the ruling class (known as the 'hegemonic culture') – structures and shapes the nature of society, some people can challenge and resist this structural force. This is 'common culture' – a place of resistance where the dominant culture cannot reach.
- *Subculture.* Each subculture (although it makes more sense to think in terms of a collection of different subcultures) is a specific example of a common culture. It is a 'counter hegemonic' culture since it is based on resistance to the ideas of the ruling group or groups.

Gramsci, the CCCS and hegemony

The Italian thinker Antonio Gramsci, writing in the 1930s, took the traditional Marxist accounts of 'ideology' and 'false consciousness' (see Chapter 3) further with his own concept of 'hegemony' (see Gramsci, 1971, 1977, 1978). This idea has proven very influential with many modern-day neo-Marxists, especially those in the CCCS. The starting point for the idea of hegemony is Gramsci's observation that ruling-class domination and control in capitalist society do not simply rest on the use of force and violence, but also operate at the level of ideas. The masses can be fooled or tricked into thinking that society is fair, when in fact it is against their true interests. This is the traditional Marxist conception of 'ideology' – that false ideas are used by ruling-class groups to hide the true nature of class inequality and exploitation.

The idea of hegemony goes further than this. It refers to the ways in which people in society actively consent to their domination. In this way ruling-class power is allowed to continue, without the need for physical force to maintain it.

Hegemony means that culture is the result a war of ideas between different groups, each with its own idea of what society should be like, depending on its own interests. If one side wins this struggle or battle and its ideas come to be seen as 'common sense' by groups who may not benefit from them, then this is 'hegemony'. In this way the world-view of society is shaped by one specific set of ideas and the majority of cultural products will, in time, reflect and reinforce this world-view without the ruling class having to maintain strict control over them. Thus people go along with their domination, since their world-view tells them that this is how society must be, and it simply would not make sense for it to be any other way. The CCCS sees subcultural groups as attempts to fight the dominant world-view; that is, they are 'counter-hegemonic'.

The CCCS and semiology

The members of the CCCS have also been influenced by 'semiology' – the study of signs (see Chapter 9). In particular, some members of the CCCS have been influenced by the ideas of the French cultural commentator and semiologist Roland Barthes (1993). Barthes depicts ordinary life as a 'text', which just like a poem, novel, play or painting can be studied to find the hidden meanings that lie beneath the surface.

The idea behind semiology is that day-to-day cultural activities should not simply be taken at face value. They are not simply 'how they appear to be', or 'just are'. Instead, Barthes and other semiologists look for the signs or symbols hidden in everyday life. What does an activity really mean? What are people really trying to say about themselves? When looking at youth subcultures, it is not simply a matter of considering their favourite music and what they wear. We need to go beyond this and ask 'what does it *really* mean'? Why this particular style of music? What does this sort of fashion mean? Why do they use these words and not others?

We need to 'break down' or to 'deconstruct' the hidden meanings behind youth subcultures – a theme that, combined with Gramsci's notion of hegemony, appears in Dick Hebdige's book *Subculture: the meaning of style* (1979). Hebdige writes about the ability of 'alternative' subcultures to create oppositional subcultures that allow the subordinate to develop counter-hegemonic life-styles, symbols and 'spaces'. These subcultures work against the ideology of the dominant cultural groups in society (the capitalist class), in the minds of the members of the subcultural groups and through the styles of dress they wear. Youth styles are 'meaningful'. They can be used to challenge, to resist.

Exercise 8.7

Choose a favourite song of yours and deconstruct it. Make a presentation to your class explaining what the song means and what are the hidden messages and references in the lyrics.

By 'style' Hebdige means the many methods of symbolic expression open to subcultural groups. For example:

- Dress.
- Haircuts.
- Behavioural patterns.
- Patterns of language.
- Ways of 'carrying oneself', including walking/standing, facial expressions and body language.
- Dance styles (or even the decision not to dance!).

All these forms of expression are seen as 'symbolic' – they are more than just 'being fashionable'. They can stand for oppositional values. They might attack hegemony.

Exercise 8.8

This exercise requires you to think about how youth cultural 'style' can contain hidden messages or symbols. For each of the six forms of style listed above, provide an example of a youth culture that places emphasis on that style and explain what it means.

Hebdige argues that hegemony is like a 'moving equilibrium'. In this respect he shares with Gramsci the notion that hegemony is powerful, but not stable. It is not fixed, but changing. Challenges to hegemony can arise that can prove difficult for ruling groups to suppress; but other challenges can be redefined and incorporated into the dominant culture, where they pose no real threat. For example alternative life-styles can become part of the accepted mainstream through overexposure on television, which strips them of their underground and radical qualities. These previously challenging counter-hegemonic subcultures simply become another product to consume, and to line the pockets of the capitalist media owners.

Willis *et al.* (1993) argue that even if they are popular, mass and based on the consumption of low-culture products, youth subcultures are still massive feats of creativity, particularly in respect of the manipulation of old symbols, the invention of new ones and the redefinition of previous cultural practices:

we insist that there is a vibrant symbolic life and symbolic creativity in everyday life, everyday activity and expression – even if it is sometimes invisible, looked down on or spurned. . . . Most young people's lives are . . . actually full of expressions, signs and symbols through which individuals and groups seek creatively to establish their presence, identity and meaning. Young people are all the time expressing or attempting to express something about their actual or potential cultural significance. This is the realm of living common culture. Vulgar sometimes, perhaps. But also 'common' in being everywhere, resistant, hardy (ibid.)

Willis *et al.* point out that although this is highly creative, it is also 'ordinary' – not in the sense that it is mundane, boring or unworthy of artistic consideration, but in the sense that it is day-to-day: it is inescapable:

We are thinking of the extraordinary symbolic creativity of the multitude of ways in which young people use, humanize, decorate and invest with meanings their common and immediate life spaces and social practices – personal styles and choice of clothes; selective and active use of music, TV, magazines; decoration of bedrooms; the rituals of romance and subcultural styles; the style, banter and drama of friendship groups; music-making and dance (ibid.)

As an example of such common, day-to-day yet creative uses of symbols for the purposes of identity, consider how and why young people decorate their bags, school books, folders and bedroom walls with posters, stickers, drawings and messages to and from friends. Why does this occur? What does this cultural practice mean? For Willis this is a creative activity in which one plays with meaning and tries to establish who one is.

Weinstein (1991) borrows the term 'bricolage' from structural anthropologist Claude Lévi-Strauss (see Chapter 9) to discuss how subcultures borrow, redefine and use styles and symbols from cultural groups other than their own. Bricolers are social actors who create meaningful cultural myths, stories and so on in order to think about and understand the world around them. The process of creating such myths and stories is highly creative and based on the manipulation of symbols. It borrows from traditional interpretations of symbols and reclassifies them. It uses old cultural signs and symbols in fresh ways. Although this concept was used to describe how myths are created in small-scale, non-literate cultures, the term is often used to refer to the creative symbolic interpretations made by groups in today's society. What this means is that to establish an original place in the world, subcultural groups create for themselves a unique sense of style. To fight against the hegemony of a dominant cultural group, they borrow, redefine and reuse past and present cultural symbols in new ways. This is what is meant by 'bricolage' – the mixing of symbols by reclassifying them and actively creating new and meaningful subcultures based on resistance to dominant values.

Henry Giroux (1983, 1994, 1998) argues that if subcultural activities by alienated youth are serious attempts at counter-hegemony, then they must be being undertaken in a conscious fashion. Giroux sees this as a paradox of youth subculture – a contradiction, but one that is almost impossible to avoid. On the one hand, many youth subcultures are attempts to reject a dominant hegemony – especially, by definition, a dominant *adult* hegemony. That is, they wish to separate themselves and their history from adult society. However, when rejecting the dominant adult hegemony these youth groups end up turning to the consumption of products largely controlled by adults, especially the media and the music industry. Giroux, when discussing the 1970s punk movement in Britain, notes that when truly antagonistic and counter-hegemonic subcultures emerge they are quickly swallowed up by the capitalist culture industry, sometimes amid cries of 'sell-out' by the original fans.

Exercise 8.9

Copy out and complete the following table to help you evaluate the ideas in this section.

Writer	Basic argument on popular culture	Strengths	Weaknesses
Stanley Cohen			
John Fiske			
Paul Willis			
Dick Hebdige			
Weinstein			
Henry Giroux			

The historical rise of youth culture

For many commentators the 'teenager' is a recent social phenomenon. This specific age group – a symbol for young adulthood – has its origins in the rise of affluence and the emergence of a culture industry in the West in the aftermath of the Second World War. During this period there was a move away from an economy based on the production of goods from raw materials, and towards one based on the consumption of goods and the provision of services. The emerging communications industry – television, films and music – is considered to have invented the typical teenager in order to create a market for its goods. Youth music dates back to the development of rock 'n' roll in the

United States, the subsequent expansion of the music industry into soul, jazz and pop music, and finally the beginnings of rock with bands such as the Beatles and the Rolling Stones. All these styles of music caused a moral panic among white (adult) society at the time. They were seen to stand for:

- Rebellion by the young.
- The rejection of traditional values, especially religious and family-based ones.
- A rise in anti-authoritarianism.
- A rise in recreational drug taking and sexual permissiveness.
- The politicisation of youth and student movements.
- The replacement of the work ethic with pleasure-seeking.

Although it seems that every generation has questioned the behaviour of its young, the Second World War is regarded as a watershed for popular culture because of the creation of a multiplicity of youth cultures.

Youth culture and television

In many youth subcultures emphasis is placed on the consumption of popular culture. Given this, the growth of TV viewing in the last twenty years or so has been particularly bound up with the creation and rise of youth culture. They go hand in hand, since young people make up a vast proportion of the TV audience and images of youth – especially sexual images – are used to sell numerous commodities. The media also targets the young as a subject. A great number of programmes are not just aimed at young people, but also promise to expose the true lives of the young (as is seen with the 'docusoap' format and highly sensationalist documentaries in general), which are then used to create moral panics.

Neil Postman (1985) suggests that TV is causing a 'disappearance of childhood' since very young TV viewers are being increasingly exposed to images of sex, violence and other adult behaviour that children were sheltered from before the arrival of TV. For Postman, TV robs children of their innocence and causes them to grow up too quickly. Against this, without the rapid growth of TV viewing youth culture would not be as widespread or as varied as it is. TV may not strip children of their childhood, rather it may create 'youth' for the young.

Postmodern TV?

In contemporary social theory and cultural criticism a great deal of attention has been paid to the rise of postmodern ideas (see Chapters 6 and 7). Given the emphasis by postmodernist, on audiences' creative use of 'low' or popular culture (see Chapter 7), we should consider the relationship of youth subcultures to popular cultural forms such as TV and music.

Postmodern TV shows can be seen as sharing the characteristics of the wider postmodern culture in society. They are based on irony, self-reference and pastiche, and frequently convey ambivalent meanings that can be interpreted in many ways. For example the American TV show *Baywatch* – the most watched television show in the world at the end of the 1990s – is a perfect example of the postmodern sensibility in the sense that the narrative structure of the programme is broken down and based on pastiche – combining many different elements together. The average episode contains slow-motion sequences, frequent use of flashbacks, music video-like sequences and a vast array of 'perfect', highly sexualised bodies. It is unclear exactly what *Baywatch* means to its audience, that is, how the audience experiences the meanings represented. Is it a drama about lifeguards, or a crime show, or is it used in a pornographic way by adolescents – displaying as it does images of 'impossibly perfect' women shaped by plastic surgery and breast implants?

Postmodern programmes frequently depict postmodern youth as nihilistic, hedonistic, drug-taking, interested in popular throwaway culture, and especially obsessed with TV and video games. Such postmodern youth are what American commentators frequently refer to as the 'MTV generation': short attention spans, interested in cultural products that offer little substance but a great deal of style, consuming today's products now – instant gratification, over in a flash, gone tomorrow.

For example one of the characters in the animated American TV show *The Simpsons*, 10 year-old Bart, has grown to love TV more than his family, is totally desensitised to TV violence and is interested only in 'being cool'. Although we might argue that this is only a cartoon (which it is), it is interesting to think about the image of youth presented to us in such cultural products. While programmes such as *The Simpsons* are based on satire, they can be seen both as a representation of popular attitudes of the time, and as a massive source of meanings for the audience – meanings that might help them to construct their particular view of the world around them.

Steven Best and Douglas Kellner (1998) suggest that another popular American cartoon series – *Beavis and Butt-head* – offers a quite disturbing vision of the youth of tomorrow. The two central characters spend all their time as 'couch potatoes': time-killing spectators of a media-based 'reality' of which they lack the ability to be critical – the most they can manage is to say that something 'sucks' or is 'cool'. There appears to be a similarity here to the postmodern concept of the 'hyper-real' (see Chapter 6). Beavis and Butt-Head are more embedded into their media world than they are into the real world, based on their own experiences. The most ironic thing of all is that while such programmes might intend their image of the postmodern young to act as a warning to society that it is losing its children to TV, they are also part of the problem since they are a part of the media-saturated world that the audience is being lost to – and as such they present a 'reality' for tomorrow's postmodern children to copy!

Exercise 8.10

Take a popular television programme of your choice and think about the ways in which it might be an example of 'postmodern television'. Make a presentation to your class on your findings.

Youth culture and the music industry

Youth subcultures do not simply consume music, they are often based on a very particular form of music. Yet the relationship between the symbolic actions of individuals and commercial forces is not clear. When music scenes are 'underground', individuals establish and keep them alive by highly creative means – including word of mouth, via pirate radio broadcasts (as with the early development of raves and warehouse parties) and through photocopied fanzines and information sheets. However, when musical styles and scenes become more widely known they are often taken up the wider, profit-seeking music industry and a hence become 'commodities' – bought for a price.

Although a great deal of subcultural activity is based on the consumption of cultural products made for profit by the music industry, the meanings and motives behind the choice of consumption – and the way that the music is 'used' after consumption – can still be active and creative. As Willis *et al.* (1993) note, while pop music is sometimes seen as low-culture and throwaway and the audience is seen as passive, this ignores the massive feats of symbolic creativity on the part of those who consume such music:

> Most musical activity . . . begins as and from consumption, from the process of listening to music. But consumption itself is creative . . . it depends too on consumer abilities to make value judgements, to talk knowledgeably and passionately about their genre tastes, to place music in their lives, to use commodities and symbols for their own imaginative purposes . . .
>
> For many young people the purchasing of records and tapes is an important sphere of cultural activity in itself, one that can range in intensity from casual browsing to earnest searching for particular records. It is a process that involves clear symbolic work: complex and careful exercises of choice from the point of initial listening to seeking out, handling and scrutinizing records (ibid.)

The consumption of music is often fundamental to youth subculture and identity. Music is often an ever-present feature of life in the home, serving as a background sound-track to other activities. Equally, music is a source of entertainment outside the home and a topic of conversation and debate. Finally, because of home-taping it is often a personalised record of daily life – carried around from place to place via audio-tape and CD players. Many of the technological developments in the world of music encourage such creative consumption. The invention of audio tapes, CDs, mini-discs, recordable CDs and MP3s can be seen as providing technological liberation from the days when music came from a large radio in the home or from records: not portable, unable to be rerecorded and manipulated, unable to be ever-present. Paul du Gay *et al.* (1997) consider that the use of personal stereos is a highly meaningful cultural practice. The personal stereo is 'cultural' since:

- It is a product that we can buy and consume.
- It is represented in advertising using cultural images.
- It has a cultural image of its own – as developed by advertisers.
- It is seen to have recognisable significance in everyday life – we see people using them all around us.
- The film industry often uses images of people using a personal stereo to represent certain cultural groups – often youth.
- It is used by individuals in a creative way to consume music how and where they wish.

Du Gay *et al.* (ibid) argue that, as a cultural product, the use and popularity of the personal stereo raises some key issues and themes of contemporary life, based on its ability to offer 'private listening in public places'. It suggests:

- The lonely figure in the crowd.
- The use of media to screen out the boring, routine aspects of everyday life.
- An emphasis on mobility and choice.
- The self-sufficient individual wandering alone through the city landscape.

Du Gay *et al.* suggest that the popular use of the personal stereo in everyday life is both a part of modern culture and a symbol of it. Like cash cards and mobile phones it has become an easily recognisable image for those of us who live in the contemporary world, and it enables us to understand what it means to live in such a world:

> If we can conjure up a picture of what 'modernity' is like as a distinctive way of life, with an image of, say, the Manhattan skyline or some other similar urban landscape – as many television programmes and films do – we could do the same by tuning in to

the typical sounds of the late-modern city. They would include not only snatches of recorded music but other familiar sounds, like the wailing siren of ambulance, fire-engine or police car, the endless murmur of traffic, the exhalations from sooty exhausts, whezzing engines and chugging juggernauts – the modern sound-scape (ibid.)

The personal stereo is lightweight, small and portable – a true reflection and representation of modern technology. It is made to be 'worn' – it is part of one's identity: an extension of the body, carried wherever we go. Finally, it is designed to be mobile – to be used by people who are rushing around.

Exercise 8.11

id in What other technological objects might be seen as a symbol of modern times? Listed below are five examples. Describe how each one symbolises our contemporary world and what it might say about those who use or carry it.

- Mobile phone
- WAP phone
- Portable tape/mini disc/CD player
- MP3 player
- Digital watch

Is there a postmodern youth culture?

We shall now discuss some recent developments in youth subcultural styles and evaluate them from the point of view of postmodernises. When sociologists describe popular culture as 'postmodern' they are referring to the hybrid, pastiche, pick-and-mix nature of the use of contemporary cultural signs and symbols in fashion, architecture, music and so on. Postmodern ideas are not just the province of academics and social theorists commenting on the young and their activities – the media have latched onto the term as a fashionable device and use it to reflect on themselves.

Variations of dance-based musical styles – such as jungle, big beat, techno, drum-and-base and garage – are often described as postmodern since they emphasise ambiguity, ironic and 'knowing' references, the borrowing of other styles and sounds, and a sometimes pessimistic, sometimes hedonistic atmosphere. These styles of music frequently blur the boundary between so-called 'high' and 'low' cultures by sampling from both and mixing the two together. Such samples might include an eclectic mixture of the spoken word, rap, chanting, snatches of famous historical speeches, news reports and film soundtracks, 'fake' distortion and feed-back sound effects, and even a deliberately created 'hiss' from a record player needle – despite the fact that the recordings are digital and could be cleaned up if wished.

For example, the music magazine 'Q', in a review of the 1998 album 'Hello Nasty' by the white American rap group the Beastie Boys, tells us that 'frat boy goofiness has been replaced by what we might have to call post-modernism: old-school hip hop beats and scratching vie with mantric buddhist bells, latin, 60s garage-psych vignettes and rhyme-swopping mayhem' (Q magazine, no. 148, 1999). In this sense this type of music is postmodern since it plays around with style, form and meaning in a way that would never have been accepted or even imagined in the past. In popular music the postmodern rallying cry of 'anything goes' is at the root of much of what is produced. Q magazine (no. 155, 1999) describes Madonna as a postmodern icon. Madonna's projection of style (though usually reflecting the mainstream world of American white rock) is based on frequent reinvention of herself, the use of many different cultural forms and ethnic musical styles, a sexualised display of the body or, conversely, the masking of the body through body piercing and tattooing, and playing around with religious images, sexuality and so-called 'deviant' sexual practices. This is very postmodern since it is a hybrid of many different cultural forms and signs.

Pre-postmodern youth culture was traditionally seen as 'exclusive'. Membership of a movement or group involved not just liking some styles of music, but passionately disliking others. In postmodern youth culture and music there has been a blurring of musical styles as never before. For example 'white' guitar-based rock music takes from urban 'black' music the use of drum machines, record decks and sampling to create something in between the two. The indie band Kula Shaker combines the 1960s guitar rock of while bands such as the Beatles and the Rolling Stones with Hindi musical sounds and Hindu religious images and references, and adds to this sampling and other sound effects.

Some examples of postmodern youth cultures

Slacker/grunge

According to Jonathon Epstein (1998) the members of what is known as the 'slacker' or 'grunge' culture are twenty-somethings born between 1964 and 1979 – often of 'baby-boomer' parents who grew up in the 1960s. 'Slackers' tend to be middle class and white, and they have adopted a rather nihilistic approach to the time they live in – seeing their future as bleak. The grunge or slacker look has borrowed a great deal from some aspects of punk and has in turn influenced the indie-kid look. The movement as a whole is post-punk and has been taken up by American 'art school' bands, as was the case with punk in Britain in the 1970s. The musical style of the Seattle band Nirvana is considered to encapsulate grunge culture.

In the album 'Mellow Gold' by Beck, the chorus in the opening track describes very clearly the slacker world-view: 'I'm a loser baby, so why don't you kill me?' The members of this subculture might be described as postmodern since they are pessimistic about the future and therefore give up on the present. Unlike punks, however, slackers are not angry about the drying up of the future – they simply see this as a rational and realistic response to a changing world. Many commentators refer to them as 'Generation X', meaning affluent, middle-class people who are highly educated and could be highly successful but instead decide to drop out and take 'dead-end' jobs: what postmodern author Douglas Coupland refers to as 'McJobs'.

Rave and techno

Lori Tomlinson (1998) notes that 'Chicago house music' (the forerunner of rave, techno, trance, acid house and so on in Britain) was originally based in clubs frequented by the gay community. Techno or rave thus originated from the cultural practices of a disadvantaged group. Tomlinson quotes Andrew Ross (1994), who suggests that dance music genres can be classified according to the class of those who follow them – with techno subscribed to by working-class youth, and 'ambient' followed by more middle-class devotees.

Tomlinson (1998) deconstructs rave as a genre or subculture based on the concept of 'age'. She suggests that rave culture is about reclaiming childhood: it is based on primary colours and small clothes; the use of toys as props at rave events is common, especially whistles and dummies; females often put their hair into child-like pigtails; and many rave tracks include themes from TV shows aimed at children. In fact, as was claimed by the Britain media at the time, the initial popularity of the children's show the *Teletubbies* was due to ravers coming home from clubs in the early hours of the morning and watching the programme as part of a psychedelic experience.

Rave also offers a culture of community since the pleasure of attending a rave event is based on having physical contact with others when dancing on one's own. This is reflected in the often anonymous nature of rave musicians. Many do not seek pop-star fame and publicity, and prefer to remain 'faceless'.

In *Club Cultures* Sarah Thornton (1995) states that the young clubbers involved in the rave and techno scenes have a highly developed sense of style and taste, and use this to judge who is an insider or outsider of the clubbing scene. Insider membership, and the sharing of common subcultural values and fellowship, is based on the possession of what Thornton calls 'subcultural capital': having the ability to know what is 'in' or 'hip' and what is not – ranging from styles of dress, to language, to dance steps, and even to the music itself and the DJs who play it. An important credential for an insider is a long-standing relationship with the dance-scene community (not just jumping on a fashionable bandwagon) and an understanding of the underground rave scene – not just the commercial and popular clubs. This could be seen as representing some sort of search for authenticity in the postmodern age. In a time when all claims to taste, art and identity are deemed to be no more worthy than any other, are some people seeking a sense of security and membership of a scene that is perceived to have 'roots', rather than just being a cultural throwaway?

Hip-hop and rap

Angela McRobbie (1986) and Kobena Mercer (1995) both claim that rap music – and in particular the act of 'scratching' – is a highly postmodern phenomenon and the ultimate expression of postmodern cultural values:

- The music is a pastiche of many elements.
- It is immediate and for pleasure, and lays no claim to ultimate artistic taste.
- It often mixes high and low cultures together.
- It is frequently self-referential, using samples in ironic ways.

Hence the hip-hop DJ conforms to Strauss's concept of a 'bricoleur' (someone who performs the process of 'bricolage'), since they are borrowing cultural symbols and styles, reclassifing them and using them for their own means. In the ultimate example of postmodern ironic expression, the dancing partner to hip hop music – breakdancing, which orginated in the poor ghettos of inner-city America as a symbolic representation of gang warfare – is now part of the staple diet of white, commercial dance groups and is frequently used by advertisers to sell products such as trainers to the white, surburban, affluent middle class in Britain.

Willis *et al.* (1993) suggest that the cultural significance of rapping can be likened to the oral tradition of passing on stories in small communities. With its emphasis on the immediate environment, day-to-day life and an awareness of the political nature of class, urban and ethnic experiences, rap music represents an attempt to reflect on the nature of life and one's place in the community.

'Wiggers'

The term 'wigger' is a contraction of 'white nigger'. It is used sometimes as a racist insult, and sometimes by white lower-middle-class youths to refer to themselves. Wiggers take on and incorporate into their own cultural practices the style adopted by inner-city, usually American, black youths. In this case 'style' includes dress, language, music and so on. Some commentators see this type of youth subculture as highly postmodern since it involves mixing and playing with traditional ethnic identities in new ways.

Hardcore

David Locher (1998) has studied what in Britain called 'hardcore' and in the US is known as 'industrial' or sometimes 'industrial hardcore'. With its roots in guitar-based music such as punk, grunge and speed-metal, and its borrowing of techno-based sampling, break-beats and drum machines, this style of music can be seen as mirroring the postmodern cultural practice of picking-and-mixing from previous cultural movements. Other variations combine Ska (a reggae-based musical style) with speed metal or punk, and sometimes rap with heavy metal guitar work. This is often referred to under the broader heading of 'nu-metal'. Like the music of some slacker bands, hardcore music is often taken up by urban 'street-skaters' and 'boarders'.

Exercise 8.12

Select a song from a musical style of your choice and consider the ways in which it might be an example of postmodern music. Make a presentation to your class on your findings.

Conclusion

Youth subcultures are the source of many moral panics in society, providing even more reason for sociologists to take seriously what others in society might dismiss as unimportant – just a phase that young people are going through. It is important for sociologists to understand why young people behave as they do, how they use seemingly trivial media products as a source of identity and creativity and how such creativity is symbolic, meaningful and at times political. All this will be ignored if we dismiss such cultural groups as unimportant because they are based on fun!

A dominant theme in contemporary subcultural study is the idea of creativity or agency – an idea that takes us back to the action approach discussed in detail in Chapter 4. This concept is used in an interesting way by many thinkers. It is often combined with a Marxist-based approach, uniting structural and action sociologies together.

Examination questions

Use the advice on pages 28–9 to answer the following questions:

(a) Assess the sociological explanations of the rise of youth culture since the Second World War

(b) To what extent can youth culture be seen as a popular rebellion against the powerful in society?

9 Semiology, structuralism and poststructuralism

> By the end of this chapter you should:
>
> - understand the method of semiologial analysis;
> - be able to apply the ideas of structuralism to culture and identity;
> - be able to use the semiological method to think about youth subcultures;
> - be able to compare structuralism with poststructuralism.

Introduction

Sociology is a distinctive way of thinking about the world and it has a recognisable world-view that allows us to identify issues of concern to sociologists, yet ideas, concerns, methods and theories from other social sciences and related subjects can influence the development of sociology, and *vice versa*. So at one level sociology is a distinct subject, but at another it contributes theories to a wider 'resource pool' of theories taken from other subjects, such as psychology, philosophy, anthropology, cultural studies and so on. For example the ideas of the postmodernists (see Chapter 6) have influenced all these subjects as well as sociology, and in this book we can see that some of the ideas of philosophers and anthropologists are of interest to sociologists. Given that this book is about culture and identity it is necessary to look at what these subjects have to say since the themes of culture and identity are important to all subjects that study human life, even if they do so in different ways.

In this chapter we shall look at some of the ideas from linguistics, anthropology, media studies and philosophy that have influenced sociologists when attempting to answer the essential question of what human behaviour really means.

The answer to this question can be seen as the end goal of sociological study. The business of those who 'do' sociology is not just to theorise, but also to say something about what life is like and what it really means. A dominant theme in sociology is the idea of a 'sociological imagination' – a term coined by the American sociologist C. Wright Mills (1959) (see Chapter 2). In our 'sociological imaginations' we aim to see and then understand the world by detaching ourselves from 'common-sense thought' – the ideas of the culture in which we have been brought up. Although common sense enables us to be capable actors in society, it may stop us truly thinking about 'why' we do the things we do in our culture.

Exercise 9.1

What are the problems of common-sense thought for the sociologist, and how does common-sense thought differ from sociological knowledge? Copy out and complete the following table – you might like to refer back to the ideas of C. Wright Mills in Chapter 2 for some help.

What are the features of common-sense thought?	What are the problems of common-sense thought?	What are the features of sociological knowledge?	Why is sociological knowledge better than common-sense thought?

The use of theories allows us to go beyond what common sense tells us society is like. For example Marxists use their theories to argue that although society might appear quite fair to those involved, it is actually highly unequal. The task – and the promise – of sociology is not just to see what humans do, but to try to understand why – to search for the meaning behind what we see happening. For example why might some people have their body pierced? What does this mean? Why doesn't everyone do it? Why has it suddenly become popular? One way of thinking about what things really mean, about the hidden meanings behind the action, is known as 'semiology', which was originally developed for use in the study of language – called 'linguistics'.

Semiology and structuralism

Thinkers who adopt a structural approach tend to believe that what we see doesn't always tell us what is really going on. Structuralists believe that we have to look beyond the surface action and study the hidden patterns that make this action meaningful. These hidden patterns are the structures that unite all the surface variations together. Once we can identify the structure and understand how it works, we can understand better what human social life means. If we only observe society directly, we may see glimpses of the pattern but we shall never achieve a full understanding.

The philosophical ideas of structuralism are linked to the method of analysis known as semiology – the scientific study of 'signs'. Semiology and structuralism have been influential in sociology because they have raised three key observations/concepts:

• The idea of reality being a 'structure' or pattern beneath the surface.
• The importance of symbols in human society and culture.
• The importance of the idea of 'difference' or 'otherness' in the creation of cultural meanings.

Saussure

Semiology is associated with the work of Ferdinand de Saussure, a linguist lecturing at the University of Geneva at the start of the twentieth century. Saussure's *Course in General Linguistics* (1983) marked the start of a new and highly influential way of thinking about language. Before Saussure, language tended to be studied in a historical fashion. Changes in words, sounds and meanings were studied in the order they developed in the culture that spoke the language in question. Saussure proposed something very different – an idea that led to the philosophical position of 'structuralism'. Saussure drew a distinction between:

• *structure*: 'langue' – the system of differences between signs; and
• *surface*: 'parole' – the use of these signs in day-to-day speech.

Saussure thought that language should be seen as a pattern or a structure that unites all the individual acts of speech within a language into a regular whole. This is the true but unseen 'reality' of how a language exists. Acts of speech are simply the surface. The true reality of language is the rules that make all the variations in speech possible. Saussure saw all language as made up of a collection of 'signs', that is, collections of symbols that stand for, represent, 'symbolise' something outside the language. For example the sound we make when we utter the word 'tree' is simply a symbol for something that our particular language calls by the sign 'tree'.

Each sign has two parts to it, known as a 'dyad':

• a *signifier*: the 'sound image', the actual word itself; and
• a *signified*: the concept, in our minds, of the object that the sound image represents.

According to Saussure the allocation of these signs to actual objects is purely arbitrary. There is no real reason why the object we call a 'tree' should actually be called 'tree' at all. This is why different societies and cultures have different ways of speaking. They have assigned different signs to objects. However once the signs have been allocated, then those who are born into the language have no choice but to use that sign.

Why and how are signs allocated to objects in the first place? For Saussure it does not matter what signs are used, only that there is agreement about the rules and examples. The most important thing is that signs only become 'meaningful' because they are different from other signs. Therefore when we use the sign 'tree', because it is different from the sign 'dog' we can make sense of it. If however what we call 'dog' and 'tree' had the same sign, there would be no difference and thus no meaning could be established. It is important to note that while language is thus a structure – or a system – it is also abstract and communal. The rules of language make it real and allow it to shape and regulate all acts of speech, but it exists only in the minds of a collective group, and it thus unites all their individual acts of speech into a whole.

Charles Sanders Peirce

The American philosopher Charles Sanders Peirce (1991), writing at the same time as Saussure, divided 'signs' into three possible types:

- *Icon*. This type of sign is identical to that which it stands for, for example a picture of a tree.
- *Index*. This type of sign is built upon a link to the senses, for example if we were blindfolded the feel of the bark on a tree would tell us we were touching a tree.
- *Symbol*. This is a sign that only links to an object through symbolic means. For example the written word TREE only reminds us of the object 'tree' because this is the arbitrary symbol we have learnt.

Peirce explored the link between the sign and the object it represents by suggesting that rather than a dyad, the sign is a triad: divided into three parts:

- *The sign*: the actual symbol that represents something else.
- *The object*: the 'something else' the symbol represents in the material world.
- *The interpretant*: not the person doing the thinking, as such, but the way in which we use our experience of signs and objects from the past in order to use and recognise signs more easily.

Roland Barthes

So far we have discussed how language can be seen as structured into a system that controls the individual examples of human speech by uniting them into a wider pattern. It is through the work of the French cultural commentator Roland Barthes (1967) that we can see the connection between these ideas of semiology and the meaning of culture (see Chapter 8). Barthes divides the process of signification – when the signifier and the signified relate together – into three 'orders' or levels:

- First order: *denotation* – the meaning of the sign that our common-sense thought gives us.
- Second order: *connotation* – the association our culture gives to each sign, which in turn links to others that are not directly 'seen' when we experience the first order. For example if I saw a sports car, in the first order I would think to myself 'that is a car'! However in the second order I might invoke other signs such as 'powerful', 'fast' or even 'sexy'.
- Third order: *myth* – this usually occurs at the same level as the second order, and can be seen as the chain that links together all the signs one uses. Thus in the example above, the myth of sports cars is that they are all fast, sexy and powerful. Myths are culturally based and tend to be well known, but this is not to say that they are 'true' – they are only true because the culture says so!

Exercise 9.2

Answer the following questions, using the information presented so far in this chapter to help you.

1. Why is language important for group identity?

2. How do symbols help us to create a meaningful reality in which to live and engage with each other?

3. How might symbols bond the individual to the group?

4. How would functionalists interpret the role of language in human societies?

5. How would action sociologists interpret the role of language in human societies?

6. How would structurational sociologists interpret the role of language in human societies?

Applying the semiological method

In his book *Mythologies*, Roland Barthes (1993) takes features of ordinary life and demonstrates how they can be studied in the same way as Saussure studied language. In other words, our entire culture is like a massive 'text' made up of symbols and signs that enable us to expose the meaning underlying our culture. Barthes argues that a system of signs in culture structures all meaning into a pattern that exists as a 'reality' beneath the surface of these cultural texts. Culture creates 'myths' – collections of signs that are present in the cultural products we encounter in day-to-day lives.

As an example of myths creating meanings in society that are understood but largely hidden, Barthes looks at the significance of 'steak and chips'. Barthes says that steak and chips signify – represent – 'Frenchness' itself (we could make the same claim in terms of their 'Englishness'). He argues that 'steak' signifies heartiness, simplicity, freshness, strength, going back to nature. It is both the food of those with exotic and expensive tastes, and the simple food of the peasant. It thus unifies all French people.

Barthes provides another example by 'reading' (interpreting the signs) an advertisement for pasta produced by a company called Panzani. The advertising image used is a string bag containing some tins and some packets of Panzani pasta, together with fresh ingredients such as tomatoes, mushrooms and so on. Barthes suggests that the advertisement consists of signs denoting freshness, return from the market and Italianness – the latter because of the product's name and the Italian-flag colours of the bag's contents.

Exercise 9.3

Summarise the ideas of Saussure, Peirce and Barthes in a copy of the following table. Try to demonstrate the similarities and differences between them.

	Time period writing in	Key ideas	How did this author extend the semiological method used by his predecessors?	Strengths of this approach	Examples of argument
Saussure					
Peirce					
Barthes					

Exercise 9.4

Conduct your own semiological 'reading' of an ordinary aspect of day-to-day life, in the same way that Barthes looked at steak and chips. Write about 200 words in all.

Exercise 9.5

While the semiological method might allow us to uncover hidden meanings, it is quite unreliable since it is highly subjective. Using this statement as a guide, list four advantages and four disadvantages of this method.

Dick Hebdige

Neo-Marxist researchers at the *Centre for Contemporary Cultural Studies* (CCCS) have extensively employed the semiological method to analyse the meanings behind the styles adopted by youth subcultures (see Chapter 8). Dick Hebdige (1979) suggests that the styles adopted by subcultural groups – such as punk, grunge, indie, rave, hip-hop and so on – are not accidental but are highly meaningful attempts to create identity. Therefore such styles can be 'read' as signs, which can be interpreted by sociologists.

Signs and human agency

Many structuralists refer to what is known as 'the death of the author', meaning that we have the freedom to 'read' texts in creative ways. Our interpretation or 'reading' of the signs may not be that intended by the author, hence the 'authorship' of cultural products – such as those of the media – has 'died' and the audience are free to interpret the products in any way they wish – a situation of relativism also noted by many postmodern thinkers (see Chapter 6).

The idea that humans interpret signs in different ways is reflected in the work of Stuart Hall (1993) and David Morley (1980) (see Chapter 7 for a further discussion). Hall makes a distinction between the 'encoder' and the 'decoder' of signs. The encoder is the creator/producer/author of the sign; the decoder is the object/receiver/audience. When decoders receive signs and decode them they do not do so passively, but take one of three approaches or 'readings' (interpretations):

- Dominant/intended reading.
- Negotiated reading.
- Oppositional reading.

The type of decoding that takes place depends on the background and experiences of the person doing the decoding.

Structuralism and anthropology: Claude Lévi-Strauss

The anthropologist Claude Lévi-Strauss (1969, 1978) takes the idea of linguistic structuralism and applies it to the study of non-Western, small-scale societies and tribal communities. In his book *The Savage Mind* (1972), Lévi-Strauss differentiates between societies at two different stages of historical development. There are 'hot societies' – literate societies – where rapid social change has been experienced and massive, complex social hierarchies have emerged; and there are 'cold societies' – preliterate societies – where social change has either been resisted or is occurring at a slower rate. The latter maintain their social system in a state of unchanging equilibrum or balance. For Lévi-Strauss, cold societies offer an excellent opportunity to investigate how human social life is shaped, regulated or structured by the cultural system.

Lévi-Strauss is highly critical of the functionalist anthropology of writers such as Malinowski (1922, 1954) and Durkheim (1982) (see Chapter 3). In *The Elementary Forms of the Religious Life*, Durkheim suggests that Western thought is superior to that of tribal societies because Western knowledge is based on rational scientific knowledge. However Lévi-Strauss argues that although 'hot' and 'cold' societies do use different forms of knowledge they are only different on the level of surface variation, and that there is a deeper structure that unites these two ways of thinking.

The 'savage mind'

At a deep structural level the thoughts of the 'savage mind' are not that different from the ways of thinking in the Western world. This savage mind, despite how it might appear to functionalist thinkers, is not inferior, less organised or more open to irrationality. Rather it is based on a 'science of the concrete'; that is, it uses analogies to think about the world and to develop massive and complex systems of classification – just as Western science does. For example the 'organic analogy' (see Chapter 3) used by functionalists is no different, as a mechanism to aid thinking, from a myth or legend in a tribal culture.

Therefore all human thought, while appearing different on the surface, can be seen as united by the deep structure that runs through all human thinking: the mechanisms of organising, classifying and thinking about differences or opposites. An excellent example of the way in which human thought classifies the world around it is provided by kinship patterns in tribal societies. Many such communities have complex rules on who can and cannot marry whom, and who is related to whom and how. These kinship patterns are found in many different types of society and are an indication of an underlying logical structure in the way that all humans classify the world, their relationships with each other, and therefore their own identities. Kinship tells you who you are, and who you are not. Like Barthes and Saussure, Lévi-Strauss uses the concept of 'difference' to explain how cultural myths and patterns of kinship work. Myths tend to be based on stories or legends that categorise, group and organise systems of knowledge by indicating what is the same and what is different, or 'other'.

Exercise 9.6

It is often useful for the sociologist to step back from his or her own culture and think about what other cultures are like. Use anthropological textbooks, CD-ROMs, the Internet and any other sources available to you to find out about the culture of two societies other than your own. In a copy of the table below, note the obvious differences between these cultures in respect of each of the key social features listed.

	Present-day Western society	Society 1	Society 2
Kinship			
Religious practice			
Knowledge			
Entertainment			

Bricolage

When describing how culture and cultural signs are created and given meaning, Lévi-Strauss uses the term 'bricolage' (see Chapter 8). This concept is used to discuss the role played by humans in the creation of cultural meaning. 'Bricoleurs' – individuals or group of individuals who perform the act of 'bricolage' – can be seen as working in the manner of artists or handymen. They collect many different elements of cultural meaning and fuse them together to create new meaning; that is, they take a whole collection of signs and work on them as though they are materials and tools to create new cultural meanings. As with objects of art or other material objects, these cultural meanings have form and texture – they are multilayered, sign upon sign, forged together in an ad hoc fashion.

Bricoleurs create new cultural meanings from the vantage point of existing meanings within the cultural system, from which they borrow their raw materials. Accepted cultural meaning is 'played with' and changed, but from within the structure. Meaning cannot come from 'nothingness'. It has to use what is already there, but in different forms and combinations. This process of bricolage – the creation of symbolic cultural meanings – is the same for a work of art as it is for a tribal cultural myth, a sociological theory or even a Western scientific law.

Structuralism and Marxism:
Louis Althusser

Louis Althusser (1971, 1976) takes the principles of structuralism and uses them to update or reassess the original ideas of Marx (see Chapter 3). However this is a very different update from that offered by the 'humanist' neo-Marxist Antonio Gramsci (1971, 1977, 1978) (see Chapter 8). Gramsci argues that the class system of capitalism can be resisted and actively combated through the self-conscious and self-aware cultural activities of ordinary people. The dominance of the ruling class is the result of a 'war of ideas' in which their ideas take precedence over all others and shape how people see reality around them. This is known as 'hegemony'. The hegemony of the ruling class can be fought through the 'agency' of the working classes.

Althusser (1968) argues that a distinctive break or rupture can be observed in the ideas of Marx if they are read in a structuralist fashion. The '*early Marx*' was preoccupied with the humanistic concerns of ideology and alienation (see Chapter 3), while the '*late Marx*' was concerned with the way in which production structures and shapes the inner logical workings of society. Althusser refers to this break as an 'epistemological break' and he adopts the second position, which he sees as a scientific version of 'mature Marxism' produced by a 'sympathetic rereading' of the economic determinism in Marx's book *Das Kapital*.

In *For Marx*, Althusser (1969) stresses the role of class conflict in the shaping of human history. Gramsci locates class conflict in individual consciousness, but according to Althusser we should look instead at the structure of the wider class system, which is made up of numerous groups of people, not just individuals. The true determining or structural force in human social history is economic production. This is the force that directs society and social change – it makes society what it is, and what it is likely to become. Althusser does not adopt a simplistic view of the economy, where class forces alone shape society. Instead he argues that in the final instance the economy does shape society, but at most times the social system is determined by many different forces – not just economic but also cultural. Ultimately, however, it is the conflicts caused by the way in which production is organised that lead to change in the structure of the system.

Althusser suggests that there are three structural levels in a class-based society: economic, political and ideological. Although the political and ideological levels have a degree of autonomy from the economic, in the end it is still the economic structure that is dominant. In the same way the class system can be seen as layered, and while all the layers are interconnected they also have some autonomy. Collectively they constitute the 'structure' into which humans are born, and by which humans are shaped.

Unlike Gramsci, who attributes some free-will ('agency') to individuals, Althusser believes that individual self-identity is not independent of the structure of the system. Since we are born into a society that predates us, its structure makes us its subject. The structure of society moulds us, and allows us to 'know ourselves' only from within it. Althusser refers to the simultaneous existence of an 'ideological state apparatus' and a 'repressive state apparatus', which shape us into who we think we are. The state can use ideology to control us – we can be socialised by institutions such as the family, religion and the media into thinking that our society is 'normal' and accepting it as it is. However if ideology fails the state can control us physically through the use of force and violence. For example the police have the legal right to use force against us, and we can be locked up in a prison or an asylum.

Exercise 9.7

List six similarities and six differences between the ideas of Gramsci and Althusser.

Exercise 9.8

k u in a e

This exercise requires you to consider the key arguments and ideas of Lévi-Strauss, Hebdige and Althusser, as discussed above. Record your findings in an extended version of the table below.

	What hidden structures do they look at?	Basic ideas	Strengths	Weaknesses	How useful do you find their ideas? Explain your answer.
Lévi-Strauss					
Hebdige					
Althusser					

Structural feminism

As we have seen, writers such as Althusser use structuralist ideas to update Marxism. Other writers have applied similar ideas to feminist sociology. These writers argue that a particular structure controls and unites society – the structure of gender.

Hélène Cixous

Hélène Cixous (1980; Cixious and Element, 1986) observes how culture often designates a gender to objects, words, attitudes and other concepts through the use of language. For example being strong is seen as an attribute of masculinity, whereas being irrational is seen as feminine. Cixous takes up the idea of the 'birth of difference' from the work of Saussure and Lévi-Strauss. She notes that cultures often contain pairs of opposites – one of which is seen as male, the other female. For example:

Masculine	Feminine
● Strong	● Weak
● Rational	● Irrational
● Economically productive	● Sexually reproductive
● Emotionally 'hard'	● Caring and nurturing
● Emotionally detached	● Over-emotional

Although humans are controlled by such 'differences', socialised into common-sense thought, they can and do fight against it. This means that inequality is not natural, but the product of learnt and cultural behaviour (see Chapters 2 and 11). In her essay '*Sorties*', Cixous (1980) lists, among others, the following examples of binary opposities frequently found in Western cultures: culture/nature, head/heart, form/matter, speaking/writing. As a feminist, for her the most powerful binary opposite is the male/female one and she suggests that this division structures – or patterns – everything else in society. Although one of the two has more power – in this case 'male' – both need each other in order to exist. They are defined as much by what they are not as by what they are.

Lucie Irigaray

Lucie Irigaray (1985, 1992, 1993), who originally trained and worked as a psychiatrist, suggests that schizophrenic patients are not biologically ill, they are merely defined as being 'ill' by the cultures they live in. Irigaray is particularly interested in how language structures and defines reality for humans within their culture and governs their sense of self-identity. Some people become 'overwhelmed' by language – they become the subject of language and are controlled by it, rather than being able to use it in a reflexive and active fashion. Such people, frequently women, are unable to create a stable sense of self-identity and as a consequence are defined as schizophrenic. Irigaray argues that women in particular find it difficult to create a sense of self, because language has a masculine bias that dominates them and what they see as reality.

Julia Kristeva

Julia Kristeva (1981, 1986) – also a psychiatrist – criticises Saussure's structural linguistics for treating language as a structure that controls humans, rather than being open to human creative manipulation. Her work is based on a reworking of Freudian psychoanalytic theory (see Chapters 2 and 3), combining this with some aspects of symbolic interactionism (see Chapter 4) and structural linguistics.

Kristeva draws a distinction between the semiotic (the informal, preverbal language developed in infancy and based on the uncertainty surrounding our biological desires and drives) and the symbolic (the adult verbal language, based on rules and a common structure). Kristeva states that both types of thought and communication exist within us when we interact in everyday life, and that when we do so we manipulate signs both consciously and unconsciously. Self-identity is established and reinforced by the transition from semiotic to symbolic communication. It is vital for their self-identity that children learn the concept 'I' and therefore develop a sense of their 'difference' from others – they come to see themselves as a separate being. In adult life these two aspects of humanity – the culturally created structure of language, and early preverbal biological drives – exist in tension with one another, and the conflict between the two – the cultural structure and the biological – can result in mental illness and identity problems.

Exercise 9.9

List the key concepts used by each of the structural feminists discussed above (Hélène Cixous, Lucie Irigaray and Julia Kristeva) and the key features of their arguments.

Exercise 9.10

Consider structural feminism as a whole. Identify two strengths and two weaknesses of this approach.

Postmodernism and signs

Jean Baudrillard

Baudrillard (1981) takes some ideas from Marxism and uses them to further his argument about the new role that signs have taken on in postmodernity. Marx (see Chapter 3) saw the production of objects for consumption as being controlled by those who own the means of production. This 'economic determinism' – where the nature of production influences and determines everything else in society – is reflected in the general Marxist idea that the ruling class rule because they control the productive forces, and this gives them power over everything in society.

For Baudrillard, capitalism continues to rule society because it has created false desires that are fulfilled by consumption. Although many Marxists would agree with this statement, Baudrillard goes one step further and suggests that it is the manipulation of signs that makes us think that we need these objects in the first place. Baudrillard argues that objects that are commodities – such as televisions, washing machines, videos, trainers, mobile phones and so on – have both a 'use value' and an 'exchange value' associated with them as part of their sign:

- Use value is the purpose ('utility') to which we put objects – in other words, why we might need something, and what we would do with it.
- Exchange value is how much something is worth in terms of how much we are prepared to pay for it – also referred to as 'commodity value'.

Baudrillard states that the use value of the sign of the object hides its exchange value. Capitalism tells us to buy this or that product because it is the 'best' or the 'newest' or even the 'smallest', and this use value is seen to relate to a human need and desire for the object. Baudrillard says that this is really the other way round: use values are ideological. We do not really need the commodities we buy. In fact we only want them because we are told by advertisers that we do need them. We think that use and need come first and then a commodity is created to meet that need – but actually it is the other way round. We only need that commodity because it has been made! Therefore the ideological illusion of the so-called use value of the sign hides the fact that such objects only exist because of their exchange value – because they make a profit for capitalists.

Writing from the postmodern perspective Baudrillard argues that in the present age symbols or signs have become commodities. They have taken on a reality of their own, over and above the objects they represent (see Chapter 6). For example, when purchasing an item of designer clothing we are not buying the object for what it is, rather we are buying the sign – we are consuming signs and images, trying to represent ourselves with them.

The hyper-reality of signs

Baudrillard suggests that if we separate the signifier from the signified (if we separate the sign from the object) we soon see that signs create culture, not the other way round. Signs *give us* meaning, they are not *given* meaning by culture. All we have left to consume, in postmodernity, are signs since there is no reality, no absolute truth, no way of seeing the world in such a way that we can create a dominant meaning. Signs not only become real – because this is all there is – they become 'more real than real' – 'hyper-real'. Since we have no means to get at the truth, we simply accept the signs given to us by the media and use these to create meaning.

Jacques Derrida

Baudrillard's ideas have been greatly influenced by Jacques Derrida's idea of 'deconstruction'. Derrida (1973, 1977, 1978) argues that we need to pull signs apart to see what they are hiding from us, to separate the sign from the object in order to see more clearly what the real truth of the matter is. This is what he calls 'deconstruction'. We must deconstruct ideology and illusion. Derrida wishes to move beyond the structuralist idea that structures control human action and give meaning to human life. In Derrida's view structures have no meaning apart from that given to them by humans through the use of language, and that it is the use of words by some people to create meaning that leads to the lack of power of others. Derrida suggests that we should study how words – in speech, writing and sets of communication-based interactions, known as 'discourse' – limit those whose identity is controlled by them. This idea has been highly influential in the creation of the perspective known as 'poststructuralism'.

Exercise 9.11

Identify two strengths and two weaknesses of the postmodern approach to the study of signs.

Poststructuralism

The term 'poststructuralism' originally referred, to the work of a collection of French philosophers writing in the wake of structuralists such as Althusser, Lévi-Strauss and Barthes. These poststructuralists include Jacques Derrida and Michel Foucault, although the term 'poststructural' is sometimes rejected by these writers themselves. In many respects the views of poststructuralists represent a blending together of ideas already covered in this chapter: ideas from some structuralist thinking and some postmodernist thinking.

Poststructuralism argues that:

- Language is the key feature of power in society and it shapes and controls human action.

- Signs have become detached from the objects they represent, and have become 'real' themselves through language.
- Since signs are detached from reality we are no longer able to speak of a single 'truth' since we have no basis upon which to establish this. We are simply left with many different interpretations.
- Humans are not controlled by invisible structures, but are defined and given identity by 'discourses' – sets of languages – with which they can fight, resist and seek self-identity.
- What we consider to be 'reality' is created for us by language, and is based on the construction of 'difference'. In other words, for something to be seen or defined as real or true its opposite has to be defined as untrue or unreal, at the same moment of definition.

Within these claims we can see elements of a wide range of ideas from other sources:

- Saussure's emphasis on 'difference' as the basis of meaning.
- Baudrillard's view that signs have become detached from reality.
- The general postmodernist view that there is no truth – only relativitsm.
- The structuralist idea of the 'death of the author'.
- Derrida's view that language controls humans.

According to post-structuralism the signifier has priority over the signified; that is, the signifier controls and shapes the signified by giving it meaning and identity. In addition there are more signifiers than signified in culture, and thus signifiers take on a reality of their own. This means that truth is relative, since the languages we use are not linked in any concrete way to the objects of the material world. Power is the ability to control and use sets of languages – called 'discourses' – to define others. This idea is associated with the work of French historian and philosopher Michel Foucault.

Michel Foucault

Michel Foucault (1984) is influenced both by the structuralist notion of 'difference' and by Derrida's idea of 'deconstruction' and the role of discourses in society. Foucault takes as his starting point a critique of the ideas of a French intellectual, wartime resistance fighter and political campaigner: Jean-Paul Sartre.

Sartre's particular version of philosophical thought – known as 'existentialism' – was in turn based on Husserl's phenomenology (see Chapter 4) and it suggests that the 'essence' of humans succeeds the 'being' of humans. In other words, unlike objects we cannot say much about the nature of a particular person before that person has been born and grown up. If we consider an object – say a chair – we can be sure of a number of things about the 'essence' of this object even before it is made, before its 'being'. The chair will have a seat and a back, and it will be raised from the ground in some way. We cannot do the same with humans. We cannot say that a yet to be born person will be kind, or clever or good at mathematics. Therefore for Sartre 'being' precedes 'essence' for humans.

Sartre goes on to suggest that humans only become the people that they do – individuals with an identity – because they make it happen themselves. We have free will to decide who we are, so if we feel unhappy with our life and our being – our identity – we are living in a state of 'bad faith' if we blame anything or anyone other than ourselves for this. We have the power to be who we wish. We have agency (see Chapters 4 and 5). Foucault disagrees with this. He suggests that identity is formed by the combination of languages that are used to observe and to define us. These languages are referred to as 'discourses'.

Discourses and power

We can see discourses as sets of ways of thinking about, knowing about, classifying and speaking about a subject that takes priority in being used to control and observe people involved in different bits of social life. They are sets of specialist or technical languages that define, control and observe – or as Foucault says, 'gaze'. For example medicine is a discourse that is used to control the body in our society, and it is seen to have specialist knowledge with which to think about the body. The knowledge associated with this way of thinking and speaking is powerful as it can be used to limit and to control. If you are defined as being sick or ill by the gaze of your doctor, you might not be allowed, legally, to go to work until you are re-defined as being well or healthy again!

Other discourses include:

- Pedagogy: thinking and speaking about how children learn.
- Penology: thinking and speaking about how we should control prisoners.
- Criminology: thinking and speaking about how we should stop crime.
- Economics: thinking and speaking about how we should organise production in society.
- Psychiatry: thinking and speaking about how we should treat mentally ill people.

The structure of society, then, is seen as a complex and vast web of many different discourses. Power is thus multilayered and each individual might be under the gaze of many different discourses at any one time.

Truth and power

Like postmodernists such as Baudrillard, Foucault does not believe in a single, identifiable, absolute truth. Knowledge is simply a way of thinking that allows the exercise of one's will against others. This idea is based on the ideas of the German philosopher Fredrich Nietzsche, who spoke of a '*will to power*' whereas Foucault speaks of a '*will to truth*'. For Foucault, different discourses present different truths and different ways of thinking about, speaking about and knowing the truth. The truth thus becomes a site or battleground over which different discourses exercise their will – their desire to take control, to have power. In Foucault's words: 'There is a battle "for truth", or at least "around truth" – it's a matter not of a battle "on behalf" of the truth, but of a battle about the status of truth and the economic and political role it plays' (Foucault, 1984).

What he means by this is that powerful groups have the opportunity to define the particular sets of ideas and ways of thinking that come to be seen as the truth. This must mean that 'the truth' rather depends on where you stand. Discourses create the truth – they provide ways of seeing, thinking and speaking about the world and our experiences of and in it. Culture is thus made up of a variety of discourses and our identities are the result of them defining who we are. Foucault reserves the term 'power-knowledge' for the particular way in which truth is a feature of those who have knowledge.

Discourses and the birth of difference

Foucault adopts a historical method drawn from the ideas of Nietzsche – a method known as 'genealogy'. This is based on the idea of 'the birth of difference'. Whenever a discourse invents or creates – gives birth to – a new way of thinking about the world, it does so through the creation of binary opposites. For example, when we have sanity we also have insanity. The same goes for health/ill-health, normal/deviant, decent/pervert.

In his historical studies *Madness and Civilization* (1989a) and *The Birth of the Clinic* (1989c), Foucault notes that the introduction of the mental asylum, which promised to help and to cure 'sick' people, was actually responsible for defining and controlling both the insane and the sane, since each was defined within the discourse by its opposite. The job of the historian should be to identify the historical break or rupture that causes the birth of difference. This is often referred to by Foucault (1989c) as an 'archaeological' method, and he is critical of historical accounts that ignore the birth of difference since he sees this as contributing to the sort of discourses that try to define 'how things are' and in doing so gain power – knowledge.

Foucault seeks to develop a history of the hidden and the silent in historical studies: to understand those who are on the 'forgotten', 'silent' and 'powerless' side of these differences – to try to see how they have their identities created for them by the complex fields of discourse into which they are born. Foucault sees the structure of discourses as both enabling and constraining, and in this respect his ideas echo those of Anthony Giddens on structurational sociology (see Chapter 5). Although one's identity is created and defined by the multilayered structure of the discourses that hold the individual under their gaze, one can nonetheless fight, resist and subvert. But one can only fight this structure within the structure itself since one simply cannot live outside it.

Exercise 9.12

Copy out and complete the following table. Match each statement to the author(s) most likely to make that statement.

Statement	Who would say this?
Clothes act as signs to other people	
People who are schizophrenic have become 'overwhelmed' by language	
Signs have become hyper-real	
Language is like a set of rules that enable us fit into a group	
Some groups can gain power since they control knowledge	
We can uncover the hidden meaning behind everyday images and objects	
Western science and tribal religions are united by a common, hidden, structure	
There is no truth separate from that which we decide is the truth	
We are what we buy	
Symbols can be manipulated in a creative way to create new identities – an act of bricolage	
National identities are often created through the manipulation of shared signs and symbols	
Discourses control us – they label and define us	
Class forces are the underlying structure of all societies	
Language contains symbols that are used to perpetuate female subordination	
The media audience is free to interpret signs as they choose	

Conclusion

Structuralist and poststructuralist ideas raise important issues about how people think about the world around them, about how people create reality and about the role of power in the creation of what we regard as 'truth'. These ideas allow us to think about identity as an issue of 'difference' and power in a similar way to Marxist ideas, as explained in Chapters 3, 7 and 8. The role of power in culture, identity and language is a theme that dominates the work of Michel Foucault and his ideas have influenced a great many sociologists. His ideas are being taken up by other branches of sociology, such as Marxism and some feminisms, and in this way sociology is moving forward – new and interesting ideas are being built on the backs of previous ideas.

Examination questions

Use the advice on pages 28–9 to answer the following questions:

(a) How useful are the ideas of structuralism in helping us to think about how identity is created in society?

(b) To what extent can we say that in the contemporary age 'signs' have changed as sources of identity?

10 Class and consumption

By the end of this chapter you should:

- understand the relationship between class and identity;
- have knowledge of the changing nature of class identity in contemporary times;
- be able to evaluate the idea of class identities from New Right and postmodern perspectives;
- understand the idea of a consumer culture;
- be able to relate the idea of a consumer culture to postmodern views on identity;
- understand how class and consumption relate to patterns of lifestyle choice;
- understand the role played by new social movements in identity formation.

Introduction

For many sociologists the concept of class is the idea 'par excellence' of sociology: it is seen by many as the major contribution sociology has made to academic thought on the nature of society and social relations, and it is one of the most powerful tools at the sociologist's disposal. Discussions of the nature of class – and of class culture and identity – are often vehicles with which the key themes of sociology – *power, inequality, domination, social control* and *ideology* – are presented in a clear way. Class itself is most associated with the insights made by Marxist sociology and the great variety of theories that have been influenced by Marxist ideas.

In more recent times the idea of class has undergone a quite profound reassessment. Many sociologists have subsituted the concept with 'consumption' and/or 'life-style'. This is seen as reflecting changes in sociology since the Second World War, based on observations of actual changes to the class structure in Western societies. We shall explore both traditional and contemporary views on class culture and identity, but first we shall review some theoretical interpretations of the role of class in society.

A theoretical review of class identity

Exercise 10.1

Using other sociological sources, look up the concept of class and write your own definition.

Exercise 10.2

Using your own definition of class, in what way and why do you think the concept is important in today's society? Answer this question by filling in a copy of the table below.

Does class matter in the following areas of social life? Justify your answer for each one.

Voting	Consumption	Life-style	Identity	Politics

Traditional theoretical interpretations

Functionalists (see Chapter 3) see class division as natural to the smooth running of society. Distinct class cultures create distinct class identities since those in a similar class position are similar people with similar values and life-styles. Equally, class allows individuals to 'know their place' in the pecking order – the 'best people' occupy the highest position and have the most 'refined' cultural backgrounds.

Traditional Marxists see class culture and identity as a tool of ideological domination. For example Frankfurt School members Adorno and Horkheimer (1979) argue that the working classes, being deprived of education and therefore critical thought, are subjected to a stable diet of popular/low culture that serves to perpetuate their class position over time (see Chapters 3 and 7). This is known as 'cultural reproduction' – the way that culture helps to reproduce the class structure with each succeeding generation.

Neo-Marxists such as those working at the CCCS are interested in how subcultures – which are oppositional to the dominant culture of the ruling classes – develop as pockets of resistance. A class identity is created that enables the development of true class consciousness, through struggles with the hegemony of those who rule (see Chapters 7 and 8).

Exercise 10.3

The traditional Marxist interpretation of political action in society would be to claim that class is the basis of all political action – such as strikes, demonstrations, protests and so on – and that this is due to the importantance of class in defining our sense of group identity. Conduct some research to see whether this is still true today. You will need to use newspapers, CD-ROMs or the Internet in order to obtain the most up-to-date information.

Theoretical reassessments of class

The New Right claim that in modern society class identity and culture are fragmentating or decompositing. For example Peter Saunders (1990) suggests that class is irrelevant to people's lives, it is no longer a meaningful factor in their life-styles. Saunders cites home ownership as a more important factor in both inequality and identity formation today. These ideas are reflected in the claim by the former Conservative Prime Minister John Major that Britain had become a 'classless' society.

Equally, some New Right thinkers argue that people who to work hard can be any class they wish. Those in the 'underclass' deserve to be there since they are lazy and ill-motivated. In this view class is not important since those who work hard will move upwards in an open or meritocratic society. Those who do not work hard and are in the underclass pose a significant problem, but one that can be solved by the withdrawal of state benefit.

Many feminists argue that the overemphasis on class within sociology has led to the creation of a 'malestream' sociology that ignores, and renders invisible, women and gender as a source of identity and inequality. Abbott and Wallace (1997) argue that:

> the feminist challenge to malestream sociology is one that requires a radical rethinking of the content and methodology of the whole enterprise, one that recognises the need to see society from the position of women as well as from the standpoint of men.

Finally, postmodernists such as Crook *et al.* (1992) suggest that present-day identities are much more fluid and ambivalent than they were under the rigid constraints in class identity in the past. Now individuals are free to become who they wish, through consumption and the creative adaptation of life-styles.

We shall use these basic theoretical approaches to consider the ways in which class, life-style and consumption shape identity. Before we do this we need to conduct a brief historical review of how class culture and identity have been treated within sociology.

The historical treatment of class culture and identity

The traditional working class

Paul Willis (1990) sees culture as the routines and patterns of everyday life. Culture in this sense exists everywhere, and it orders or makes sense of every aspect of social reality:

> Culture is not artifice and manners, the preserve of Sunday best, rainy afternoons, and concert halls. It is the very material of our daily lives, the bricks and mortar of our most commonplace understandings, feelings, and responses. We rely on cultural patterns and symbols for the minute, and unconscious, social reflexes that make us social and collective beings: We are therefore most deeply embedded in our culture when we are at our most natural and spontaneous: if you like, at our most work-a-day (ibid.)

Given the emphasis on work as a defining feature of one's life and identity, the nature of our culture is most evident in our work: how we organise, interpret, make sense of and cope with our daily routine. Willis associates traditional working-class culture (which may have changed today) with the following values, which were meaningful responses to life in the factory:

- Mental and physical bravery (when working in hostile workplace conditions).
- Physical strength.
- Masculinity.
- Skills obtained through experience, not education.

Willis (1977, 1990) suggests that a key feature of working-class culture in everyday life is the use of humour – 'having a laugh' – in order to get through the day and to make meaningful the long periods of relentless boredom, whether on the factory floor or at the work site. Many commentators suggest that in postmodern or post-industrial society this traditional working-class culture is in decline.

Exercise 10.4

Does class still matter? Drawing on all that you have read and investigated so far, explain the position taken on this question by each of the following theoretical branches:

- Functionalism
- The New Right
- Traditional Marxism
- Feminism
- Neo-Marxism
- Postmodernism

Walter B. Miller (1962) suggests that working-class culture is made up of a number of 'focal concerns': masculinity, immediate gratification (instant pleasure seeking), excitement and a willingness to leave one's life open to chance, not to plan ahead. Some sociologists suggest that such focal concerns create a 'culture of dependency' that prevents the working class from being upwardly mobile. These focal concerns hold back the working classes by placing no real value on education. Opportunities are thrown away in favour of immediate pleasure seeking. They encourage poverty and being 'happy with one's lot' rather than trying to 'better oneself'. Finally, reliance on these focal concerns may encourage rule breaking, which may lead to delinquent and criminal behaviour.

Exercise 10.5

Compare the ideas of Willis and Miller. Identity and list five similarities and five differences between what they have to say about working-class culture and identity.

The main criticism of Miller's ideas is that he is very judgemental about working-class life. He seems to see working-class life-styles and tastes as inferior to those of the middle classes. Such attitudes tend to 'pathologise' the working classes. They make the working classes seem different from everyone else and dysfunctional, which holds them back. The association of working-class people with crime is also highly suspect. If crime statistics do show a preponderance of working-class criminality it might be due to selective policing practices and the more visible nature of their crimes, rather than because they are more prone to criminal activities than anyone else.

Other sociologists, such as Paul Willis (1977) and Stanley Cohen (1987), see working-class culture as containing a great deal of creativity, given that the society they live in is highly exploitative of them. John Lea and Jock Young (1993), adopting a position they describe as 'New Left Realism', warn against the tendency of writers such as Cohen and Willis to romanticise the criminal and delinquent activities of working-class youths by portraying them as 'Robin Hood' figures, engaged in a symbolic and creative fight against capitalism. Such portrayals provide little comfort to the victims of nasty and ignorant crimes, victims who themselves are often working-class people living in inner city areas.

Some of Miller's ideas, especially his claim that the culture of the working class is responsible for their position in society, are reflected in the thinking of the New Right and the New Left. For example New Right thinker Charles Murray (1984) is highly critical of the 'underclass' – the long-term unemployed – who he regards as lazy, intellectually inferior, criminal and responsible for their own position due to their dependence on state welfare. Such ideas caused the Conservative governments from 1979 to 1997 to reduce state spending on welfare amid moral panics over 'social security scroungers'. New

Labour, under Tony Blair, seems to have adopted a very similar policy towards and image of the underclass in the welfare reform referred to as 'welfare to work'. According to one Marxist-based interpretation of this, the underlying assumption is that the majority of the unemployed are simply too idle to look for work and therefore should only be given benefits if they start to do so!

Exercise 10.6

Using the Internet, CD-ROMs and newspapers, collect information on the present government's views on poverty, class and welfare. What do you think this information suggests about how class is seen by politicians today?

The fracturing of class identity

Since the Second World War, and especially during the 1960s, there has been a sociological debate about the changes the traditional class structure has undergone and what the consequences of restructuring might be for work, inequality, culture and identity. An early contribution that shaped ideas on the 'death' of class identity was the work of Zweig (1961). Zweig argued that due to a process of 'embourgeoisement' there had been a reduction in the size of the traditional working class and the growth of a 'new', more affluent, service-based middle class.

In opposition to this idea, Goldthorpe *et al.* (1968) claimed that rather than a new middle class, a new working class had emerged. This new working class had rejected the class-based labour politics of their forefathers and adopted what was described as a more 'instrumental orientation' to both work and politics. This class would readily vote Conservative (described at the time as 'deviant voting') if they thought that doing so would bring them financial benefits. This new working class adopted a life-style that was home-centred, and thus the family became an important site for consumerism. This was an early sign of the rise of a 'consumer society' and the decline of class identity in postmodern times.

Mike Savage *et al.* (1992) point to the 'fracturing' or decomposition of the middle class into a number of middle class*es* with different life-styles and identities. Firstly, there are new consumer identities based on life-styles and a concern with the body as source of and object for such life-styles. Secondly, there are identities based on 'cultural capital' – the highly educated who work in the service sector of the economy or in the caring professions and who possess high cultural tastes. Finally, there are the more 'traditional' middle-class life-styles based on the family, home ownership and foreign holidays.

The rapid expansion of non-class identities has been explored by Harriet Bradley (1996). Bradley suggests that class does still exist –

something that many postmodernists and members of the New Right might challenge. However she notes that it is no longer regarded as important by people themselves. It is frequently rejected by those very people who could objectively be classified as working class but have chosen to adopt a consumer orientation towards the world that is more reminiscent of the middle classes.

Exercise 10.7

To conclude our discussion of the relevance today of class identity, and to support the Marxist position against the postmodern views above, look up the current statistics on poverty in Britain. Do *you* think that class is still important?

Clark Kerr *et al.* (1973) and Daniel Bell (1973) suggest that the postwar rise in affluence, the creation of the welfare system, the growth of consumerism and the decline of traditional class identities signalled a profound change in society: the dawn of the 'post-industrial society'. Such a society is characterised by:

- Increased affluence.
- Increased consumption.
- The decline of primary industry.
- The rise of a service-based economy.
- The rise of knowledge as a commodity to be used as a basis for status and power.
- The rise of new managerial and professional classes.

Exercise 10.8

How might increased affluence lead to changes in life-style and identity? Copy out and complete the following table. A few examples are provided to get you started.

Feature of affluence	How might this lead to changes to identity and life-style?
1. Having more money to spend 2. e.g Credit cards 3. e.g Increase in affordable domestic appliances 4. 5. 6. 7.	1. 2. 3. 4. 5. 6. 7.

The optimism inherent in this image of Western capitalist nations is based primarily on the belief that capitalism has 'delivered the goods'. This claim has influenced a diverse range of writers, including writers from the New Right and postmodernists. For example New Right thinker Francis Fukuyama (1992) suggests that capitalist societies in the 'late', 'advanced' or 'mature' stages of development have seen the erosion of class and the fracturing of traditional class cultures and identities. Likewise many postmodernists suggest that with the shift towards a service economy and mass consumption, society has become very different.

Exercise 10.9

The following thinkers claim that class has 'declined' or 'fragmented'. Summarise their views in an extended version of the following table.

Name of thinker	According to this thinker, what change has occurred in society?	What, in this thinker's opinion, has this done to class?
Zweig		
Goldthorpe		
Savage		
Bradley		
Kerr		
Fukuyama		

From production to consumption

The alleged decline or death of class as a factor in identity formation has been traced back to the decades after the Second World War and three key developments:

- The rise of a much more affluent new working class/new middle class.
- The expansion of popular cultural products.
- The shift from an economy based on production to one based on consumption.

These three developments have been important for a wide range of theories with very different ideas, such as the New Right, the theory of 'post-industrial society' and postmodernism.

The origin of mass consumption lies in the mass production that took place during the American 'wonder years' of the 1950s: the mass production of popular Ford motorcars for the 'average man', television sets, washing machines and so on – and the rapid growth of the advertising industry. With the rise in affluence, those previously denied the opportunity to consume could become consumers too.

Two other historical developments took place that went hand in hand with the three identified above:

- The creation of large multinational companies that developed brand-name products and invested massively in advertising.

- The rapid expansion of the music industry and the development of 'youth' as a distinct cultural group (see Chapter 8).

This was a time of massive expansion in the availability of popular culture and popular products, many of which we take for granted today: fashion, pop music, consumer durables, the home entertainment provided by record players, and so on. This early consumption was still structured by the class system. Although many working-class people were more affluent than ever and more products were available, there were distinct differences between the tastes and desires of the different classes. These tastes were both structured and played upon by the advertising industry, which marketed their customers' products according to market research based on class categories. Today we have a 'consumer culture' – detached from traditional class identification.

In his book *Keywords*, Raymond Williams (1983) observes that the word 'consume', which has been present in the English language since the fourteenth century, originally meant 'to destroy' or 'to use up'. The word 'consumer', which dates from the eighteenth century, was also associated with 'waste', in the sense that a consumer was someone who used something up. The word is now used to denote the purchase and use of cultural products. Implicit in the term is the idea that once a product is used up, once it is 'spent', then it no longer has any value and is thus thrown away.

Therefore a consumer culture is one where people regularly purchase and use a wide variety of cultural products as a matter of everyday life. The consumer culture has the following elements:

- Consumption is bound up with a capitalist economy based on the production of commodities.
- The commodities consumed come from popular cultural sources.
- Consumption is immediate, based on the instant gratification of needs.
- Advertising plays a large role in the creation of wants and desires.
- Once products are consumed they are thrown away and rapidly replaced by the next – the 'newest' and the 'best'.

With the arrival of postmodern ideas in sociology we can add the following to the list of characteristics of a consumer culture:

- We are consuming not just the material products themselves but also what they stand for. We are consuming 'signs'.
- The process of globalisation has led to an increase in the type and range of products available to be consumed.
- The act of consumption involves the manipulation of symbolic meaning in a creative fashion.

- What we consume is a source of our identity: we are what we buy!
- Consumption plays a part in life-style formation.

Exercise 10.10

Provide an example of each of the four points listed immediately above.

According to many sociologists, consumption patterns have changed dramatically since the 1950s and 1960s. Consumption has become a 'reality' in its own right, not structured by class but superseding class as a way of defining who we are. As Paul Willis and his colleagues (1993) observe:

> The early history of marketing was precisely about separating consumer groups into socio-economic categories so that products could be aimed at them more exactly. Modern marketing, however, has moved on from delineating socio-economic groupings to exploring 'new' categories of life style, life stage, and shared denominations of interest and aspiration.

Many sociologists insist that it makes little sense to speak of distinct class cultures or tastes. This is not to deny the importance of financial and economic structures in consumption, but to illustrate that traditional class differences are no longer as clearly identifiable as they once were. As Robert Bocock (1993) observes, for many identity is in a state of 'flux' whereas before it was stable and fixed due to the importance of class in society. Individuals can develop their own identity, or add to their identity through consumption. They can buy fashionable or designer label goods that symbolise something about them. However Bocock stresses that the freedom to consume and create an identity still rests on the amount of money you have. In which case, is the significance of class really dead?

The traditional Marxist view of consumerism is based on Marx's idea of 'commodity fetishism'. Marx (1989) believed that the money we pay for the commodities our economy creates – their 'exchange value' – is based on a false conception of our need for such things/objects/commodities. We do not really need many of these things, but this is obscured by the fact that they are perceived to have a 'use' and their cost is a reflection of their perceived usefulness. This simply hides the true nature of production – working-class people are the ones whose labour creates these commodities, yet they do not own them and have to pay money for things they themselves have made in the first place. This money is paid to the ruling class, who have contributed no labour at all! Marx referred to this 'isolation' of workers from the products of their labour as 'alienation'.

Marx saw commodities as 'false idols' that are worshipped by the very people who produce them with their labour power, but do not own them. According to the traditional Marxist view of consumption, consumers are tricked by the ideologies of the capitalist economy into buying things they do not really need and, when doing so, feeling happy about the society that is exploiting them. Although consumption may be open to ideological manipulation, this view depicts the consumer as a passive robot, and advertising/marketing as an all-powerful, manipulative tool.

With the rise of postmodernist ideas the nature of consumption has been reassessed. It is no longer seen as a 'trick', but as the result of human agency. Consumption is seen as a highly creative act, involving the active manipulation of symbols. Advertising is a highly important aspect of popular culture. It may be true that advertising manipulates and creates 'false needs' – that is its purpose – but it is also a read source of popular images. It creates, but it uses others and taps into the popular cultural ideas of the times.

Exercise 10.11

Draw up a copy of the following table and in it summarise the ideas of Willis, Bocock, traditional Marxism and postmodernism on the role of consumption in society.

	Key ideas on consumption	Is consumption creative or is it a 'trick'?
Willis		
Bocock		
Traditional Marxism		
Postmodernism		

Types of consumer culture

There are many types of consumption in the postmodern age, and many types of consumer:

- The *passive cultural robot* 'duped' by the power of advertising.
- The *creative actor*, constructing his or her life-style and identity from consumption, exercising free choice.
- The *deviant consumer*, manipulating dominant popular cultural messages, signs and commodities to create a new life-style meaning based on the rejection of popular, consumption-based capitalism; still fighting the class struggle, still resisting the dominant hegemony, using consumption as a political act.
- The *postmodern consumer*, playing with meanings and styles, picking and mixing, creating throwaway identities, forever

recreating her- or himself, concerned only with outer image and style, not inner substance.

Exercise 10.12

In your own words, define each of the four types of consumer listed above, and state how realistic you find each of the four interpretations of consumption.

In *The Consumerist Manifesto* Martin Davidson (1992) notes that both the politically oriented deviant consumerism and the playful, pick-and-mix postmodern consumerism have been held up by some feminists as offering female liberation from traditional gender roles. For example, when discussing the image of (post) modern femininity presented in contemporary women's magazines, feminist Andrea Stuart (1990) argues that the magazine *Elle* is targeted at liberated female readers who take pleasure from consumption and are able actively to manipulate their own identities. The contents of *Elle* indicate that its readers have postmodern 'fractured identities' – liberated, sexually ambiguous and racially varied. These 'new women' may have confused identities but these are 'played with' in order to construct meaning.

Davidson himself seems doubtful about the claim that consumerism within the capitalist system can lead to freedom from it. He sees this as 'having your cake and eating it'. It is an excuse to have fun and not worry about the politics of identity and life-style formation, while at the same time feeling that one is not a 'cultural dupe' – that one is still in charge. Many Marxists would also be sceptical about this claim. They would insist that such 'playing' with consumption means that the capitalist economy is still being supported and inequalities in wealth and power will continue. Any pleasure from such consumption is merely a state of false pleasure created by ideology.

Mike Featherstone and Mike Hepworth (1991) have identified three aspects of postmodern culture in which consumption plays an important role:

- The pursuit of pleasure.
- The rise of a throwaway culture: the 'playful' use of throwaway popular and low cultural products and venues such as theme parks are pleasurable *because* they are throwaway.
- The emergence of an important role for new social movements in identity construction.

Featherstone (1991) also notes that political action, life-style creation and consumption are frequently focused on the body as an object to be moulded, shaped and redefined as one wishes. Body images are everywhere in popular culture and many symbols for identity are based on doing things to or with one's body, such as so-called 'deviant sexual practices', body piercing and tattooing. These are called 'body practices', and those who manipulate their bodies in this fashion are seen as active and creative. The body has become politicised within these life-styles since body practices are often used to symbolise alternative life-styles or counter-cultures against dominant hegemonic values (see Chapter 8).

Exercise 10.13

List the things that people can do to/with their bodies in order to express their individuality. How might each of the items on your list contribute to identity formation?

'DIY' postmodern politics

Postmodern politics can be seen as having less to do with traditional political parties and voting, and more with how one lives one's life at the more local, everyday level. In this sense politics can be seen as making creative choices about style, sexuality and the body, and such politics operate through informal networks, gatherings and subcultures. In this sense people 'do' postmodern politics themselves, on themselves.

Although not a postmodernist, Anthony Giddens (1991) writes about 'life-style politics' as the basis for 'projects on the self': moulding one's identity and trying to deal with the insecurities inherent in having to take responsibility for oneself. This is further reflected in Ulrich Beck's (1992) idea of a 'risk society'. Due to the 'manufactured uncertainties' of the present age, largely caused by science, we are prompted to adopt life-style practices that help to avoid harm – such as harm from environmental pollution and so on. These practices in the risk society are focused on the body, for example wearing sunblock to avoid skin cancer, and practicing safe sex to avoid AIDS. These body practices are political since they are based on criticising the world, and seeking to improve one's life and protect oneself.

Exercise 10.14

Listed below are a number of items that threaten to cause us harm. Consider each one and suggest how it can be avoided by a change in lifestyle.

- HIV/AIDS
- Genetically modified food
- Pollution
- Skin cancer
- Crime
- Heart disease
- CJD

New social movements

As Kevin Hetherington (1998) shows, new social movements frequently incorporate the above observations. These movements are life-style politics based on the body, and are localised and identity forming. New social movements are non-class-based, and are frequently formed by those on the margin who feel that they, their life-styles and identities are not represented by the traditional politics of the ballot box. New social movements develop around issues such as:

- Sexuality.
- Ethnic identity.
- Gender.
- Environmental concerns.

The rapid rise of such movements since the 1970s is seen as further evidence of the death of class and the rise of post-class formations in society. Heller and Feher (1988), however, argue that modernist, class-based politics coexist with the more postmodern variations based on the body, life-styles and new social movements. The decision to embrace postmodern politics comes from a willingness on the part of individuals to accept society and their place in it as pluralistic and fragmented. In other words, postmodern politics are about the awareness of others, the understanding that one's body and life are political, and the realisation that political struggles can exist at both the local (community-based) and the national level. Politics can be about freeing one's street from traffic, protesting about the building of roads through wooded areas, exploring one's sexuality in new ways and even engaging in body practices such as tattooing and body piercing. Postmodern politics are therefore about fighting for who you are. Identity is a key political issue in the postmodern age.

McAllister-Groves (1995) uses Goffman's idea of 'framing' in order to explain why people join new social movements and how they might help in the process of identity formation. These movements are seen as providing 'frames' or 'frameworks' – sources of meaning – with which to make sense of personal, emotional and intimate feelings. The life-styles and views associated with each new social movement allow individuals to think about their feelings and make sense of them. Thus vegetarians might join groups or movements against GM food or animal testing since they provide a set of ideas with which to express the feelings they have.

In *Beyond Left and Right*, Giddens (1994) argues that the rise of new social movements represents a move towards the further democratisation of society and identity since more views, life-styles and people are being 'included' in the processes of power and decision making. They have created new 'spaces' – arenas or areas – for debate on political issues. These new political spaces include intimacy, identity and life-style. Giddens calls this a 'life politics'.

Exercise 10.15

In a table copied from the one below, summarise the theoretical ideas on new social movements (NSMs) covered in this chapter.

	Beck	Hetherington	Heller and Feher	McAllister-Groves	Giddens
Basic beliefs about the rise of NSMs					
Key concepts					
Any examples of NSMs given?					

Conclusion

The concept of class (along with gender and ethnicity – see Chapters 11 and 12) has shaped the sociology we have today. It would be very different without it. However, although class has been seen as a major source of identity, this is now being questioned. Postmodernists, feminists and reflexive modernists question the role of class identity in contemporary society, and therefore its role in sociology. With the rise of consumption, new social movements and globalisation (see Chapter 13) the centrality of class is questioned. As a tool it does enable sociologists to think about the key features of capitalist societies, but it is also vital for sociologists constantly to question and reevaluate older but strongly held ideas.

Examination questions

Use the advice on pages 28–9 to answer the following questions:

(a) Assess the view that different classes develop different subcultures.

(b) How has class identity changed in contemporary society?

11 Feminism, gender and sexuality

By the end of this chapter you should:

- understand a variety of feminist theories;
- be able to evaluate feminist ideas;
- understand the process of gender-role socialisation;
- understand the role played by gender in the construction of identity;
- understand how gender roles have changed in recent years;
- be able to relate feminist ideas to the sociologies of sexuality and the body.

Introduction

Feminist sociology is an example of 'critical sociology'. What this means is that feminism seeks to re-evaluate the way we understand society. Unlike functionalist theory it does not seek to protect the status quo – the way things are – but rather to challenge and change society. The ideas of feminism often complement those of Marxism since both are critical of the way society is. Feminist ideas also complement action sociology since feminists often use micro or ethnographic methods in their research.

For many feminists the relatively recent introduction of feminist ideas into sociology and their widespread adoption in textbooks and syllabuses is evidence of the past invisibility of women sociologists in sociology – mirrored by the devaluation of 'female knowledge' in other academic areas, especially science. Many feminists feel that feminism has been ignored for too long. The invisibility of female writers is reflected in the fact that sociology often talks about 'the founding *fathers*', but never about founding *mothers*. This mainstream or traditional sociology is referred to as 'malestream' since it is dominated by male sociologists and the male world-view. It is, in the words of Abbott and Wallace (1997), *'by men, for men and about men'*. This applies in particular to positivist methodology since its scientific nature is seen to represent – through the experimental method – patriarchal ideology. It devalues female knowledge and treats the social actors involved in its research as 'objects' to be thrown away once used. This mirrors the way that men treat women in society.

Feminist thinkers such as Mackinnon (1982) and Callaway (1984) note that priority is given to the male world-view over the female one and the gathering of female knowledge. This is a position of power that male sociologists enjoy over their female colleagues – the power to define the key issues to be discussed within the subject; the power to say what are and what are not acceptable avenues for sociological investigation.

Exercise 11.1

1. Why do you think sociology started as a male-dominated discipline? List your reasons.

2. What evidence can you find for this still being the case today? Borrow an older sociology textbook from your teacher and write a list of the ways in which such a book might (if at all) disadvantage women and feminism.

Through the criticism of malestream sociology a number of feminist thinkers have come to advocate a whole range of feminist viewpoints. It is important to recognise that there is no such thing as *a* feminism, rather there are many *feminisms*. We shall discuss these varieties of feminist sociology first.

Varieties of feminism

While there are many different types of feminism, they all share a number of assumptions in common. This is the feminist 'world-view'. Firstly, society is seen as male dominated and this domination is based on ideological and coercive forms of social control. Secondly, the aim of sociology is to highlight social injustice against women, and to try to challenge and change this. Such a male-dominated society is often described as 'patriarchal'. This means 'rule of the father', but is frequently taken by feminists to mean male dominated. Finally, it is considered that women have been ignored within sociological discussion until recently, both as thinkers and as topics of study. As Abbott and Wallace (1997) note: '*sociology has been at best sex-blind and at worst sexist*'.

Ann Oakley (1982) argues that sociology is founded on sexist assumptions and that these assumptions were a fundamental part of the origin of the subject in the nineteenth century. This means that unlike other theories, feminism has twice as much to do! It not only wishes to challenge the nature of society, but it must first fight an internal battle within sociology. This is not the case with theories based on male knowledge, such as Marxism. The major contribution made by feminism to modern sociological thought is to encourage an awareness of the positions of inequality of a whole range of previously 'invisible' groups. Many types of feminist theory discuss a wide range of issues, not just those relating to sex, gender and sexuality. For example many feminists have raised awareness of issues of race and ethnicity, and issues relevant to disabled people.

In discussions of the history of the various types of feminism a distinction is usually drawn between two 'waves' of feminism – two historical stages in the development of feminist thought and feminist campaigns in society. The first wave of feminism started at the end of the nineteenth century and was almost totally ignored by the founders of sociology. At that time feminism was concerned with the establishment of equal rights for women – political and legal rights in particular. Feminist groups included the *Women's Social and Political Union* (WSPU), which aimed to reverse women's standing in society as 'second class' citizens. The early feminists were often part of the suffragette movement and were fighting for women's right to vote. It was not until 1928 that the vote was granted to all adults (men and women) over the age of 21 in Britain.

Exercise 11.2

With the help of history books or other appropriate sources, make some further notes on the aims and campaigns of the suffragette movement.

The second wave of feminism began in the mid to late 1960s with the rise of the consciousness-raising movement known as 'women's liberation'. During this second wave feminists began to be characterised in a number of derogatory ways in the popular imagination, fuelled by media moral panics about 'lesbian bra-burners'. Such insulting, sexist, patronising and incorrect stereotypes still exist today and are a barrier against which feminists fight to gain respectability and popularity. Feminists claim that this is as true of the social scientific community as it is of society as a whole. Mary Maynard (1998) notes that this in second wave feminist views were narrowly categorised into what she calls the 'big three': liberal feminism, Marxist feminism and radical feminism. The concentration on these three views at the expense of other versions of feminism has led to almost all feminists being categorised in this way, the rich variety of other feminist ideas being ignored.

Exercise 11.3

For the duration of your study of this topic, compile a folder of newspaper cuttings, that discuss feminist ideas and issues of female liberation. To what extent do these stories and reports categorise feminist ideas and to what extent are they based on the use of sexist and homophobic assumptions?

Liberal feminists seek to resolve female inequality through the legal system. They wish to bring about Acts of Parliament that improve the lives of women in every sphere of society, but especially in the world of work – Acts such as *The Equal Pay Act* of 1970. The liberal nature of this perspective is usually contrasted with what is described as 'radical feminism', which is often associated with the ideas of Shulamith Firestone (1979). This view is 'radical' since it argues that power and domination is an inherent aspect of all males. All men are viewed as prone to violent and physical domination of all women. Heterosexuality is seen as further exploiting and oppressing women since men are able to dominate women's bodies through the act of reproduction. Men benefit from the fact that women give birth and men do not. Finally, Marxist feminism suggests that capitalism and patriarchy are interlinked. Patriarchy serves the interests of a capitalist economy. For example female housework benefits capitalism since those who undertake it represent an unpaid workforce doing essential – yet undervalued – jobs. The solution to male domination and female subordination is seen by Marxist feminists to lie in the overthrow of capitalism – without capitalism there would be no need for patriarchy to continue in society. This is why they are 'Marxist feminists' and not 'feminist Marxists'.

As Maynard (1998) notes, although these three versions of feminism are important – and have made a great contribution to sociology – they are just the beginning of the feminist story, not the end of it. Heidi Hartmann (1981) has described Marxist feminism as an 'unhappy marriage', as in this particular form of theorising class is given priority over gender. In other words, Marxism takes the lead and feminism follows. Hartmann argues that this is the sort of malestream thinking that feminism should be criticising, not supporting. Instead, Hartmann and others offer a 'dual systems' theory, where both capitalist exploitation and patriarchy are seen as symbiotic, feeding off each other. They are interlinked and in some historical situations one might take precedence over or even contradict the other, but it should not be assumed that in every case the class system takes priority over gender inequality. This is very similar to a point made by Abbott and Wallace (1997), who argue that even if class is more important than gender, this has yet to be adequately proven by malestream sociologists.

The idea of interconnected forms of inequality is reflected in the development of what Sylvia Walby (1989, 1990) describes as a 'triple systems' approach. In this view patriarchy and capitalism intersect and sometimes overlap, and they also intertwine with racism. All three forms of power combine to shape society and make it as it is. Black feminism and Third World feminism also seek to understand the relationships between patriarchy and racism in society. Many black feminists claim that just as day-to-day life in society is experienced differently depending on whether you are a man or a woman, it is also experienced differently by different ethnic groupings. Amina Mama (1989) suggests that discussions of the experiences of ethnic groups should not just be 'tacked on' to feminism, but should be seen as an opportunity to reassess the whole theory. In a similar fashion Stanlie James and Abena Busia (1993) argue that the concepts of class, patriarchy and racism do not exist separately in a person's life and therefore simply cannot and should not be separated in sociological study. All three operate simultaneously and therefore should be studied as a single, integrated concept.

Exercise 11.4

Summarise the main types of feminist theory in an extended version of the table below.

	Key thinkers	Why did this theory develop?	Basic beliefs	How can inequality be challenged and changed?
Liberal feminism				
Radical feminism				
Marxist feminism				
Dual systems theory				
Triple systems theory				
Black feminism				
Third World feminism				

Exercise 11. 5

Identify two strengths and two weakness of each of the feminisms discussed so far in this chapter:

- Liberal feminism
- Radical feminism
- Marxist feminism
- Dual systems theory
- Triple systems theory
- Black feminism
- Third World feminism

Postmodern feminists seek to give a voice to a whole range of marginal and previously 'silenced' groups in society. Like other postmodernists they argue that definitions of 'truth' are merely the result of power struggles that some groups have won over others. Postmodern feminists emphasise plurality and ambiguity in society. That is, they believe that gender – what it is to be 'masculine' or 'feminine' – has been 'deconstructed'. Its definition as a fixed, either/or category of 'truth' has changed and has been replaced by a whole variety of femininities and masculinities. This means that what it is to be a man or a woman in society is more plural and ambiguous than ever before, and such definitions are still rapidly changing. They are identities or masks to be played with, rather than absolute, fixed biological facts.

Evaluation of postmodern feminism

The strength of postmodern feminism is that it moves beyond simplistic notions of identity based on distinctions between opposites – such as being either male or female, or black or white. It suggests that identity is more pluralistic. For many feminists this strength is also the main weakness of postmodern feminism. For example Susan Bordo (1990) notes that postmodern feminism rests on the assumption that there are no more absolutes in society, no definite ways of getting at a single 'truth'. This means that if identity has become fragmented or 'fractured' into a plurality of identities it will be difficult if not impossible for women to unite under a collective feminist banner to change society. Increasing fragmentation of identity means that women are less likely to feel close to other women, and the whole project of feminism might therefore be in danger of collapse.

Exercise 11.6

Copy out and complete the followig table.

Statement	Associated with which type(s) of feminist theory?
All men are rapists	
Class and gender are as important as each other	
All men as a global class dominate all women, due to the global expansion of capitalism	
If the problems of capitalism are solved, sexual discrimination will be solved too	
Marxist feminism is an 'unhappy marriage'	
By nature all men wish to dominate all women	
Patriarchy serves capitalism	
Ethnic identity may lessen the problems of patriarchy for some women	
Western women enjoy greater equality than women elsewhere in the world	
Gender identity is no longer fixed: women can be who they wish to be	

Statement	Associated with which type(s) of feminist theory?
Changes to the law can bring about equality for women	
Class, gender and ethnicity overlap as forms of inequality	
Society is male-dominated	

Exercise 11.7

Reread the descriptions of the varieties of feminism above and list six similarities and six differences between the different forms.

Exercise 11.8

Which version of feminism do you find most convincing? Explain your view in 150 words.

Sex, gender and socialisation

Traditionally, sociologists are more interested in studying 'gender' than 'sex'. The distinction here is that sex refers to the biological features that differentiate men from women, while gender refers to the culturally learnt characteristics of what it means to be masculine or feminine. Feminists argue that since gender is a product of society and not of biology, matters of gender are not fixed. Hence, discrimination against women is a cultural creation and can therefore be changed.

The 'normal' way to act as a man or as a woman has nothing to do with one's reproductive organs but rather with how one is taught to act. We are socialised into learning how to behave in a masculine or feminine way through the instilling of 'gender roles'. The process of gender role socialisation starts in the early years in the family home and continues through the education system and into the world of work, reinforced by media representations.

Those who adopt a sociobiological approach (see Chapter 2) claim that how men and women behave is a matter of their genetic codes and natural urges rather than the result of how they are brought up. According to this approach, men and women have different roles in society due to their reproductive organs and so from birth they are preprogrammed to behave in different ways. In this sense inequality and difference between men and women is a natural feature of all human societies. A similar claim has been made by the functionalist Parsons (1951, 1971) who suggests that men and women are predisposed to behave in different ways and learn different sets of roles, based on their natural instincts. Parsons makes a distinction between the 'expressive roles' taken on by women in society and males' 'instrumental roles'. What he means by this is that cultural roles differ between men and women because women are naturally more expressive and emotional and men are more task-orientated. Parsons therefore concludes that women are more suited than men to caring roles. Many feminists view Parsons's ideas as patriarchal ideology – his views justify male oppression and excuse inequality and discrimination in society.

Due to the devaluing of many early feminist ideas in academic thought, some feminists have turned to the work of the early Marxist thinker Engels as a source of feminist ideas. Engels considered female roles and their general subordination to be the result of nurture (upbringing) rather than nature. He argued that the traditional view of women as best suited to a domestic caring role had only existed since the introduction to society of private property. This is an example of the Marxist idea of 'economic determinism': changes in the economy determine or cause cultural changes. Before property became private, Engels claimed, there were no 'families' in the modern sense or monogamous marriage. However, with the increase of property ownership a system of inheritance was needed and so marriage – in the present-day sense – was invented to control the sexual behaviour of women and give power to men. If women's sexuality was controlled, it was easier to identify who the father of the child was send therefore easier to say who should inherit property. In support of this argument, feminists point to anthropological evidence that in earlier societies 'women's work' was defined differently from our present understanding of it. They therefore conclude that gender roles must be social and not biological.

Feminists note that discrimination in society is often the result of society equating sex with gender when in fact they are not the same. For example, just because women can bear children it does not mean they have to wear skirts! Equally, just because men have a penis it does not make them good drivers! These examples are rather obvious ones, and the links between sex and gender are not always so straightforward. For example, just because women give birth does not necessarily mean that they are naturally more suited than men to look after children. What happens, argue many feminists, is that biological sex differences become confused with learnt cultural differences. Such an argument is found in the work of Ann Oakley (1972), who notes that in other societies women perform heavy manual work and men engage in childcare – the opposite of the so-called 'natural' way described by Parsons and those who adopt the sociobiological view.

Exercise 11.9

List 16 stereotypical sexist assumptions in society about the differences between men and women (for example men are thought to be better drivers than women; women are thought to be more suited to childcare than men).

Exercise 11.10

Working as a feminist, design a piece of research aimed at proving that the assumptions in Exercise 11.9 are incorrect.

In *Different for Girls*, feminist writer Joan Smith (1997) argues that culture makes females different from males – it treats them as separate simply because they have different reproductive organs. Like many other feminists she is critical of this and does not consider that there is any real link between sex and gender other than that created by culture itself. It is a 'social construction', a product of society.

Smith makes five propositions about the nature of femininity in society and the relationship between sex, gender and identity:

- Men and women become different because they are treated differently.
- Religious values and other theories about male and female difference, such as those from science and medicine, are used in society as evidence or proof of the difference between men and women.
- The difference between men and women is believed by many in society to be a natural phenomenon, yet the evidence suggests that this is not the case – that nurture is more important than nature.
- Being defined as a 'woman' by society is not simply a matter of biology but also involves restrictive moral judgements about how one should behave as a woman.
- Because of the emphasis on sex or biology in common-sense patriarchal thought, all women are seen as fundamentally different from all men, yet similar to all other women. In other words, sex differences are seen in society as a vital source of difference.

Kirby (1999) points to a growing body of evidence that the concept of 'sex' is not a fixed biological reality but the product of social creation. For example Hood-Williams (1996) notes that the biological determination of whether an individual is a male or a female is not always clear cut and a choice sometimes has to be made by adults about the sex of a child. For example some males have more female chromosomes than the scientific definition of 'being male' prescribes (one male and one female chromosome), yet because they look male at birth they become categorised as male – not a very scientific basis upon which to make a judgement.

Exercise 11.11

List the arguments that feminists would use in order to criticise the claim that inequality between men and women is natural.

Understanding 'motherhood'

For Maureen O'Hara (1996) there is no such thing as an essential, biological female 'reality'. Rather, this depends on how those in power decide, in a particular historical time period, to use females. For example during the Second World War women performed heavy physical work that was traditionally associated with men. However, with the end of the war and the arrival of men back from the armed forces the 'reality' of what a women was reverted to what O'Hara describes as the 'cult of motherhood' – the view that the best place for women was in the family home engaging in childcare. This means that categories of feminine and masculine behaviour are not absolutes since they change with the cultural and economic circumstances of societal change. This view is influenced by postmodern ideas in that O'Hara claims that the 'truth' of being a woman is defined by those in power rather than by objective, absolute criteria. The truth is therefore a site for power struggles.

This view is reflected in the work of Kathryn Woodward (1997), who suggests that while motherhood as a source of identity might appear fixed, stable and rooted in natural biology, it is in fact a social construction. Woodward notes that everyone can relate to the idea of motherhood and knows what this means in society – even those of us who are not and cannot be mothers still have mothers and can therefore understand what this concept means. To be a mother is seen first and foremost as a biological act since it is based on the ability to reproduce. It is seen as natural. However in today's society bearing children is not necessarily the 'natural biological act' it was once seen as. There is artificial insemination, there are surrogate mothers and there are lesbian mothers – all of which suggest that motherhood is not a single, absolute, 'natural' concept. Motherhood also implies childcare as well as childbirth, yet this can vary considerably within and between cultures. Finally, there are 'good' mothers and there are 'bad' mothers, and many of the latter are blamed by the media for causing delinquency in society by failing to exercise discipline in the home. If motherhood is natural, why is it so difficult to get right?

Woodward (ibid) points out that feminists adopt different positions on the nature and role of motherhood as a source of identity. On the one hand motherhood might be seen as serving to control the female body and female sexuality, whereas on the other it could be seen as a liberating way for women to embrace who they are, to understand their bodies, and to distinguish themselves from men.

For example Kate Millet (1970) and Shulamith Firestone (1979) see the family – and the woman's role within it as a child bearer and a child carer – as the prime source of gender inequality and female oppression. The physical act of bearing children limits what women can do and are allowed to do, and their role within the home limits their day-to-day actions. This consideration has informed a great deal of the recent feminist criticisms of the New Right's view of the role of women in society. For example during the prime ministership of Conservative Margaret Thatcher women were seen as essential to the provision of care in society and such care was located in the family home – the 'natural' place for women to be. This policy – called 'care in the community' – echoed the ideas of sociobiology and the views of functionalists such as Parsons. In this way, ideological images of 'motherhood' are used by society to define what women should be like and are often used by women themselves to define who they are.

Woodward (1997) suggests that Western society uses 'myths of motherhood' to socialise and control the activities of women by defining what and who women are and should be. Such myths include the view that being a mother involves giving up one's personal identity/independence for the good of one's offspring – to be self-sacrificing. Or in other words, a woman is defined as a woman not by who she is, but by who she looks after. Many feminists see this as a distorted and false view of motherhood in particular and womanhood in general, a view that operates to control women in a male-dominated society.

The postmodernisation of gender

Along with class and ethnicity, gender has traditionally been seen within sociological thought as a structural constraint upon the individual and a major source of personal identity. All three sources of identity are now being challenged by the postmodern idea that class, gender and ethnicity are being pluralised and are no longer the rigid structural constraints they once were. The importance of the postmodern feminist view in modern-day sociology has led some to describe it as a 'third wave of feminism'.

Some thinkers from the postmodern perspective have taken the sex–gender distinction further. For example Butler (1990) suggests that it is impossible to talk in any meaningful way about a femininity or a masculinity. These are so plural as to be meaningless. All there is are biological sex differences and the many different ways that people choose to live their lives. As soon as we speak of femininity we are attaching, by definition, a narrow set of characteristics to women, and suggesting that such characteristics are much more woman-like than they are man-like. By using the concept 'gender' we are shaping the world around us, and in doing so we are creating female oppression by limiting women's opportunities. This means not only that the question 'what does it mean to be a women' is impossible to answer, but also in asking the question we are drawing a distinction between men and women that is oppressive and restrictive.

The influence of postmodern ideas has led to the observation that gender identity is a matter of active creation and at times liberation. A similar theme is explored in *The Company She Keeps* by Valerie Hey (1997). Hey's ethnographic fieldwork was influenced by post-structuralist ideas (see Chapter 9) and especially the idea that to establish one's sense of identity one thinks about others and their 'differences'. While conducting a 'participant observation' study of school girls in a secondary school, Hey reflected on the meaning of note-passing during lessons. She argues that the writing and circulation of such notes is a symbolic activity in which young teenage girls reflect on the nature of friendship, intimacy, sexuality and their own self – their personal identity. By writing these notes, which are like ongoing conversations between a number of parties, girls create for themselves a private 'space' in which they consider what it means to be a young female in today's world. This is seen as an active and creative process of gender identity formation rather than something that is handed down ready-made from culture as a structure of constraint.

Exercise 11.12

During her research Hey used the technique of participant observation. This exercise requires you to assess the usefulness of this technique by answering the following questions.

1. Define what participant observation means.

2. What is the difference between covert and overt observation?

3. List five advantages of observation.

4. List five disadvantages of observation.

5. When applied to the study of girls' friendship patterns, what are the problems with observation?

6. When applied to the study of girls' friendship patterns, what are the strengths of observation?

Exercise 11.13

Consider your answers to Exercise 11.12. Design a way of doing Hey's research that does not use the observation method. Write down your proposal in approximately 200 words.

Linda Nicholson (1999) suggests that the concepts of 'sex' and 'gender' hold a contradictory place in feminist thought. For example, whereas feminists are critical of 'biological determinism' they advocate a form of it themselves. For sociobiologists biology (nature) determines how one behaves – it makes us who we are. Humans are seen as little more than the product of biological urges. This biologically determinist view is rejected by those feminists who claim that we are who we learn to be. Culture places norms and values upon us and in doing so it moulds who we become. Therefore, so the argument goes, women and men might behave differently, but this does not mean that by nature they are any more different than the simple difference in reproductive organs. However Nicholson notes that many feminists then go on to express the view they claim to have rejected. Such feminists suggest that although women might act differently in different cultures, underneath they are all women and therefore have common bonds of womanhood between them. Such arguments, for Nicholson, are not really about gender – they are actually about sex since they do not recognise that people of the same gender might nonetheless have many differences. This emphasis on differences within gender illustrates the influence of postmodern ideas on Nicholson's argument.

Sexualities

Whereas 'sex' refers to the biological – often reproductive – differences between being male and being female, 'sexuality' refers to one's sexual desires and participation in the sex act. Billington *et al.* (1998) suggest that although sexuality might at first seem natural it is still shaped by culture:

> If sexuality is something deeply rooted in our 'nature' how is it that we need to learn how to do it and develop a variety of religious, moral and even legal rules and regulations about who it is appropriate to do it with, when, where and how?

They note that the idea of 'sex' is in fact highly problematic – even the word itself is confusing. It can be an act, a biological type or a gender. Given that the sex act is regulated so much, and that some means of sexual gratification are defined as acceptable and others as deviant (and that this changes over time), sexuality must be understood as a cultural process. For Billington *et al.* the question 'is sex and sexuality natural or cultural?' is a false question. It is impossible to answer. That is because sex, sexuality and sexual identity are often seen as 'either/or': they are due either to nature or to nurture. This is not the case, they argue. Sexuality is a complex interplay between culture and biology, plus there is an element of free choice in the type of sexual acts one engages in and the life-style one adopts. Billington and her colleagues see sexuality as a prime source of power. Those who have power are able to proclaim the 'truth' of sexuality that everyone else must follow.

Lynne Segal (1997) notes that academic interest in sex and sexuality moved from a biomedical model based on scientific studies of why and how sexual pleasure occurs, through psychoanalytic theories that looked at male and female sexual activity, to feminist interpretations that either sought to encourage women to achieve sexual pleasure for themselves and to embrace their sexuality and sexual desires, to feminist theories that advocated non-penetrative sex and lesbianism as a way to challenge male sexual power. Today sociologists tend to discuss sexualities – a wide range or diversity of sexual acts, pleasures, meanings and behaviours. There is also, due to the influence of postmodern ideas in sociology, the observation that many develop life-styles that 'play' with sexuality and traditional images of masculinity, femininity, heterosexuality and homosexuality. This is further reflected in recent popular cultural images and representations that use highly ambigious masculine/feminine images.

Exercise 11.14

1. Write a list of advertisements you have seen that 'play with sexuality' – that present ambiguous images of sexuality and gender that break away from the more traditional understanding of how males and females should behave and physically look like.

2. Why do you think advertisers use such images? (One paragraph.)

3. What effect do you think such images might have on audiences? (One paragraph.)

Segal observes that discussions of sexuality – both popular (in the media) and academic (within sociology) – are 'complex' and 'contested'. Young children are sexualised in themselves and for adult audiences, and male bodies have become sexualised for the viewing pleasure of a female audience.

There has been a large number of moral panics over sexuality and the risks of sex, especially for young people and children. The position of 'child sexuality' in these moral panics is especially problematic. On the one hand we have witnessed the widespread use of sexualised images of young teenage girls in the fashion industry, in beauty advertisements and in advertising in general, yet on the other hand the newspapers have expressed great concern about single mothers, underage sex, illegitimacy, child pornography and child sexual abuse.

Adolescent and sometimes prepubescent girls are often presented in a sexualised way in the media by the advertising industry. Such girls are portrayed as adult male fantasy figures, as objects of the 'male gaze'. Many feminists feel that such representations provide role models for the young girls who make up the media audience. These images suggest that certain forms of sexual behaviour are the norm for young adolescents, and that certain body shapes are more desirable than others.

The argument that representations of women are designed to fulfil male sexual fantasies is a familiar theme in feminist media and cultural studies. For example Laura Mulvey (1975) suggests that the female body is characterised in media representations in a very narrow way. Females are often depicted as sexual toys for men – as objects to be used – and, as with adolescents, certain body types are held up as the 'ideal' for women to strive for.

In discussions of sexuality, many feminists identify what they call a 'compulsory heterosexuality' within the wider patriarchal picture of the nature of society. For example Diane Richardson (1993) notes that heterosexuality is seen as biologically 'natural' – a 'normal' state to be in – and therefore every other type of sexual behaviour is deemed unnatural. It was only recently that sexuality came to be seen as a choice, as a basis for life-style creation rather than something that is fixed at birth. William Simon (1996) suggests that in the postmodern age gender and sexual identity are important to each individual and are not handed down by society 'ready-made'. Instead they are a product of negotiation between the individual and the wider culture she or he lives in. There are many different and changing identities to draw from. For some this might lead to confusion, personal anxiety and uncertainty but for others it might be liberating. Simon makes the same claim for sexuality as a source of identity. He argues that sexuality is increasingly becoming less a matter of biology and 'normality' and more a matter of life-style and choice.

In *The Transformation of Intimacy* Anthony Giddens (1992) argues that contemporary sexuality is very different from earlier forms. He describes the emergence of what he terms 'plastic sexuality', where sexual pleasure is separated from the act of reproduction. Instead sexual desire is a source of personal pleasure, liberation and a significant feature of one's life-style. In this way sexuality has become a matter of identity – it tells us about who we are and who we wish to be. Giddens notes that plastic sexuality is an outcome of, and in turn has led to an increase in, women's liberation in society. Unlike in earlier times, women's sexual pleasure is not seen as a deviant act, but as a natural and important part of a healthy relationship. Such changes in sexuality have led to a move towards a 'pure relationship' for many 'ordinary women' – an emotional and intimate relationship based on equality between the partners, not violence or domination. Sexuality is no longer something to be hidden or denied, especially for women – it is based on increased democratisation between men and women in the intimate sphere of private life. It is bound up with our identity, and who we wish to become. Giddens calls this 'life politics': matters of personal identity that we have active control over.

Sexual identity and 'sabotage'

As Segal (1997) notes, cultural identities – including gender and sexual identity – are more open and fluid in today's society, which for some writers is evidence of the postmodernisation of social life. Such identities can also be seen as political acts. For example many gay and lesbian life-styles are based on 'gender sabotage' – redefining what it means to be 'straight' or 'gay', using and playing with images and cultural identities from one gender and sexuality from the viewpoint of another. Such political life-styles based on sexuality and gender identity seek to push back the boundaries of what is considered the norm in modern society. They seek to redefine what is considered 'deviant', and in doing so to create new meanings and identities.

These acts of gender redefinition are based on the political ideas of Michel Foucault (see Chapter 9) and the idea that invisible or silenced identities can fight back against their invisibility by changing the existing structures from within.

Gender and popular culture

A great deal of feminist discussion on popular culture concerns the way in which women and girls are represented to the audience. Such representations are seen as highly ideological and as serving to reinforce patriarchy. For example women are considered to occupy a limited number of roles – usually sex object, mother and housewife.

A great deal of feminist research into representations of femininity has concerned the nature of teenage girls' magazines and women's magazines. For example Marjorie Ferguson (1983) and Angela McRobbie (1983) have identified an ideology of femininity in media products aimed at women. Such products depict female gender identity as based on romantic love, finding and keeping a man, marriage, being a good wife, being a good mother and so on.

Early feminists saw media audiences as largely passive (see Chapter 7). Men and women were thought to 'soak up' ideological images and to see these as a true picture of society. While many feminists still suggest that representations of femininity are ideological, there is a tendency within sociology to recognise that media audiences are more active. For example Ballaster *et al.* (1991) have argued that although women's magazines might portray women in limited ways, women themselves get pleasure from them and 'read' or 'decode' them in a variety of ways. Having said this, Ballaster *et al.* note that magazines

– and popular cultural products in general – allow both men and women to make sense of the world around them, and do so using highly ideological images.

Images of masculinity

Exercise 11.15

Collect copies of so-called 'new lad' magazines aimed at teenage males – how do they portray femininity and masculinity? Compare one 'new lad' magazine to one young women's and one teenage girls' magazine. How are sexualised images used, and what do these magazines say about what it is to be male or female in modern society? Is this similar or different from the ideas of Ferguson above? Discuss your findings in 200 words.

Perhaps one of the most noticeable changes in popular culture in recent years has been the growth of the male life-style magazine and the new lad culture that many seem to be advocating. Such magazines frequently include highly sexist stories and sexualised images of women. However at roughly the same time there has also been an increased sexualisation of the male body for female audiences. This can be been in TV adverts, films and between the covers of teenage girls' magazines offering sexual tips and independence to 'modern young women'. This phenomenon has led many sociologists to consider not just images of femininity but images of masculinity as well.

Angela McRobbie (1994) argues that although the male body – like its female counterpart – has become sexualised this does not mean that sexual equality has been achieved. In fact far from it. Gender inequality and oppression continue, but now both men and women are portrayed in limited roles and are oppressed by ideological representations.

Is feminism dead? Has it gone too far?

In *Backlash*, Susan Faludi (1992) argues that there has been an antifeminist backlash against the rise of the female voice in society. Women have made considerable and significant inroads into the dismantling of an unequal society, but many men feel that their masculinity and male identity are threatened by such social change. This suggests that there is still a patriarchal struggle in society and gender is still a source of difference between men and women and an important source of identity.

Within sociology, perhaps as part of this antifeminist backlash, there has been a rise in 'postfeminist' ideas and rational-choice theory.

This movement is often associated with the ideas of Catherine Hakim (1995), who suggests that women's lives have been significantly improved and hence there is no longer a need for feminism. Its job is over. Hakim suggests that women are totally free to make whatever choices they wish and are not in any way held back by their status as women. They can be mothers, have full-time careers or even combine the two. She suggests that women are not disadvantaged in the labour market but *choose* to engage in poorly paid, part-time employment – it is a conscious decision. Not as many women have entered the labour force as might be thought, but this is because they choose not to. Women wish to get married, have children and look after them in the family home. If they do not, then there are opportunities in society for them to do whatever they wish to do. This view has come under attack by other feminists who still see patriarchy as putting a powerful structural constraint on women.

Andrea Stuart (1990) also questions whether feminism is alive or dead, but her answer is different from that of Hakim. Stuart notes that many women still feel strongly about feminist issues, many see gender as an important source of identity and many feel that society is still unequal. Yet they feel that feminism as a movement is irrelevant. It does nothing actually to help them. She suggests that the feeling of togetherness that accompanied previous waves of feminism has been all but lost in modern-day society. Women do not feel part of a wider whole, united by their common experiences and gender. A gulf has developed between 'feminism the profession' – in universities – and the popular feminism that is found in many women's magazines – advocating antisexist legislation, giving advice on sexual pleasure, presenting the male body as an object for the female gaze (rather than the other way round) and providing images of strong, career-oriented, independent women. Women are still finding strength in such messages and still understand what it means to be a woman in society, yet these identities are transmitted through popular media rather than a clearly defined feminist movement. Stuart sees this as a product of the increasing postmodernisation of society – an increasing plurality of identities for women to adopt.

Conclusion

There are a number of dominant themes in modern-day feminist sociology, despite the wide range of approaches. These themes are based on the observations that the feminist movement has come a long way from its early origins; that women's lives in society are very different today than in the past; that feminist sociology is beginning to receive the recognition it deserves, although a great deal of 'malestream' sociology still exists; and that gender remains a massive source of personal identity. Contemporary feminists have also noted that the nature of gender identity is changing for both women and men. Women are still disadvantaged in the patriarchal society, but they are no longer totally passive victims – they are creative users of popular culture even though they are portrayed in a sexist way by this popular culture.

Examination questions

Use the advice on pages 28–9 to answer the following questions:

(a) To what extent do the media construct masculine and feminine identities differently?

(b) How useful are the insights of feminism for a sociological understanding of identity?

12 Ethnicity and identity

By the end of this chapter you should:

- understand the problems involved in the definition and use of terms such as 'race', 'ethnicity' and 'black';
- understand the role played by ethnicity in identity creation;
- understand the arguments for increased ethnic hybridity in modern society.

Introduction

Early sociological discussions of ethnic identity tended to portray ethnicity as a problem. Immigration after the Second World War was discussed in terms of the 'assimilationist model', which argued that in the interest of order and harmony it was important for ethnic groups to fit or blend into the wider 'host' culture. With the growing awareness of racism in society and race riots in urban areas, ethnicity was treated as even more of a problem. The early sociological study of race relations aimed to solve the problems of a multicultural society, rather than valuing difference.

The sociological study of ethnicity and ethnic identity today is very different from its early predecessor. For a start, 'ethnicity' is something everyone has, not just 'others', and difference is seen as important to the creation of who we are.

Problems with the term 'ethnicity'

According to Yinger (1976), ethnicity has three defining characteristics:

- The perception by others that the group in question is different.
- The perception by those in the group itself that they are different from others.
- The fact that that those defined as being in the same group – with the same identity – share activities based on their 'sameness', whether real or imagined.

What this means is that ethnicity is about awareness, identity, belonging, culture and difference. Membership of an ethnic group suggests that there are others who are not similar.

Yinger goes on to identify four general characteristics of a multicultural or multi-ethnic society:

- The society might be based on a collection of different ethnic groups who are equal.
- The society might have a majority 'national' group alongside a number of smaller ethnic groups.
- The self-identity of some ethnic groups might be based on a 'mother' society outside the host society.
- Some ethnic groups might be disadvantaged in relation to other groups in the same society.

Matters of ethnicity – especially its definition – are open and subject to change. This is a key theme in the definition of ethnicity. Sociologists often disagree about which key terms should be used to describe a given aspect of social reality, and the meaning of the same term often varies between theories and theorists. This is especially true of the terms associated with the study of ethnic identity, including the following:

- Race
- Ethnicity
- Coloured
- White
- Black

Paul Gilroy (1997) provides a good example of the problem of definition:

> Think, for example, of 'black' as a shared identity. Does it refer to the notion of genetic differences between people or to the colour of their skins? Is it a descriptive term or a political one? Can you be 'black' and 'British'? Identity has clearly become a core component in the scholarly vocabulary designed to promote critical reflection upon who we are and what we want. Above all, identity can help us to comprehend the formation of that fateful pronoun 'we' and to reckon with the patterns of inclusion and exclusion that it cannot but help to create. This may be one of the most troubling aspects of all: the fact that the formation of every 'we' must leave out or exclude a 'they', that identities depend on the marking of difference.

Exercise 12.1

k u in a

Reread the above extract from Gilroy (1997) and then answer the following questions. Explain your answers.

1. Does 'black' refer to the notion of genetic differences between people or to the colour of their skins?

2. Is 'black' a descriptive term or a political one?

3. Can you be 'black' and 'British'?

Exercise 12.2

What does Gilroy mean by 'that fateful pronoun "we"'? Answer this question in approximately 100 words.

Traditionally the concept of 'race' is biological whereas 'ethnicity' is cultural – much the same distinction as that made in Chapter 11 between sex and gender. However the term race has become problematic in modern-day sociology. Classifications of race according to different biological types often ignore the vast diversity of human life. Such classifications have sometimes conformed to racist views themselves since these biological types are seen as all-powerful biological realities that are fixed. Many have rejected the term ethnicity on similar grounds. Ethnic differences are seen as being as fixed in cultural differences as races are fixed in biological differences. Paul Gilroy (1987) describes this situation as 'cultural racism', while Martin Barker (1981) uses the term 'new racism' to describe the same problem – that cultural differences are treated as 'essentialist'. They are used to reduce the diverse and multiple characteristics of varied and changing groups to a limiting set characteristics that account for every aspect of behaviour and identity. This leaves no room for the idea that ethnic identities are constantly readjusted as society changes.

Many sociologists try to use the terms and labels to define groups that those groups use themselves. In the 1970s and early 1980s the term 'coloured' was rejected by many in favour of 'black'. The argument put forward was that everyone was coloured, that white was as much a colour as black. By calling people who were black coloured, you were denying their true colour – hiding it as if it was something to be ashamed of. At that time 'black power' movements were fighting a conscious battle against white racism.

The term black, however, has had a problematic history. As Tariq Modood (1988, 1992) notes, the word black might have been adopted by some people of African descent but it has been rejected by many of Asian descent. Modood argues that 'black' – as was argued above in the case of 'coloured' – denies the existence of ethnic diversity and difference, and instead lumps all non-white peoples together. It is often the case that differences of identity within and between ethnic groups make the use of a single term unacceptable. This is because it sets up a very simplistic distinction between black ancd white, causing many identities to be ignored, lost or silenced. Similarly Brah (1992) suggests that while Afro-Caribbean and Asian peoples might all experience racism and inequality in Britain, they experience different types of racism based on different racist assumptions, stereotypes and ideologies. Therefore we should use different terms because their experiences and the causes of those experiences are different.

Exercise 12.3

List the problems associated with each of the following terms:

- Race
- Ethnicity
- Coloured
- White
- Black

As we can see, definitions of ethnicity in particular and identity in general are the result of political acts, both when such definitions are imposed by dominant cultures onto minority groups and when they are adopted by the members of ethnic groups themselves. As Jeffrey Weeks (1990) notes:

> Identities are not neutral. Behind the quest for identity are different, and often conflicting values. By saying who we are, we are also striving to express what we are, what we believe and what we desire.

Ethnic hybridity is sometimes referred to as 'new ethnicity' – an awareness that notions of difference do not simply limit and characterise, but that difference can be positive and powerful. Such notions can be used by ethnic groups themselves in order to be who they wish to be, and to have valued about their cultures what they wish to have valued. For Stuart Hall (cited in Woodward, 1997) ethnic identities can be 'located' within the lines of the past and the future. In other words, ethnic identity is a matter of finding a 'real' or 'authentic' past – a sense of history and tradition – but also a sense of future. In the words of Woodward, ethnic identities are about both 'being' and 'becoming'. Gilroy (1993) suggests that ethnic identities are constantly undergoing change. There is no such thing as a 'pure' ethnic identity, rather groups create their own sense of identity in relation to social structure, their sense of history (real or imagined) and what they envisage for the future. As he notes, 'The "raw materials" from which identity is produced may be inherited from the past but they are also worked on, creatively or positively, reluctantly or bitterly, in the present' (ibid.)

Exercise 12.4

Why are notions of difference important to the establishment of who we are – to establishing our identity? Answer this question in approximately 100 words.

Identity and resistance

Paul Gilroy (1997) argues that although black people are disadvantaged in society they should not simply be characterised as helpless victims – black cultures often involve political resistance against racism. As Hebdige (1979) (see Chapter 8) notes, subcultural styles and the creation of identity through group membership are symbolic means of resisting oppressive dominant values and ideologies in society. Forms of music, styles of dress and even ways of speaking can be used as symbolic tools to fight against powerlessness and alienation. In this sense 'style' is counter-hegemonic. It can be used to resist dominant ideologies and to maintain sense of difference, which in turn allows the members of a group to think about who they are and who they wish to become.

This idea of cultural resistance through style has been taken up by Kobena Mercer (1995), who notes that ethnic groups use style as a political tool. Establishing one's membership of an ethnic cultural group can be a liberating and political act. Mercer takes as an example of such identity politics the part played by hairstyles in black culture. The 'Afro' of the black power movement in the 1960s and 1970s and the 'dreadlocks' of Rastafarians are examples of identity construction through the use of symbols and resistance to a racist and oppressive society through symbolic style. Both hairstyles symbolise pride, unity and difference from an essentially racist society. They are forms of resistance to dominant ideological values.

Exercise 12.5

Consider the symbols used by black hip-hop artists and black reggae artists. For each group, list the ways in which style is used as a form of resistance and to create a sense of identity.

Diaspora, hybridity and globalisation

In *The Black Atlantic*, Paul Gilroy (1993) uses the word 'diaspora' to refer to the effect that ethnic identity and culture can have on others. Although ethnic identities are frequently based on the notion of being different, they can provide others with symbols that can be mixed together to create 'hybrid cultures'. In this sense 'diaspora' refers to how ethnic cultures come to influence others as a result of migration. As members of an ethnic group move from nation to nation their culture spreads and may be adopted by people from other ethnic groups. For example in Britain we have seen the adoption of black musical styles by white youths, the adoption of black styles by Asian youths, the adoption of white styles by black youths and so on. This transportation of cultural styles can include music, styles of dress, patterns of speech and even political ideas and symbols.

Exercise 12.6

in id a

Choose a band or another contemporary musical act that 'plays' with ethnic identity and influences. In a presentation to your class, describe how it does this. Include samples of the music played and images of how the musical act dresses. Use the Internet to help you with your research.

The rise of hybrid identities is linked to issues of globalisation (see Chapter 13). Kevin Robins (1997) notes that although 'globalisation' refers to the global narrowing of space and time it does not, paradoxically, refer to the loss of local identities or cultures. Rather it refers to the spread of the 'local' to the global stage. In other words, we become more aware of the difference of others through the spread of regional and local differences across time and space. We are not moving towards a common global culture shared by all, but towards greater awareness of the variety of ethnic identities. The end result of globalisation is not global similarity, but increased awareness of global difference.

For Robins this globalisation of difference raises questions about present notions of identity and those of the future. International travel and the popularity of tourism as a pastime, the expansion of global communications, the globalisation of popular culture and media, and the creation of world markets through the spread of multinational corporations call into question previous notions of national identity, ethnic identity and the boundaries between groups. Such questioning of the boundaries of identity is both disorientating and liberating. It can lead to increased anxiety and conflict, or to increased tolerance and harmony. In a similar argument Les Back (1994) notes that we in the West are experiencing global musical styles based on a pastiche of many cultural and ethnic symbols.

Global hybridity is often cited as evidence of the onset of postmodernity in contemporary society. In this view, postmodernity has opened up global boundaries and blurred previously rigid distinctions (geographical and symbolic, real and imagined) between cultures, and has brought with it a plurality and diversity of ethnicity, culture and identity. We are more aware of the 'other' than ever before, and are able to borrow from this 'other', styles and symbols to use in fresh and creative ways.

According to David Morley (1994) the postmodern interpretation of globalisation as liberation from traditional cultural and ethnic boundaries must be accompanied by a word of warning. What many postmodernists ignore is that there has always been a global awareness of others and of difference, especially as a result of the colonial and imperial past of many European nations. When postmodernists write of the increased awareness of others in the contemporary age, what they are really referring to is the increased recognition by those in the rich, industrialised First World of the experiences and cultures of those in the Third World. Due to slavery, religious missionary work and colonialism the ordinary members of Third World societies have been aware of the difference of Western others for a lot longer than ordinary Westerners have been aware of them. In this sense the interconnectedness of global cultures and identities is nothing new at all!

bell hooks (1996) writes of the development of a 'postmodern blackness'. By this hooks means that although postmodern views are frequently those of white, middle-class academia, the idea of cultural hybridity raises important issues for black people and can provide an important voice for black people, particularly black women. Within sociology there is much talk about the opening up of people's awareness of difference, but the views of black female sociologists are still relatively unheard in relation to those of their male and white counterparts. hooks suggests that postmodern ideas and postmodern society offer a context within which black people can think about their culture, history and themselves, and in doing so can value who they are. They can use this to struggle against racist ideologies that seek to devalue black identity.

What writers such as Stuart Hall (1992) have found useful about postmodernism when applied to issues of ethnic identity is the idea that identity has become 'fractured' or 'fragmented' into a vast plurality of possible identities – what we called a 'new ethnicity' earlier in the chapter. This is referred to as a process of 'decentring'. In other words, identity is a matter of personal creation, it is not fixed or handed down by others.

Exercise 12.7

 In a copy of the table below, summarise the ideas discussed in this chapter.

Name of thinker	Basic concepts	Argument
Gilroy		
Barker		
Modood		
Brah		
Weeks		
Hall		
Mercer		

Name of thinker	Basic concepts	Argument
Robins		
Morley		
Hooks		

Conclusion

As we have seen, notions of race, ethnicity and 'black' and 'white' are highly problematic and are open to considerable debate and discussion. As we have seen from the work of Hall and Gilroy, notions of ethnic identity are based on resistance and difference, and are frequently matters of hybridity. Ethnicity is a creation – it is based on political struggles. This raises issues not only for ethnic identity but also for national identities – a theme taken up in the next chapter.

Examination questions

Use the advice on pages 28–9 to answer the following questions:

(a) How has globalisation changed the way in which we see ethnic identities in the contemporary world?

(b) With reference to ethnicity, discuss the way in which identity is a form of resistance in society.

13 Community, nation and globalisation

By the end of this chapter you should:

- be able to define the concepts of community, nation and globalisation;
- be able to identify how community and nation can establish identity;
- understand why writers such as Giddens wish to replace the idea of 'community' with new terms;
- understand the importance of notions of 'time' and 'space' for issues of identity;
- understand the role of symbols in the creation of community identity;
- be able to apply theoretical perspectives to the issue of globalisation.

Introduction

It is 150 years since the word 'sociology' was first used, and we could be forgiven for thinking that both society and sociology are very different from what they were in the days of the founders – Comte, Durkheim, Marx and Weber. For some sociologists the founders' project of 'modernity' (see Chapters 3 and 6) has come to an end and we now live in a time of postmodernity (see Chapter 6), whereas for others great social change has taken place in our late-capitalist or postindustrial society, but not as envisaged by the postmodernists.

A central feature of contemporary sociology, whether trying to deny modernity or to update it, is the idea of globalisation, which has had profound implications for culture and identity. The onward march of globalisation has implications for how we conceive the communities we belong to, and for how nations maintain their distinctive identities in an age where ordinary people are being exposed to new cultural ideas from places that were once far away, but now seem ever nearer due to air travel and mass communications.

Modernity and the decline of community

Along with the rise of science, rationality and technology, a key feature in the image of modernity held by the founders was urbanisation: the creation of towns and cities, and migration from rural areas to these new industrial centres. Modernity was fundamentally tied to industrialisation, and urbanisation played a vital role in this. Workers were needed in the new factories and agricultural production declined. The move to towns and cities heralded the dawn of a new age – one that would have a profound effect on traditional culture and identity.

Exercise 13.1

In what ways do you feel that the modern-day community has changed from earlier forms? For each of the following aspects of society, compare and contrast the community of today with the community of the past.

- Religious practice
- Nature of the family
- Family meals
- The relationship between work and home

Exercise 13.2

1. Conduct an open-ended, oral-history-based interview with an elderly person whom you know. Try to establish how modern life in towns and cities is different from before. Use your answer to Exercise 13.1 as the basis for the questions you ask.

2. Write up your findings in approximately 500 words and include a brief section on the advantages and disadvantages of the interview method.

Many of the founders considered that the industrial age was accompanied by the 'decline of community'. An early expression of this idea is contained in the work of Ferdinand Tonnies (1963), who wrote at the end of the nineteenth century. Tonnies drew a distinction between traditional society (based on '*Gemeinschaft*') and modernity (based upon '*Gesellschaft*'). These are two different ways of organising social life, relationships and the creation of individual self-identity.

Gemeinschaft means 'community'. In rural areas individuals were bonded into close-knit communities where everyone knew each other and had personal contact in all areas of life. Relationships were based on daily, face-to-face interaction:

> The prototype of all unions of Gemeinschaft is the family. By birth man enters these relationships: free rational will can determine his remaining within the family, but the very existence of the relationship itself is not dependent on his full rational will. The three pillars

of Gemeinschaft – blood, place (land), and mind, or kinship, neigh-bourhood and friendship – are all encompassed in the family (Tonnies, quoted in Kumar, 1986).

Gesellschaft means 'contractual association'. In other words, in an industrial society relationships are based on impersonal forces. Instead of daily, face-to-face interaction with everyone, there are limited interactions with just some people, based on role speciali-sation of where some people have work relationships, others family relationships and others neighbourly – relations. Tonnies, who char-acterised *gesellschaft* as a state of isolation and tension between indi-viduals, seemed to regret the decline of community. Even though *gesellschaft* allows people the freedom to choose the relationships they wish in their lives outside work, it nonetheless isolates them from those around them.

Emile Durkheim explored a similar theme to Tonnies in his book *The Division of Labour in Society* (1938), where he made a distinc-tion between two types of 'solidarity' (see Chapter 3), that is, ways of organising individuals into a cohesive group: mechanical solidarity, found in rural areas where individuals were bonded by similarity and the sharing of tasks, and where everyone knew everyone else; and organic solidarity, which emerged with industrialisation and urbani-sation and was based on the division of labour and specialised, work-related roles. The latter was a new form of solidarity and was based not on similarity, but on difference. Society became interconnected because people came to rely on others to perform tasks and roles that they could not perform themselves. Although Durkheim was con-cerned about a potential increase in 'anomie', he believed that this new form of community would re-enforce solidarity, not reduce it.

Exercise 13.3

Design and carry out a piece of research to investigate Tonnies' claim that there has been a 'decline of community'. You will need to establish:

- A hypothesis.
- A research method.
- A sampling technique.
- The sampling frame to be used.

Include in your research report a discussion of the advantages and disadvantages of your method, as well as what was successful or unsuccessful about your actual research. Target word length: 1000 words.

The 'dark side' of city life

The idea that urban areas might not be conducive to a sense of com-munity and self-identity can be found in the work of Georg Simmel

(1950) (see Chapter 4). Simmel sees urban areas as having both advantages and disadvantages. On the one hand they allow greater freedom of expression, but on the other they bring about a feeling of isolation and loneliness since one feels most isolated when surrounded by lots of strangers. Simmel was concerned with the impersonal and anti-communal nature of life in the city.

According to Kumar (1986) the views of the founders and other classical sociologists about the communal nature of city life differed dramatically, offering different ways of looking at the city and its effects on identity, relationships, community and culture. Consequently there developed over time very different ways of thinking about 'community' and different defininitions of the concept.

Exercise 13.4

kuinida

Consider the five quotations below from a range of classical thinkers (quoted in Kumar, 1986). Identify which quote or quotes can be associated with the three general positions listed after the quotations. Explain why you have allotted the quotations as you have (about 200 words).

1. Marxist thinker Freidrich Engels: 'We know well enough that the isolation of the individual – a narrow-minded egotism – is everywhere the fundamental principle in modern society. But nowhere is this selfish egotism so blatantly evident as in the frantic bustle of the great city. The disintegration of society into individuals, each guided by his private principles and each pursuing his own aims has been pushed to its furthest limits in London. Here indeed human society has been split into its component atoms.'

2. Ferdinand Tonnies: 'The city consists of free persons who stand in contact with each other, exchange with each other and cooperate without any Gemeinschaft . . . these numerous external contacts, contracts, and contractual relations, only cover up as many inner hostilities and antagonistic interests.'

3. Georg Simmel: 'The reciprocal reserve and indifference and the intellectual life conditions of large circles are never more strongly felt by the individual in their impact upon his independence than in the thickest crowd of the big city. This is because the bodily proximity and narrowness of space makes the mental distance only the more visible. It is obviously only the obverse of this freedom if, under certain circumstances, one nowhere feels as lonely and lost as in the metropolitan crowd. For here as elsewhere it is by no means necessary that the freedom of man be reflected in his emotional life as comfort.'

4. Louis Wirth: 'The city consequently tends to resemble a mosaic of social worlds in which the transition from one to another is abrupt. The juxtaposition of divergent personalities and modes of life tend to produce a relativistic perspective and a sense of toleration of differences . . .'

5. Emile Durkheim: 'great cities are the uncontested homes of progress; it is in them that ideas, fashions, customs, new needs are established and then spread over the rest of the country . . . life is there transformed with extraordinary

rapidity: beliefs, tastes, passions are in perpetual evolution. No ground is more favourable to evolutions of all sorts.'

- Position one: the city as unrestrained individualism.
- Position two: the city as both enslavement and liberation.
- Position three: the city as opportunity.

Problems with defining 'community'

For the founders – and especially for Durkheim and Tonnies – the concept of community was almost interchangable with the idea of solidarity. Being in a community implied the subordination of the individual to the wider group. This view has come under attack in contemporary sociology for three reasons:

- It suggests a romanticised and nostalgic 'golden age' of community where everyone was bonded together. This is an unrealistic image.
- Living in a community might not be the same thing as experiencing solidarity. Within communities there is conflict, as well as the opportunity for creative social action.
- To claim that 'community' has died is an extreme view. It may have changed, but many consider that a sense of community still exists in society. Perhaps it makes more sense today to speak of communities.

Howard Newby (1980) identifies three main approaches to how different sociologists have tried to define the idea of community:

- Community can be seen as defined by geographical boundaries between different territories.
- Community can be seen as a localised area: a network of interrelations.
- Community can be seen as people's sense of 'togetherness'.

Despite the problems with the idea of community we should emphasise the effect that one's place in the community and one's relations hips with others have in the formation of self-identity. As Durkheim notes in *The Elementary Forms of the Religious Life* (1982), group membership and the experience of community are vital to knowing who you are and knowing who you are not. Thus group membership gives one a sense of having place into which one can fit. This idea of group membership is not just the concern of functionalist sociologists. Interactionist sociologist William Foote Whyte (1955) writes of the feeling of 'street-corner community' held by youths in Chicago's Italian slum areas during the Second World War. He notes that community membership and self-identity were a matter of everyday life and interaction, and that this included hanging around on street corners engaging in banter.

Exercise 13.5

List six ways in which life and life-styles differ between the city and rural areas.

Exercise 13.6

Consider your answer to Exercise 13.5 above. Write a couple of paragraphs on the consequences that living in the city might have on identity formation.

Bauman (1990) argues that notions of community or togetherness are about sameness and otherness. Bauman suggests that while groups may be divided into 'us' and 'them', one cannot exist without the other:

> 'Them' are not 'us', and 'us' are not 'them'; 'we' and 'they' can be understood only together, in their mutual conflict. I see my in-group as 'us' only because I think of some other group as 'them'. The two opposite groups sediment, as it were, in my map of the world on the two poles of an antagonistic relationship, and it is this antagonism which makes the two groups 'real' to me and makes credible that inner unity and coherence I imagine they possess (ibid.)

Bauman sees this sense of difference as helping us to structure who we feel ourselves to be – our identity. This difference is both symbolic and relational: it is a sign of the exclusivity of our group in our consciousness, but also it relates to the people one does and does not associate with in society in day-to-day life.

Anthony Cohen (1989) rejects the notion of 'community' as a physical geographical boundary. Instead he thinks in terms of 'imagined' or 'symbolic communities' – an approach that owes a great deal to postmodern views of society. This is not to say that the boundary concept is not useful to understanding what communities are and how they contribute to identity formation. However for Cohen such boundaries are not geographical features, nor are they imposed by politicians and the state. Rather they are in the mind of the beholder. Such boundaries are 'inherently oppositional' in that they structure the world into groups, based on their difference from each other. In this sense communities are symbolic creations – they enable further symbols to be learned, acquired and manipulated, through interaction with others who share a common idea of reality:

> Our argument has been, then, that whether or not its structural boundaries remain intact, the reality of community lies in its members' perception of the vitality of its culture. People construct community symbolically, making it a resource and repository of meaning, and a referent of their identity (ibid.)

Similar to the ideas of Cohen, Anderson (1983) suggests that 'nation' and 'nationhood' are symbolic constructions. This is true if we think about the expanse of the geographical area that is home to a 'nation'. Any sense of national identity and togetherness must be largely symbolic or 'imagined' since no national is ever likely to know each and every other national with whom he or she identifies!

The symbolic nature of national identity has also been considered by sociologist Timothy Crippen (1988). Crippen is influenced by Durkheim's *The Elementary Forms of the Religious Life* (1982) in which Durkheim makes a distinction between the 'sacred' and the 'profane'. Whereas the sacred are symbols that are treated as distinct and special, the profane are ordinary symbols of 'this world'. According to Durkheim, while sacred symbols undergo a process of renewal from time to time, they are a vital feature of group membership since they represent the group and its identity. Crippen (1988) argues that the principal sacred symbols in the present age are those connected with nation, nationalism and national identity.

Exercise 13.7

In an extended version of the table below, summarise the ideas on community discussed so far in this chapter.

	When writing?	Basic concepts	Argument
Tonnies			
Durkheim			
Simmel			
Engels			
Wirth			
Bauman			
Cohen			
Anderson			
Crippen			

Exercise 13.8

List the strengths and the weaknesses of the ideas of each of the following writers:

- Tonnies   - Durkheim   - Simmel   - Bauman   - Cohen   - Anderson

The importance of time and space

Anthony Giddens' 'structurational sociology' allows us to reconsider the notion of community, with reference to the structures that both enable and constrain us in our life (see Chapter 5). Giddens (1984) suggests that while we are born into a ready-made social reality that shapes and structures what we do, within such structures we have the freedom to think, reflect and shape our identity. Daily acts of social action and interaction occur in both time and space. Giddens states that:

- Action has a tempo associated with it that governs its duration.
- Action and interaction are 'located' at different times – some actions are considered normal at some times but not at others.
- Actions take place in spaces: some actions are considered normal in some spaces but not in others.
- Individuals are born into a space that structures and shapes their early lives, and initially the individuals have no choice as to where or what this particular space will be.

Giddens suggests that by considering the ways in which action and interaction are structured by time and space, we are led to reconsider the notion of community. He stresses that we should not 'romanticise' the notion of community, especially when discussing the past, but should think about the importance for society of local regions and the places/spaces in which humans act and interact.

Giddens points out that premodern societies were more 'fixed' in their space than is the case today. Most people did not – could not – travel very far, nor did they have much contact with other cultures. They were structured by their place – their 'locale'. Today time and space have been reduced due to the growth of transportation and communication networks, and consequently our sense of place is very different. Yet even though we may view the world differently, we still conduct our interactions within spaces – within locales – that dictate the pattern our interactions will take. Giddens thus replaces the notion of community with the idea of 'locale' – in both time and space.

A locale is a space that gives a context to the actions that occur within it. These spaces can be macro (large-scale) or micro (small-scale). They can also be political spaces, such as a particular government's legal territory, or physical spaces, such as a house or the various rooms in a school. In defining the idea of locale Giddens refers to 'regionalisation', an idea influenced by the dramaturgical writings of Erving Goffman (1971b) (see Chapter 5). What this means is that the spaces in which we interact – the locale – are organised into different areas or regions. Some of these regions allow us to act in some ways, others in different ways. This very much depends on whether the region in question is 'front stage' or 'back stage', to use Goffman's terminology: on whether it is public or private. The example Giddens himself gives is of an ordinary house. Different spaces, or rooms, are used for different actions and interactions at different times of the day and even on different days of the week. For example, how we behave in the privacy of the bathroom or our bedrooms is not necessarily the way we behave in communal areas such as the living room. Some-times rooms are used for different activities at different times. A front room might be a study or even homework room in the early evening, but not later on when other family members arrive. All the rules that are associated with the different regions of the locale define what we should do and how we should do it. In this sense they contribute to who we think we are.

Exercise 13.9

Using a copy of the table below, conduct a survey among others in your class and record how their rooms are used in day-to-day life.

How/when are the following rooms used, and by whom?	Respondent 1	Respondent 2	Respondent 3	Respondent 4	Respondent 5
Kitchen					
Parents' bedrooms					
Children's bedrooms					
Front room					
Back room					
Dining room					
Garden					

Understanding globalisation

The concept of globalisation has become highly significant for sociologists. It provides us with a way to think about how human societies are interconnected in time and space. Malcolm Waters (1995) defines globalisation as 'A social process in which the constraints of geography on social and cultural arrangements recede and in which people become increasingly aware that they are receding.'

Waters notes that although the word global has existed for at least 400 hundred years, the word that describes the process of becoming global – globalisation – did not come into use until about 1960. When first used, the word stood for the worldwide spread of interconnected economic relations and markets. However globalisation is not just an economic force, it is also a cultural force. Ideas, attitudes, mass media, cultural commodities and symbols have spread across vast and once unbridgeable temporal and spacial distances. Globalisation is about the reduction of time and space, and it has profound consequences for the establishment of one's identity.

Exercise 13.10

Consider the following items, and for each one provide examples of how globalisation has affected it and consequently our social lives.

- Clothes
- Food
- Music
- Television
- Religion
- Travel
- Communications
- Finance
- The environment

David Held (1991) suggests that the future of the nation as a self-contained political entity, and of national identity itself, has become uncertain. Whereas for some globalisation signals the end of national divisions in respect of political and economic action, cultural reproduction and consumption, and self-identity, others predict the maintenance of distinct differences between the 'imagined communities' that nations represent. For Held, while economic and cultural distances are being reduced, nationalist feelings may strengthen in response to a perceived loss of autonomy.

According to postmodernists the process of globalisation can be seen as either liberating or constraining. The plurality of cultural meanings on offer due to globalisation means that individuals can 'pick and mix' from them, and thus modify their identity in line with the ever changing and expanding world. However the rapid expansion of cultural influences might create uncertainty – it might lead to confusion, chaos and cultural disorder, in which a stable sense of identity will be difficult to maintain.

Exercise 13.11

Which of the above positions do you agree with most: the ideas of Held or the postmodern view? Explain your view in approximately 150 words.

Some writers suggest that increased global interconnectedness has led to the expansion of order and democracy in the world. Media critic McLuhan (1964; McLuhan and Fiore, 1967) wrote as early as the 1960s about the creation of a 'global village' and a 'global culture' based on new technology – a very early prediction of the global power of today's Internet. However it may be an exaggeration to suggest that the Internet represents a new 'global culture'.

New Right thinker Francis Fukuyama (1992) suggests that globalisation is bringing about a 'new world order' where the ideological differences between East and West are being settled. This new world order is symbolised by the collapse of the Berlin Wall and the spread of free-market economic principles into former communist states. Many Marxists are critical of this image of globalisation and see it as little more than the expansion of capitalist ideology across the globe. It is viewed as a process of global 'Americanisation'.

Globalisation and 'reflexive modernity'

Anthony Giddens (1996) describes the contemporary age as one not of postmodernity, but of 'reflexive modernity' (see Chapter 6). A new age has succeeded modernity in one sense, but it should not be confused with the ideas associated with the intellectual movement of 'postmodernity', such as the decline of truth and the rise of relativity. Giddens suggests that our new times are characterised by the feeling of 'ordinary social actors' that society has rapidly changed and the future has become uncertain. This is very unlike modernity, which was based on absolute notions of truth and certainty. In this new age we are beginning to think about the uncertainties of existence. It is an age in which we must be 'reflexive' about our lives, our relationships, our future and our very sense of self. Giddens suggests that, due to the changing nature of time and space, identity is no longer what it was in premodern times, when one's sense of place was much more fixed and localised. Because of globalisation we are now aware of the risks and dangers of modern living.

Two key features of reflexive modernity are the creation of a post-traditional social order and the acceleration of globalisation. Giddens suggests that although the dynamic of globalisation has existed for some time it is experienced differently today. We – as ordinary social actors – experience this process as both a constraint and a force for liberation, or as an all-enveloping process of decentring and independence. Giddens feels that few people are unaware that their lives are part of a wider, global process, that their day-to-day actions are influenced by remote events. However, not only are our individual actions influenced by globalisation, our actions in turn influence the spread of globalisation itself:

> Less evident is the reverse side of the coin. The day-to-day actions of an individual today are globally consequential. My decision to purchase a particular item of clothing, for example, or a specific type of foodstuff, has manifold global implications. It not only affects the livelihood of someone living on the other side of the world but may contribute to a process of ecological decay which itself has potential consequences for the whole of humanity (Giddens, 1996).

Giddens suggests that in the period of reflexive modernity globalisation has become not so much a matter of impersonal forces, but something that shapes our very self-identity. It has become 'intimate' to the very centre of our being – who we are, and who we wish to become. Giddens describes globalisation not as being 'out there' in relation to humans, but as 'in here'. By this he means that globalisation affects our intimate day-to-day lives and our self-identity. It enables us to think about other cultures and to locate ourselves within a much wider, larger 'locale' – the world itself. Since society is 'post-traditional', individuals now have to work as never before to construct those aspects of social life that were previously handed down. We have to create personal and intimate relationships, take control of our future and develop our own identity. This means that we live in a state of uncertainty, yet it is a state in which we can become free: free from tradition, free to decide who we are.

Conclusion

Giddens claims that we now live in a global age, and that this has been recognised by individuals in society. The concept of globalisation has certainly enjoyed a rapid risen in interest among sociologists. Globalisation raises questions about how individuals experience time and space, and how they experience and create culture and identity. Just how globalisation should be interpreted is still a matter of debate. Some see it as a source of liberation and creativity, others view it as presenting us with further risks and damage. Whatever the outcome of this debate, we can be certain that globalisation will remain an important feature of society as we move into the future.

Examination questions

Use the advice on pages 28–9 to answer the following questions:

(a) Assess the importance of location as a source of identity.

(b) To what extent do you agree that community is in decline as a source of identity?

Appendix: the role of culture and identity in the AS and A2 specifications

The theme of culture and identity runs throughout the AQA and OCR specification and appears in every option at both the AS and the A2 level. Chapters 2–13 of this book cover the following ideas, themes, theories and issues covered in the Curriculum 2000 specifications.

Chapter 2: key issues in the study of culture and identity

- AQA: theory and methods.
- OCR: the individual and society; youth and culture; popular culture.

Chapter 3: classical views

- AQA: theory and methods; religion; crime and deviance; power and politics; stratification and differentiation.
- OCR: the individual and society; religion; social inequality and difference; crime and deviance; popular culture.

Chapter 4: action sociology

- AQA: theory and methods; families and households; education; religion; power and politics; world sociology.
- OCR: the individual and society; the family; religion; education; popular culture; protest and social movements.

Chapter 5: individuals' agency in culture

- AQA: theory and methods; education; crime and deviance, power and politics.
- OCR: the individual and society; youth and culture; crime and deviance; popular culture; protest and social movements.

Chapter 6: modernity and postmodernity

- AQA: theory and methods; mass media; religion; stratification and differentiation; world sociology.

- OCR: the individual and society; religion; mass media; youth and culture; social inequality and difference, popular culture.

Chapter 7: mass culture and popular culture

- AQA: mass media.
- OCR: mass media; youth and culture; popular culture.

Chapter 8: youth culture and subculture

- AQA: mass media; crime and deviance; power and politics.
- OCR: mass media; youth and culture; crime and deviance; popular culture; protest and social movements.

Chapter 9: semiology, structuralism and poststructuralism

- AQA: theory and methods; mass media; power and politics.
- OCR: the individual and society; mass media; popular culture; protest and social movements.

Chapter 10: class and consumption

- AQA: theory and methods; education; wealth, poverty and welfare; stratification and differentiation.
- OCR: social inequality and difference; education; popular culture.

Chapter 11: feminism, gender and sexuality

- AQA: theory and methods; mass media; families and households; stratificaton and differentiation.
- OCR: the individual and society; popular culture; the family; social inequality and difference.

Chapter 12: ethnicity and identity

- AQA: theory and methods; mass media; families and households; stratification and differentiation.
- OCR: the individual and society; popular culture; the family; social inequality and difference.

Chapter 13: community, nation and globalisation

- AQA: power and politics; world sociology.
- OCR: the individual and society; protest and social movements.

References

Abbott, P. and C. Wallace (1997) *An Introduction to Sociology: feminist perspectives*, 2nd edn (London: Routledge).

Adorno, T. W. (1991) *The Culture Industry* (London: Routledge).

Adorno, T. W. and M. Horkheimer (1979) *The Dialectic of Enlightenment* (London: Verso).

Adorno, T. W. and M. Horkheimer (1993) 'The culture industry: enlightenment as mass deception', in S. During (ed.), *The Cultural Studies Reader* (London: Routledge).

Alexander, J. (1985) *Neofunctionalism* (London: Sage).

Alexander, J. C. (1990) 'Analytic debates', in J. Alexander and S. Seidman (eds), *Culture and Society: contemporary debates* (Cambridge: Cambridge University Press).

Althusser, L. with E. Balibar (1968) *Reading Capital* (London: NLB).

Althusser, L. (1969) *For Marx* (Harmondsworth: Penguin).

Althusser, L. (1971) *Lenin and Philosophy and Other Essays* (London: NLB).

Althusser, L. (1976) *Essays in Self-Criticism* (London: NLB).

Anderson, B. (1983) *Imagined Communities* (London: Verso).

Anderson, W. T. (ed.) (1996) *The Fontana Post-Modernism Reader* (London: Fontana).

Ang, I. (1991) *Desperately Seeking the Audience* (London: Routledge).

Archer, M. S. (1982) 'Morphogenesis versus structuration: on combining structure and action', *British Journal of Sociology*, vol. 33.

Archer, M. S. (1991) *Realist Social Theory: the morphogenetic approach* (Cambridge: Cambridge University Press).

Archer, M. S. (1996) *Culture and Agency: the place of culture in social theory* (Cambridge: Cambridge University Press).

Back, L. (1994) 'The Sounds of the City', *Anthropology in Action*, vol. 1, no. 1.

Ballaster, R. (1991) *Women's Worlds: ideology, femininity and the woman's magazine* (London: Macmillan).

Barker, M. (1981) *The New Racism* (London: Junction Books).

Barthes, R. (1967) *Elements of Semiology* (New York: Hill & Wang).

Barthes, R. (1993) *Mythologies* (London: Vintage).

Barthes, R. (1996) *Image-Music-Text*, edited by S. Heath (London: HarperCollins).

Barwise, P. and A. Ehrenberg (1988) *Television and its Audience* (London: Sage).

Baudrillard, J. (1981) *For a Critique of the Political Economy of the Sign* (St Louis: Telos).

Baudrillard, J. (1983) *In the Shadow of the Silent Majorities* (New York: Semiotext(e)).

Baudrillard, J. (1988) *Selected Writings*, edited by M. Poster (Cambridge: Polity Press).

Baudrillard, J. (1993) *Baudrillard Live: selected interviews*, edited by M. Gane (London: Routledge).

Bauman, Z. (1990) *Thinking Sociologically* (Oxford: Blackwell).

Beck, U. (1992) *Risk Society: towards a new modernity* (London: Sage).

Becker, H. (1973) *Outsiders: studies in the sociology of deviance* (New York: Free Press).

Beer, G. (1985) *Darwin's Plots: evolutionary narrative in Darwin, George Eliot and nineteenth-century fiction* (London: Ark).

Bell, D. (1973) *The Coming of Post-Industrial Society* (New York: Basic Books).

Benjamin, W. (1970) *Illuminations* (London: Collins).

Berger, P. and B. Berger (1971) *Sociology: A Revised Approach* (Harmondsworth: Penguin).

Berger, P. L. and T. Luckmann (1967) *The Social Construction of Reality: a treatise in the sociology of knowledge* (Harmondsworth: Penguin).

Best, S. and D. Kellner (1998) 'Beavis and Butt-head: no future for post-modern youth', in J. S. Epstein (ed.), *Youth Culture: identity in a post-modern world* (Oxford: Blackwell).

Billington, R. *et al.* (1988) *Exploring Self and Society* (London: Macmillan).

Blumler, J. G. and E. Katz (eds) (1974) *The Uses of Mass Communication: current perspectives on gratifications research* (London: Sage).

Bocock, R. (1993) *Consumption* (London: Routledge).

Bordo, S. (1990) 'Feminism, postmodernism and gender-scepticism', in L. J. Nicholson (ed.), *Feminism/Postmodernism* (London: Routledge).

Bourdieu, P. (1977) *Outline of a Theory of Practice* (Cambridge: Cambridge University Press).

Bourdieu, P. (1990) *In Other Words* (Cambridge: Polity Press).

Bourdieu, P. (1993) *Sociology in Question* (London: Sage).

Bowles, S. and H. Gintis (1976) *Schooling in Capitalist America* (London: Routledge and Kegan Paul).

Bradley, H. (1996) *Fractured Identities: changing patterns of inequality* (Cambridge: Polity Press).

Brah, A. (1992) 'Difference, diversity and differentiation', in J. Donald and A. Rattansi (eds), *Race, Culture and Difference* (London: Sage).

Butler, J. (1990) *Gender Trouble: feminism and the subversion of identity* (London: Routledge).

Callaway, H. (1984) 'Women's perspectives: research as re-vision', in P. Reason and J. Rowan (eds), *Human Inquiry* (New York: Wiley).

Cixous, H. (1980) 'Sorties', in E. Marks and I. de Courtivron (eds), *New French Feminisms: an anthology* (Brighton: Harvester).

Cixous, H. and C. Clement (1986) *The Newly Born Woman* (Manchester: Manchester University Press).

Clarke, J. (1976) 'The skinheads and the magical recovery of community', in S. Hall and T. Jefferson (eds), *Resistance Through Rituals* (London: Hutchinson).

Clarke, J. *et al.* (1976) 'Subcultures, cultures and class', in S. Hall and T. Jefferson (eds), *Resistance Through Rituals* (London: Hutchinson).

Cohen, A. P. (1989) *The Symbolic Construction of Community* (London: Routledge).

Cohen, A. P. (1994) *Self-Consciousness: an alternative anthropology of identity* (London: Routledge).

Cohen, P. (1972) 'Subcultural conflict and working class community', Working Papers in Cultural Studies No.2, Centre for Contemporary Cultural Studies, University of Birmingham.

Cohen, S. (1987) *Folk Devils and Moral Panics: the creation of the mods and rockers* (Oxford: Basil Blackwell).

Cohen, S. and L. Taylor (1992) *Escape Attempts: the theory and practice of resistance to everyday life*, 2nd edn (London: Routledge).

Comte, A. (1957) *A General View of Positivism*, translated by J. H. Bridges (first published in 1857) (New York: Robert Speller & Sons).

Cooley, C. H. (1927) *Life and the Student* (New York: Alfred A. Knopf).

Crippen, T. (1988) 'Old and new gods in the modern world: towards a theory of religious transformation', *Social Forces*, vol. 67 (December).

Crook *et al.* (1992) *Postmodernization* (London: Sage).

Darwin, C. (1871) *The Descent of Man and Selection in Relation to Sex* (New York: Prometheus).

Davidson, M. (1992) *The Consumerist Manifesto: advertising in postmodern times* (London: Routledge).

De Beauvoir, S. (1972) *The Second Sex* (London: Vintage).

Derrida, J. (1973) *Speech and Phenomena and Other Essays in Husserl's Theory of Signs* (Northwestern University Press).

Derrida, J. (1977) *Of Grammatology* (Baltimore, MD: Johns Hopkins University Press).

Derrida, J. (1978) *Writing and Difference* (Chicago, Ill.: University of Chicago Press).

Douglas, M. (1966) *Purity and Danger* (London: Routledge).

Du Gay, P. *et al.* (1997) *Doing Cultural Studies: the story of the Sony Walkman* (London: Sage).

Dunn, J. (1988) *The Beginnings of Social Understanding* (Oxford: Basil Blackwell).

Durkheim, E. (1938) *The Division of Labour in Society* (Glencoe, Ill.: Free Press).

Durkheim, E. (1970) *Suicide: a study in sociology* (London: Routledge & Kegan Paul).

Durkheim, E. (1972) *Selected Writings*, edited by A. Giddens (Cambridge: Cambridge University Press).

Durkheim, E. (1982) *The Elementary Forms of the Religious Life*, 2nd edn (London: George Allen & Unwin).

Elias, N. (1978) *The Civilising Process* (Oxford: Blackwell).

Elias, N. and E. Dunning (1986) *Quest for Excitement: sport and leisure in the civilizing process* (Oxford: Blackwell).

Eliot, T. S. (1948) *Notes Towards a Definition of Culture* (London: Faber & Faber).

Epstein, J. S. (ed.) (1998) *Youth Culture: identity in a postmodern world* (Oxford: Blackwell).

Faludi, S. (1992) *Backlash* (London: Chatto & Windus).

Featherstone, M. (1991) 'The body in consumer culture', in M. Featherstone *et al.* (eds), *The Body: social process and cultural theory* (London: Sage).

Featherstone, M. (1992) 'Postmodernism and the aestheticization of everyday life', in S. Lash and J. Friedman (eds), *Modernity and Identity* (Oxford: Blackwell).

Featherstone, M. (1994) *Consumer Culture and Postmodernism* (London: Sage).

Featherstone, M. and M. Hepworth (1991) 'The Mask of Ageing and the Postmodern Life', in M. Featherstone *et al.* (eds), *The Body: social process and cultural theory* (London: Sage).

Ferguson, M. (1983) *Forever Feminine* (London: Heinemann).

Firestone, S. (1979) *The Dialectic of Sex*, 2nd edn (London: Women's Press).

Fiske, J. (1989) *Reading the Popular* (London: Unwin Hyman).

Foucault, M. (1984) *The Foucault Reader*, edited by P. Rabinow (London: Penguin).

Foucault, M. (1989a) *Madness and Civilisation: a history of insanity in the age of reason* (London: Routledge).

Foucault, M. (1989b) *The Archaeology of Knowledge* (London: Routledge).

Foucault, M. (1989c) *The Birth of the Clinic: an archaeology of medical perception* (London: Routledge).

Freud, S. (1923) *The Ego and the Id*, vol. 19 of J. Strachey (ed.), *The Standard Edition of the Complete Psychological Works of Sigmund Freud* (London: Hogarth Press).

Freud, S. (1930) *Civilization and its Discontents*, vol. 21 of J. Strachey (ed.), *The Standard Edition of the Complete Psychological Works of Sigmund Freud* (London: Hogarth Press).

Fukuyama, F. (1992) *The End of History and the Last Man* (New York: Free Press).

Gans, H. (1974) *Popular Culture and High Culture* (New York: Basic Books).

Garfinkel, H. (1967) *Studies in Ethnomethodology* (Englewood Cliffs, NJ: Prentice-Hall).

Giddens, A. (1976) *New Rules of Sociological Method: a positive critique of interpretative sociologies* (London: Hutchinson).

Giddens, A. (1978) *Durkheim* (London: Fontana).

Giddens, A. (1984) *The Constitution of Society: outline of the theory of structuration* (Cambridge: Polity Press).

Giddens, A. (1990) *The Consequences of Modernity* (Cambridge: Polity Press).

Giddens, A. (1991) *Modernity and Self-Identity: self and society in the late modern age* (Cambridge: Polity Press).

Giddens, A. (1992) *The Transformation of Intimacy: sexuality, love and eroticism in modern societies* (Cambridge: Polity Press).

Giddens, A. (1993) *The Giddens Reader*, edited by P. Cassell (Basingstoke: Macmillan).

Giddens, A. (1994) *Beyond Left and Right: the future of radical politics* (Cambridge: Polity Press).

Giddens, A. (1996) *In Defence of Sociology: essays, interpretations and rejoinders* (Cambridge: Polity Press).

Gilroy, P. (1987) *There Ain't no Black in the Union Jack* (London: Hutchinson).

Gilroy, P. (1993) *The Black Atlantic: modernity and double consciousness* (London: Verso).

Gilroy, P. (1997) 'Diaspora and the detours of identity', in K. Woodward (ed.), *Identity and Difference* (London: Sage).

Giroux, H. A. (1983) *Theory and Resistance in Education* (New York: Bergin and Garvey).

Giroux, H. A. (1994) *Disturbing Pleasures* (New York: Routledge).

Giroux, H. A. (1998) 'Teenage sexuality, body politics, and the pedagogy of display', in J. S. Epstein (ed.), *Youth Culture: identity in a postmodern world* (Oxford: Blackwell).

Goffman, E. (1968) *Asylums: essays on the social situation of mental patients and other inmates* (London: Pelican).

Goffman, E. (1971a) *Relations in Public: microstudies of the public order* (Harmondsworth: Penguin).

Goffman, E. (1971b) *The Presentation of Self in Everyday Life* (London: Penguin).

Goldschmidt, W. (1990) *The Human Career: the self in the symbolic world* (Oxford: Blackwell).

Goldthorpe, J. *et al.* (1968) *The Affluent Worker* (Cambridge: Cambridge University Press).

Gramsci, A. (1971) *Selections from the Prison Notebooks*, edited by Q. Hoare (London: Lawrence & Wishart).

Gramsci, A. (1977) *Selections from Political Writings: 1910–1920*, edited by Q. Hoare (London: Lawrence & Wishart).

Gramsci, A. (1978) *Selections from Political Writings: 1921–1926*, edited by Q. Hoare (London: Lawrence & Wishart).

Habermas, J. (1981) *The Theory of Communicative Action* (London: Heinemann).

Habermas, J. (1987) *Toward a Rational Society* (includes the essay 'Technology and science as "ideology"' (Cambridge: Polity Press).

Hakim, C. (1995) 'Five feminist myths about women's employment', *British Journal of Sociology*, vol. 46, no. 3.

Hall, S. (1988) *The Hard Road to Renewal: Thatchersim and the Crisis of the Left* (London: Verso).

Hall, S. (1990) 'Cultural identity and diaspora', in J. Rutherford (ed.), *Identity: community, culture, difference* (London: Lawrence & Wishart).

Hall, S. (1992) 'The question of identity', in S. Hall *et al.* (eds), *Modernity and its Futures* (Cambridge: Polity Press).

Hall, S. (1993) 'Encoding, decoding', in S. During (ed.), *The Cultural Studies Reader* (London: Routledge).

Hall, S. (1996) *Stuart Hall: Critical dialogues in cultural studies*, edited by D. Morley and K. H. Chen (London: Routledge).

Harris, D. (1996) *A Society of Signs?* (London: Routledge).

Hartmann, H. (1981) 'The unhappy marriage of Marxism and feminism', in L. Sargent (ed.), *The unhappy marriage of Marxism and feminism* (London: Pluto Press).

Hebdige, D. (1979) *Subculture: the meaning of style* (London: Methuen).

Held, D. (1991) 'Democracy, the nation state and the global system', in O. D. Held (ed.), *Political Theory Today* (Cambridge: Polity Press).

Heller, A. and F. Feher (1988) *The postmodern political condition* (Cambridge: Polity Press).

Hetherington, K. (1998) *Expressions of Identity: space, performance, politics* (London: Sage).

Hewitt, R. (1986) *White talk, black talk* (Cambridge: Cambridge University Press).

Hey, V. (1997) *The Company She Keeps: an ethnography of girls' friendship* (Buckingham: Open University Press).

Hollis, M. (1977) *Models of Man* (Cambridge: Cambridge University Press).

Hood-Williams, J. (1996) 'Goodbye to sex and gender?', *The Sociology Review*, vol. xx.

hooks, b. (1996) 'Postmodern blackness', in W. T. Anderson (ed.), *The Fontana Post-Modernism Reader* (London: Fontana).

Irigaray, L. (1985) *Speculum of the Other Woman* (Ithaca, NY: Cornell University Press).

Irigaray, L. (1992) *The Irigaray Reader*, edited by M. Whitford (Oxford: Basil Blackwell).

Irigaray, L. (1993) *An Ethic of Sexual Difference* (London: Athlone Press).

James, S. and A. Busia (eds) (1993) *Theorising Black Feminisms. The visionary pragmatism of black women* (London: Routledge).

Jameson, F. (1983) 'Post-modernism and consumer society', in H. Foster (ed.), *Post-modern Culture* (London: Pluto).

Jenkins, R. (1992) *Pierre Bourdieu* (London: Routledge).

Jenkins, R. (1996) *Social Identity* (London: Routledge).

Jones, S. (1994) *The Language of the Genes* (London: Flamingo).

Kellner, D. (1992) 'Popular culture and the construction of postmodern identities', in S. Lash and J. Friedman (eds), *Modernity and Identity* (Oxford: Blackwell).

Kerr, C. *et al.* (1973) *Industrialism and Industrial Man* (Harmondsworth: Penguin).

Kirby, M. (1999) 'New Approaches to Social Inequality', *The Sociology Review*, vol. 8, no. 3.

Kristeva, J. (1981) *Desire in Language* (Oxford: Basil Blackwell).

Kristeva, J. (1986) *The Kristeva Reader*, edited by T. Moi (Oxford: Basil Blackwell).

Kroeber, A. L. and C. Kluckhohn (1963) *Culture: a criticial review of concepts and definitions* (New York: Vintage Books).

Kumar, K. (1986) *Prophecy and Progress: the sociology of industrial and post-industrial society* (London: Penguin).

Lea, J. and J. Young (1993) *What is to be Done About Law and Order?* (London: Pluto).

Lévi-Strauss, C. (1969) *The Elementary Structures of Kinship* (Boston: Beacon Press).

Lévi-Strauss, C. (1972) *The Savage Mind* (London: Weidenfeld & Nicolson).

Lévi-Strauss, C. (1977) *Structural Anthropology 1* (Harmondsworth: Penguin).

Lévi-Strauss, C. (1978) *Structural Anthropology 2* (Harmondsworth: Penguin).

Locher, D. A. (1998) 'The industrial identity crisis: the failure of a newly forming subculture to identify itself', in J. S. Epstein (ed.), *Youth Culture: identity in a postmodern world* (Oxford: Blackwell).

Lyotard, J. F. (1984) *The Postmodern Condition: a report on knowledge*, 2nd edn (Manchester: Manchester University Press).

Mackinnon, C. (1982) 'Feminism, Marxism, method and the state', in N. Keohane *et al.* (eds), *Feminist Theory* (Brighton: Harvester).

Malinowski, B. (1922) *Argonauts of the Western Pacific* (London: Routledge & Kegan Paul).

Malinowski, B. (1954) *Magic, Science and Religion and Other Essays* (New York: Anchor Books).

Mama, A. (1989) 'Violence against black women: gender, race and state responses', *Feminist Review*, no. 28.

Mannheim, K. (1960) *Ideology and Utopia: an introduction to the sociology of knowledge* (London: Routledge & Kegan Paul).

Marcuse, H. (1964) *One-Dimensional Man* (London: Routledge & Kegan Paul).

Marcuse, H. (1969) *Eros and Civilization* (London: Routledge & Kegan Paul).

Marx, K. (1989) *Readings from Karl Marx*, edited by D. Sayer (London: Routledge).

Marx, K. and F. Engels (1974) *The German Ideology*, 2nd edn (London: Lawrence & Wishart).

Marx, K. and F. Engels (1984) *Basic Writings on Politics and Philosophy*, edited by L. S. Feuer (London: Fontana).

Marx, K. and F. Engels (1985) *The Communist Manifesto* (London: Penguin).

Maynard, M. (1998) 'Feminists' knowledge and the knowledge of feminisms', in T. May and M. Williams (eds), *Knowing the Social World* (Buckingham: Open University Press).

McAllister-Groves, J. (1995) 'Learning to feel: the neglected sociology of social movements', *Sociology Review*, vol. 43, no. 3.

McLuhan, M. (1964) *Understanding the Media* (London: Routledge).

McLuhan, M. and Q. Fiore (1967) *The Medium is the Message* (London: Allen Lane).

McRobbie, A. (1983) 'Teenage girls, *Jackie* and the ideology of adolescent femininity', in B. Waites *et al.* (eds), *Popular Culture* (London: Croom Helm).

McRobbie, A. (1986) 'Postmodernism and popular culture', ICA Documents 4/5 (London: ICA).

McRobbie, A. (1994) *Postmodernism and Popular Culture* (London: Routledge).

Mead, G. H. (1934) *Mind, Self and Society* (Chicago, Ill.: Chicago University Press).

Mercer, K. (1990) 'Welcome to the jungle: identity and diversity in postmodern politics', in J. Rutherford (ed.), *Identity: community, culture, difference* (London: Lawrence & Wishart).

Mercer, K. (1995) 'Black hair/style politics', in E. Carter, J. Donald and J. Squires (eds), *Cultural Remix: theories of politics and the popular* (London: Lawrence & Wishart).

Merton, R. K. (1989) 'Social structure and anomie', in D. H. Kelley (ed.), *Deviant Behaviour: a text-reader in the sociology of deviance*, 3rd edn (New York: St Martin's).

Millet, K. (1970) *Sexual Politics* (New York: Doubleday).

Miller, W. B. (1962) 'Lower class culture as a generating milieu of gang delinquency', in M. E. Wolfgang *et al.* (eds), *The Sociology of Crime and Delinquency* (New York: John Wiley and Sons).

Mills, C. W. (1959) *The Sociological Imagination* (London: Oxford University Press).

Modood, T. (1988) '"Black" racial equality and Asian identity', *New Community*, vol 14, no. 3.

Modood, T. (1992) 'British Muslims and the Rushdie Affair', in J. Donald and A. Rattansi (eds), *Race, Culture and Difference* (London: Sage).

Morgan, D. H. J. (1996) *Family Connections: an introduction to family studies* (Cambridge: Polity Press).

Morley, D. (1980) *The Nationwide Audience* (London: BFI).

Morley, D. (1994) 'Postmodernism – the highest stage of cultural imperialism?', in M. Perryman (ed.), *Altered States: postmodernism, politics and culture* (publisher unknown).

Morris, D. (1968) *The Naked Ape* (London: Corgi).

Mulvey, L. (1975) 'Visual pleasure and narrative cinema', *Screen*, vol. 16, no. 3.

Murray, C. (1984) *Losing Ground* (New York: Basic Books).

New, C. (1993) 'Structuration theory revisited: some reflections on agency', *Social Science Teacher*, vol. 22, no. 3.

Newby, H. (1980) 'Community', study section 20 in *An Introduction to Sociology* (Milton Keynes: Open University Press).

Nicholson, L. (1999) *The Play of Reason: from the modern to the postmodern* (Buckingham: Open University Press).

Norris, C. (1992) *Uncritical Theory: postmodernism, intellectuals and the Gulf war* (London: Lawrence & Wishart).

Norris, C. (1993) *The Truth about Postmodernism* (Oxford: Blackwell).

Oakley, A. (1972) *Sex, Gender and Society* (London: Temple Smith).

Oakley, A. (1982) *Subject Women* (London: Fontana).

O'Hara, M. (1996) 'Constructing emancipatory realities', in W. T. Anderson (ed.), *The Fontana Post-Modernism Reader* (London: Fontana).

Park, R. (1929) 'The city as a social laboratory', in T. Smith and L. White (eds), *Chicago: an experiment in social science research* (Chicago, Ill.: Chicago University Press).

Park, R. and E. Burgess (eds) (1925) *The City* (Chicago, Ill.: Chicago University Press).

Parsons, T. (1951) *The Social System* (New York: Free Press).

Parsons, T. (1971) *The System of Societies* (Englewood Cliffs, NJ: Prentice-Hall).

Pearce, F. (1989) *The Radical Durkheim* (London: Unwin Hyman).

Pearson, G. (1983) *Hooligan: a history of respectable fears* (London: Macmillan).

Peirce, C. S. (1991) *Peirce on Signs: Writings on Semiotics by Charles Sanders Peirce*, edited by J. Hope (London: University of North Carolina Press).

Philo, G. (1990) *Seeing and Believing: the influence of television* (London: Routledge).

Poole, F. J. P. (1994) 'Socialization, enculturation and the development of personal identity', in T. Ingold (ed.), *Companion Encyclopedia of Anthropology* (London: Routledge).

Postman, N. (1985) *The Disappearance of Childhood: how TV is changing children's lives* (London: W. H. Allen).

Richardson, D. (1993) 'Sexuality and male dominance', in D. Richardson and V. Robinson (eds), *Introducing Women's Studies* (London: Macmillan).

Robins, K. (1997) 'What in the world's going on?', in P. du Gay (ed.), *Production of Culture/Culture of Production* (London: Sage).

Rorty, R. (1989) *Contingency, irony and solidarity* (Cambridge: Cambridge University Press).

Rorty, R. (1996) 'Ironists and metaphysicians', in W. T. Anderson (ed.), *The Fontana Post-Modernism Reader* (London: Fontana).

Ross, A. (1994) 'Andrew Ross' Weather Report', *Artforum*, 10–12 May.

Saunders, P. (1990) *Social Class and Stratification* (London: Routledge).

Saussure, F. de (1983) *Course in General Linguistics* (new translation) (London: Duckworth).

Saussure, F. de (1990) 'Signs and Language', in J. C. Alexander and S. Seidman, *Culture and Society: contemporary debates* (Cambridge: Cambridge University Press).

Savage, M. *et al.* (1992) *Property, Bureaucracy and Culture: middle-class formation in contemporary Britain* (London: Routledge).

Segal, L. (1997) 'Sexualities', in K. Woodward (ed.), *Identity and Difference* (London: Sage).

Simmel, G. (1950) *The Sociology of Georg Simmel*, edited by K. H. Wolff (New York: Free Press).

Simmel, G. (1955) *Conflict and the Web of Group Affiliation* (New York: Free Press).

Simmel, G. (1957) 'Fashion', *American Journal of Sociology*, vol. 62, pp. 541–8.

Simon, W. (1996) 'The postmodernization of sex and gender', in W. T. Anderson (ed.), *The Fontana Post-Modernism Reader* (London: Fontana).

Smith, J. (1997) *Different for Girls. How culture creates women* (London: Chatto & Windus).

Soja, E. W. (1996) 'Los Angeles 1965–1992: from crisis-generated restructuring to restructuring-generated crisis', in A. J. Scott and E. W. Soja (eds), *The City: Los Angeles and urban theory at the end of the twentieth century* (London: University of California Press).

Spencer, H. (1971) *Herbert Spencer: structure, function and evolution*, edited by S. Andreski (London: Nelson).

Stuart, A. (1990) 'Feminism: Dead or Alive?', in J. Rutherford (ed.), *Identity: community, culture, difference* (London: Lawrence & Wishart).

Sumner, C. (1994) *The Sociology of Deviance: an obituary* (Buckingham: Open University Press).

Sutherland, E. (1924) *Principles of Criminology* (Chicago, Ill.: Chicago University Press).

Swingewood, A. (1977) *The Myth of Mass Culture* (London: Macmillan).

Thornton, S. (1995) *Club Cultures: music media and subcultural capital* (Cambridge: Polity Press).

Tiger, L. and R. Fox (1972) *The Imperial Animal* (London: Secker & Warburg).

Tomlinson, L. (1998) '"This ain't no disco" . . . or is it? Youth culture and the rave phenomenon', in J. S. Epstein (ed.), *Youth Culture: identity in a post-modern world* (Oxford: Blackwell).

Tonnies, F. (1963) *Community and Society*, edited by P. Loomis (New York: Harper & Row).

Turner, B. S. (1984) *The Body and Society: explorations in social theory* (Oxford: Basil Blackwell).

Walby, S. (1989) 'Theorising Patriarchy', *Sociology*, vol. 23, no. 2.

Walby, S. (1990) *Theorising Patriarchy* (Oxford: Blackwell).

Waters, M. (1995) *Globalization* (London: Routledge).

Weber, M. (1961) *From Max Weber: essays in sociology* (London: Routledge).

Weber, M. (1968) *Economy and Society: an outline of interpretive sociology*, 3 vols, edited by G. Roth and C. Wittich (New York: Bedminister Press).

Weber, M. (1985) *The Protestant Ethic and the Spirit of Capitalism* (London: Unwin).

Weeks, J. (1990) 'The value of difference', in J. Rutherford (ed.), *Identity: community, culture, difference* (London: Lawrence & Wishart).

Weinstein, D. (1991) *Heavy Metal: a cultural sociology* (New York: Lexington).

Whyte, W. F. (1955) *Street Corner Society: the social structure of an Italian slum* (Chicago, Ill.: Chicago University Press).

Williams, R. (1963) *Culture and Society 1780–1950* (Harmondsworth: Pelican).

Williams, R. (1983) *Key Words: a vocabulary of culture and society* (London: Fontana).

Willis, P. (1977) *Learning to Labour* (Farnborough: Saxon House).

Willis, P. (1979) 'Masculinity and factory Labor', in J. Clarke *et al.* (eds), *Working Class Culture* (London: Hutchinson).

Willis, P. (1990) 'Masculinity and factory Labor', in J. C. Alexander and S. Seidman (eds), *Culture and Society: contemporary debates* (Cambridge: Cambridge University Press).

Willis, P. with S. James, J. Canaan and G. Hurd (1993) *Common Culture: symbolic work at play in the everyday cultures of the young* (Milton Keynes: Open University Press).

Woodward, K. (ed.) (1997) *Identity and Difference* (London: Sage).

Yinger, J. M. (1976) 'Ethnicity in complex societies', in A. Lewis *et al.* (eds), *The Uses of Controversy in Sociology* (New York: Free Press).

Zweig, C. (1996) 'The death of the self in the postmodern world', in W. T. Anderson (ed.), *The Fontana Post-Modernism Reader* (London: Fontana).

Zweig, F. (1961) *The Worker in an Affluent Society: family life and industry* (London: Heinemann).

Author index

Abbott, P. 158, 171–2, 174
Adorno, T. W. and Horkheimer, M.
    49–50, 102–3, 157
Alexander, J. 41–2
Althusser, L. 145–6, 150
Anderson, B. 203–4
Anderson, W. T. 88–90, 110
Ang, I. 105
Archer, M. S. 21, 23–4, 80

Back, L. 195
Ballaster, R. 186–7
Barker, M. 192
Barthes, R. 122, 140–1, 143, 150
Barwise, P. and Ehrenberg, A.
    107–8
Baudrillard, J. 62, 91–2, 110–11,
    148–50, 151, 153
Bauman, Z. 203
Beauvoir, S. de 19
Beck, U. 97, 168
Becker, H. 116–17
Bell, D. 162
Benjamin, W. 103–4
Bennett, T. 96
Berger, P. L. 65
Best, S. 127–8
Billington, R. 183–4
Blair, T. 161
Blumler, J. G. 108
Bocock, R. 165
Bordo, S. 176
Bourdieu, P. 68, 71–3, 83
Bowles, S. 49, 120
Bradley, H. 161–2
Brah, A. 192–3
Burgess, E. 116
Busia, A. 175
Butler, J. 181–2

Callaway, H. 172
Cixous, H. 147
Cohen, A. P. 27, 75, 203
Cohen, S. 70–1, 117–19, 160
Comte, A. 30–1, 198
Cooley, C. H. 64
Coupland, D. 132
Crippen, T. 204

Darwin, C. 13, 44
Davidson, M. 167
Derrida, J. 150, 151
Dickens, C. 100
Durkheim, E. 3, 21–2, 30–4, 35–42,
    51–2, 53, 58–9, 61, 73, 143, 198,
    200, 201–2, 204
Dunn, J. 67
Dunning, E. 14

Ehrenberg, A. 107–8
Elias, N. 15, 16
Eliot, T. S. 101
Engels, F. 31, 43, 47, 178, 201
Epstein, J. S. 131

Faludi, S. 187
Featherstone, M. 84–5, 89, 109,
    167–8
Feher, F. 169
Ferguson, M. 186
Fiore, Q. 207
Firestone, S. 174, 181
Fiske, J. 106–7, 119
Ford, H. 109
Foucault, M. 150–4, 155, 186
Fox, R. 13
Freud, S. 13–16, 18, 21, 59, 61, 81,
    148
Fukuyama, F. 162–3, 207

Garfinkel, H. 65
Gans, H. 104
Gay, P. du 129–30
Giddens, A. 18, 27, 68, 73, 74–5,
    76, 78–80, 83, 96–7, 120, 154,
    168, 169–70, 185–6, 204–6,
    208–9
Gilroy, P. 191–4, 197
Gintis, H. 49, 120
Giroux, H. A. 125
Goffman, E. 76–8, 116, 169, 205
Goldschmidt, W. 13
Goldthorpe, J. 161
Gramsci, A. 121–3, 145–6

Habermas, J. 76, 81–2, 83
Hakim, C. 188

Subject index